ROTHERHAM LIBRARY & INFORMATION SERVICES

This book must be returned by the date specified at the time of issue
as the DATE DUE FOR RETURN.
The loan may be extended (personally, by post or telephone) for a
further period if the book is not required by another reader, by quoting
the above number / author / title.

CL/132/F14

A

CHAMPION'S

MIND

PETE
SAMPRAS

with Peter Bodo

A

CHAMPION'S

MIND

Lessons from a
Life in Tennis

Aurum

First published in Great Britain
2009 by Aurum Press Ltd
7 Greenland Street
London NW1 0ND
www.aurumpress.co.uk

First published in the United States in 2008 by Crown Publishers, an imprint of the
Crown Publishing Group, a division of Random House, Inc., New York.

A catalogue record for this book is available from the British Library.

ISBN 978 1 84513 469 3

1 3 5 7 9 10 8 6 4 2
2009 2011 2013 2012 2010

Design by Barbara Sturman
Printed and bound by MPG Books, Bodmin, Cornwall

For my wife, Bridgette,
and boys, Christian and Ryan:
you have fulfilled me in a way that no number of
Grand Slam titles or tennis glory ever could

Contents

A few years ago, the idea of writing a book about my life and times in tennis would have seemed as foreign to me as it might have been surprising to you. After all, I was the guy who let his racket do the talking. I was the guy who kept his eyes on the prize, leading a very dedicated, disciplined, almost monkish existence in my quest to accumulate Grand Slam titles. And I was the guy who guarded his private life and successfully avoided controversy and drama, both in my career and personal life.

But as I settled into life as a former player, I had a lot of time to reflect on where I'd been and what I'd done, and the way the story of my career might impact people. For starters, I realized that what I did in tennis probably would be a point of interest and curiosity to my family. If and when my children (and the members of my large extended family) want to experience and understand what I was about, and what my times were like, I'd like them to experience it through my eyes. As I write this, both of our sons, Christian and Ryan, can already throw a ball straight—which my father, Sam, said was my own first sign of athletic talent. And I'd like for my fans, and tennis fans in general, to see it through my eyes, too. This book is my legacy.

And there was something else: my ability to fly pretty low beneath the public's radar was a great benefit to my career; it helped me stay focused and out of the limelight. That's how I wanted it. But that also meant that my career would only be known in a piecemeal way.

I liked the idea of pulling all the bits and pieces together, putting them in perspective, and making the connections that were ignored or not noticed.

In the course of writing this book, I realized that I led a pretty eventful career without ever letting individual events overtake it. My first coach spent time in jail; the mentor who was instrumental at the time when my mature game was really emerging was stricken by cancer and died at an early age; I lost one of the closest friends I had among the players to a tragic accident. I had some stress-related physical problems and at least one career-threatening injury—at a time when I was poised to overtake Roy Emerson as the all-time Grand Slam singles champ. I had my tiffs with fellow players and even my sponsors and the tennis establishment. Yet those aren't the things that come to most people's minds at the mention of my name. I'm glad and proud of that, but I also want to acknowledge those events and incidents, and reveal what they meant and how they affected me.

This isn't one of those score-settling books, though. From the outset, my goal was to write a tightly focused tennis book—one that tells my story in a way that also celebrates the game, and the period in which I played. Truth is, I'm a live-and-let-live guy. My lifelong tendency has been to deal with things head-on and then move on.

I played tennis during a time of sweeping changes. It started with a burst of growth in the level of international competition, and included features like the revolution in equipment, the intense commercialization of the game, the first high-profile performance-enhancing drug scandal in tennis, and the slowing down of the speed of the game—a process that began at the tournament I loved best and where I probably played my best, Wimbledon.

It was a glorious period, my time, especially for American tennis. My generation included four Grand Slam champions (Michael Chang, Jim Courier, Andre Agassi, and me), and players from other nations proved to be some of my most fierce and determined rivals.

That high level of competition has continued as Roger Federer, a Swiss who has become a good friend, has emerged to pick up Grand Slam titles at a record-breaking clip. Time seems to move slower or faster as events change, and the time came for me to add my story, told in my words, to the record.

Ted Williams, the great Boston Red Sox slugger, once said that all he wanted out of life was that when he walked down the street, people would point and say, "There goes the greatest hitter who ever lived." Early in my career, I adopted a similar attitude. It may strike some as arrogant, but that's the kind of fuel you need to really reach the heights of achievement. There were times in my career when I would step up to the service line at a crucial moment in the heat of combat in a big match and pause to drink in the atmosphere. Fired up by adrenaline, I'd look toward the crowd and defiantly say to myself, *All right, everybody, now I'm going to show you who I really am.*

Most champions have that kind of aggression, that competitiveness. It comes with the territory. You don't survive long with a target on your back without it. But there's this, too: in our sport, the best of players and fiercest competitors are often also gentlemen—good sports and role models. Just look at Rod Laver before my time, and Roger Federer after it.

This book will tell you, in a broader and less intense way, who I really am.

Los Angeles, January 2008

A

CHAMPION'S

MIND

1971–1986

Chapter 1

The Tennis Kid

I'm not sure you need to know who you are and what you want from the get-go to become a great tennis player. Different players have arrived at that destination in different ways. But me, I knew. I knew, almost from day one, that I was born to play tennis. It may not be mandatory, but knowing who you are and what you want—whether it's to play a violin in a concert hall or build great big skyscrapers—gives you a great head start in reaching your goals.

I was born in Potomac, Maryland, on August 12, 1971, the second youngest of four kids. Gus, my brother, is four years older than me. My sister Stella—the other serious tennis player among my siblings—is two years older, and the baby of the family is my sister Marion.

My father, Sam, is of Greek stock. When I was born, he was working in Washington, D.C., as a Defense Department mechanical engineer. With a wife, Georgia, and four kids to support, he also was part owner—with three brothers-in-law—of the McLean Restaurant and Delicatessen in suburban, McLean, Virginia. Although it wasn't a Greek joint per se, my family brought a Greek flair and love of good food to the establishment, so it was very successful.

I have almost no memories of life in Potomac, but I do remember getting hold of an old tennis racket and taking to it like it was the ultimate toy or something. I hit against anything I could find that was hard enough to send the ball back. Mostly it was the cement wall of a nearby Laundromat. Eventually I gravitated toward a local park that had some courts, and I took a lesson or two. I just fell into it, but I believe there was a reason I was drawn to it, just like there was a reason why Tiger Woods picked up a golf club, and Wayne Gretzky a hockey stick.

My dad remembers that some guy came up to him in the park in Potomac and said, "Your son—he looks like he can really play tennis." I think Dad took that to heart, even though he wasn't a huge sports fan and we had no real tennis tradition in the family. We were Greek Americans, firmly connected to our roots in many ways. Some small nations in the Western world, like Croatia and Sweden, have a rich tennis tradition. But Greece isn't one of them. Culturally, tennis was completely off our radar.

Dad knew nothing about tennis, so he had no aspirations for me until I displayed interest in the game. He also was utterly unfamiliar with the tennis scene, which is insular and mostly made up of people whose families have been involved in the game for multiple generations. But he noticed that I had a strong athletic bent. Even as a toddler, I could kick a ball well and throw it straight. That stuff just came naturally to me.

When I was seven, Dad had the opportunity to transfer to the Los Angeles area, a traditional hotbed for the aerospace and defense industries. Tennis was probably the furthest thing from his mind. Unbeknownst to us, but very, very fortunately, Southern California is also the epicenter of U.S. tennis culture—especially the populist branch of it. Tennis in the United States always did have two faces. It was a preferred sport of the wealthy, especially in the Northeast in places like Boston, Newport, New York, and Philadelphia, which traditionally hosted most of the major events, including the U.S. Open. The game there was laden with tradition, and up until shortly before I was born, grass was the major surface. California was a different story altogether.

The sunny climate on the West Coast made tennis a year-round, outdoor game that anyone could play with limited resources, and there were no socially intimidating overtones. There was plenty of space, so public courts sprang up all over the place. Most of those courts were made of cement, because they were cheap to build and easy to maintain. California evolved into a major tennis location. The earliest great players to come out of the West Coast were guys like Ellsworth Vines, who is still legendary for his awesome serve, Jack Kramer, Pancho Gonzalez, Stan Smith, Billie Jean King, and Tracy Austin.

The big serve and an aggressive style of play were the underpinnings of the "California game." Techniquewise, tennis is played a little differently by region and on different surfaces. The contrasts are pronounced enough so that the most common grips used in tennis—the Continental (European), Eastern, and Western—are all named for the regions where they were popular and suited the courts in use.

Part of my legacy—or so I'm told, anyway—is that I came close to being the model all-around player. I had a big serve and aggressive baseline game, which was pure, populist California. But I eventually embraced serve-and-volley tennis and did my major damage on foreign soil at the greatest—and most elite—tournament in the world, winning seven men's singles titles at Wimbledon. The only surface I never entirely mastered was slow European clay, insofar as I never won the biggest clay tournament, the French Open.

In my style and results, I transcended my regional and even national background to a greater extent than some of my predecessors as the world number one player. Take my countryman Jimmy Connors. Although he was from Illinois, he relocated to California at an early enough age to mature his game on the hard courts there. He "only" won Wimbledon twice, clinging to his all-court style, although that game was good enough to earn him *five* U.S. Open titles, three on his beloved hard courts.

The most important thing about California was the opportunity presented by that strong, diverse, deeply rooted tennis culture. Lacking a strong family background in tennis, we were going to have to play it by ear and make it up as we went along. Thankfully, we were right in the eye of the Open-era hurricane that started in 1968, when professional players finally were invited to compete with the amateurs at the four "majors," or Grand Slam events (the Australian, French, and U.S. Opens, and Wimbledon). That shift to Open tennis ensured that *all* the good players in the world could compete in the same tournaments, so you would end up with a true champ, and it launched a tennis boom that brought the game to millions of new players and potential pros.

By the time I moved to California, the state was teeming with world-class players and prospects, and it offered great development, training, and playing opportunities. It was mind-blowing—or would have been, had we been aware of all that. But we were not.

Anyway, my father cashed out of the deli business. It was getting old for him, what with brothers-in-law for partners. He had done very well and he needed a break. He finally felt secure enough to take the plunge that so many newly minted Americans and immigrants had taken before him. He was going west, following the American Dream to California. After a few trips to the coast to establish our home in Palos Verdes, he returned to Potomac and gathered us up.

One fine morning in 1978, he got us all packed into the car. I remember we had a tiny blue Ford Pinto, a bare-bones economy car (the Pinto later became famous when somebody discovered that if you rear-ended it, the car blew up). We piled into the Pinto—all six of us—and headed west. Wait, make that *seven*, because we were also taking our parrot, Jose. If you're familiar with the classic Chevy Chase movie *National Lampoon's Vacation*, you'll know all you need to know about our situation.

• • •

I hit the ground running when we arrived in Palos Verde and moved into our modest 1,500-square-foot home. As the oldest child, Gus had his own room, and I ended up sharing with Marion—in fact, I didn't have my own room until I was fifteen or sixteen. Shortly after we got to Palos Verdes, we found out that it was a tennis-rich environment. The Jack Kramer Club, which had been instrumental in developing so many fine players (including Tracy Austin), was nearby in Rolling Hills. And then there was West End, where I began taking lessons from one of the all-time great coaches, Robert Lansdorp.

I was a shy, introverted kid, but if you "took" from Lansdorp, you were right in the thick of things and a lot of people checked you out. It seems weird now, but we were told shortly after I started working on my game that I was going to be a great tennis player. Almost immediately, people were comparing me to guys like Eliot Teltscher, saying I was as good at fourteen as Eliot, a prodigy, had been at sixteen. (He went on to have a great pro career, becoming a perennial world-top-ten performer.)

By the time I reached my teens, I assumed that I was going to win Wimbledon and the U.S. Open, which was a real reach. A lot of kids are told they're great, believe it, work toward it—and eventually fall by the wayside. They may not have the right temperament or long-term physical assets; they might not be able to handle the expectations, they may have insurmountable flaws in their technique, their dedication, or approach to their career. The idea that none of the things that could go wrong *would* go wrong is borderline preposterous—except when it isn't.

But maybe the assumption that I was going to be as great as everyone suggested helped me become what I am. Deep down, I knew. I had that confidence. The amazing thing is that nothing happened to break it, tone it down, or take it away—and I went through a lot that could have robbed me of that sense of destiny.

Not long after I started playing at the Kramer club, my dad became acquainted with a member named Pete Fischer. He was a successful pediatrician originally from New York, and he looked the part and played tennis like it. He was thickly built, with a big belly, and had one of the most horrific tennis games anyone ever laid eyes on. But he was a very smart, stubborn tennis visionary—a true tennis nut.

Fischer looked at me and saw some kind of supernatural talent, so he befriended my dad, who would take me to and from lessons, and ultimately convinced Dad to allow him to become my coach. In retrospect, "coach" is not exactly the right word for Fischer, because his greatest asset was knowing what he didn't know. He was a hacker tennis player who masterminded my tennis development in a wise way—by having various coaches and specialists bring their unique skills to my development. He had grand, almost preposterous plans for me. He was like a combination of mad scientist and general contractor—one who was in charge of building the all-time Grand Slam champion.

Fischer's smartest move, by far, was convincing my dad to let him take charge of my tennis career. He became our adviser, confidant, and tennis go-to guy. In hindsight, the thing I valued most about Pete is what he did for my relationship with my dad. He kept tennis out of it. Pete was in the driver's seat. My dad, who would have been the first to admit he knew nothing about the game, did not have to take on the responsibility of my development. The lines between parent and coach would never blur; my results, or lack thereof, never caused strain or tension. My dad was always present in my development and career, but he was in the background. As Robert Lansdorp later put it, "He was the guy on the other side of the Cyclone fence, standing back, just watching."

This was an especially good approach because of the kind of man my father is. He isn't a hugger, and he's not a big communicator. Like most of the Sampras men, including Gus and me, he's reserved. It takes some time for us to warm up to people and we're more likely to linger in the background than to step out and be the life of the party. We share a sarcastic streak. It's not an ideal temperament for dealing with the nature of the pro tennis tour, where you're constantly moving, meeting new people, making chitchat, and trying to remember names. On the other hand, our natural shyness and reticence makes it easier to stay above the fray and avoid getting sucked into distractions. That's a huge asset once you become a top tennis player.

I didn't see much of my dad as a child, because he worked two jobs—he was all about supporting the family while my mother took care of us, physically and emotionally. But as I got deeply involved in tennis, the game became a way to spend time with my dad. He would take me to and from tennis lessons after work, or to junior tournaments on weekends. But even then, it wasn't like my father and I talked a lot. My confidant was my sister Stella; she was a little older, so I looked up to her, and she was the only other serious player in the family. Occasionally the entire family would travel to a junior event. For a while, we traveled around in a beat-up Volkswagen van.

Dad was somewhat intimidating, but if he wasn't my best friend, he wasn't a big disciplinarian, either. I remember one time I said a bad word, and he tried to put soap in my mouth. He wasn't physical with us—we didn't get spanked, but then we didn't do much that would have called for spanking. Parties? Recreational drugs? Delinquent behavior? We just didn't do any of that in our youth. It was especially easy for me: I was very focused on tennis, and I didn't let anything knock me off that trajectory.

The nurturer in our family was my mother, Georgia. She was the compassionate one. She would listen, be there to talk to you, and walk you through whatever was on your mind. My mom has been way under the radar as far as an acknowledged influence goes, but some of my best—and toughest—qualities probably come from her.

She's the sweetest lady on earth—she gave us lots of hugs, she felt our every adolescent pain. But underneath that warmth and deep concern for her family, she was tough.

Mom was born and raised in Salacia, a village near Sparta. She grew up dirt-poor. She had seven siblings, and slept on a concrete floor for a good part of her youth. When her oldest brother emigrated to Canada, he basically took his siblings with him. So my mom landed in North America without speaking a word of English, and ended up working with some of her sisters (she has five, all close in age) as a beautician in the Toronto area.

When Mom was in her twenties, she moved with her sisters to Washington, D.C., and that's where she met my dad—they were introduced by mutual friends. My dad's father had advised him to find a nice Greek girl to marry and start a family with, and Georgia turned out to be the one for Sam. They shared a vision based on the importance of family life and creating a home where their children could flourish.

Partly because my mom is a relatively new American, we were raised with a very strong Greek influence. We have an enormous family support group—I must have thirty cousins, although my life has made it tough for me to cultivate relationships with them. We attended Greek Orthodox church every week, and we went to all kinds of Greek festivals and outings—it was just like that movie *My Big Fat Greek Wedding*. Mom still cooks traditional Greek dishes like spanakopita (a spinach-based dish) and dolmades, and I've heard more than my share of bouzouki music. But we were on the road to assimilation. We never had to wear any of those crazy traditional costumes or anything like that, and we often had spaghetti bolognese for dinner.

When I think about my mom and how poor she was as a child, I realize she had to be pretty resilient and very strong. She immersed herself in a totally foreign culture—as a woman from a traditional society, no less—at age twenty-three. She had family to help, but still—it couldn't have been easy for her.

If I got my calm, reserved nature from Dad, I got my toughness, a share of my resilience, and a measure of my stubbornness from my mom. She helped instill my basic values—showing me that I wasn't going to get anywhere by taking shortcuts. I think I may have gotten my ability to focus absolutely and exclusively on the task at hand from my mother, too. Throughout my career, my mind rarely wandered, and I was never sidetracked by distractions, no matter what I was going through off the court.

Mom had her hands full with the four of us, and my budding talent didn't make it any easier. Stella and I, the two enthusiastic athletes, kind of overshadowed Gus and Marion, and I gradually overshadowed Stella. I guess I was the "golden child," although I've never liked putting it that way. But a lot of the focus was on me. A lot of money was spent on me. At times this led to a little resentment.

Gus was a big surfer and had an active social life, which was a good thing because I was always with Dad. Still, like any kid brother, I occasionally wanted to hang out with Gus and his friends, but you know how Toxic Kid Brother Syndrome works. In that sense, having tennis helped me; I was so focused on the game that I was immune to some of your typical sibling turbulence. I wasn't competitive with Gus in childhood; the age difference of four years meant we lived in different worlds. But I know that my privileged place sometimes bothered Gus. He would have to drive me and Stella to tennis lessons, and I could sense he didn't like that job. I think it was a reaction to not getting enough of Dad for himself; he felt a little left out because Stella and I, especially as we got a little older, were catered to in the family.

Sometimes Gus could be a little bit of a pain in the ass. I remember my dad got him this guitar, and he'd come into Stella's room, or our (my and Marion's) room, and he would start playing really loud and yelling. It was obnoxious, but I guess he just wanted a little attention—he was annoyed at me because it seemed to him that I was being spoiled, so he would just bang away on his guitar.

Stella, who now coaches the UCLA women's tennis team, could do no wrong. She was the perfect daughter, and maybe that was because she was more outgoing and expressive, and kind of up for anything—as well as talented in tennis. It was one of those deals where my parents just felt that if she and Gus were getting into a fight, it was always Gus's fault. I didn't mix it up much with Stella; our common interest in tennis made us allies.

My most powerful memory of Stella is from a day when we were taking a lesson from Robert Lansdorp. (It may come as a surprise, but I almost always shared my lessons with Stella—she had thirty minutes, and I had thirty. It was written in stone.) So this one time, she was at the net and Robert was really banging balls at her. He was being extra mean, which is saying a lot, and she was trying to fend off his shots—almost in self-defense. And she started hyperventilating, and then crying. "Why are you crying?" Robert asked in his gruff voice, feigning disgust. "Come on, toughen up." And Stella turned away from him; she couldn't take his demanding ways anymore. I remember walking over and putting my arm around her and trying to console her. I just said, "It's okay, Stella, everything is going to be all right." It was kind of funny. Here I was, this twelve-year-old kid, consoling somebody: "Aw, don't worry, it's okay." I felt so bad for her that I remember this incident as if it happened yesterday.

My other sister, Marion, played a little tennis and she was pretty good at it. But as the youngest child, she was slightly overshadowed. It wasn't surprising that it happened, because she was introverted, and I think she had a hard time trying to keep up and fit in with the rest of us. Trouble was, Stella and I were always playing tennis, and Gus was a boy and so many years older that Marion really had nowhere to turn. It was sometimes hard for her.

When Marion got a little older, she found God and really blossomed; her faith helped her get through her awkward teenage years, and she made a lot of friends through her church. She eventually became more confident, outgoing, and talkative, and evolved into a wonderful person. I believe in God, though I'm not especially religious. But in Marion I've seen how much faith can do for someone.

In the big picture, we were good kids who got along well, despite the inevitable conflicts and sibling rivalries. If our parents played favorites with Stella and me, it wasn't because they loved us more—it was because of tennis. I think that message somehow got through. I hope it did. And maybe that was why things never got rough or ugly. In some ways, we were an All-American family; in other ways, we were anything but. And we are very close, to this day.

By the age of eight, I was really serious about tennis. The days when I was content to have my mom feed me balls in her spare time were over. I was getting a strong dose of lessons. When I think about my developmental days, I have a vivid memory of my dad having to go to the ATM to take out sixty bucks, or whatever it was at the time, and giving it to me so I could pay Robert Lansdorp.

Cha-ching, cha-ching. There were lots of visits to the cash machine. My dad didn't make a lot of money, but he had put some away from his restaurant business and he had a pretty good job. He needed those resources when the big expenses began to kick in.

Soon after Fischer began advising my dad and taking on his role as the overseer of my development, I settled into a consistent training pattern. Lansdorp was the forehand and groundstroke guy, Fischer was involved in developing my serve, and another local coach, Del

Little, was the footwork and balance specialist. Eventually, I also had sessions on the volley with Larry Easley, a Kramer Club pro who was also the men's tennis coach at Long Beach State University. This was my unofficial developmental team.

The foundations of my ground game were laid by Lansdorp. He's an icon in Southern California tennis circles, legendary for his no-nonsense drill sergeant approach. His fingerprints were, and still are, all over some of the best ground strokes in the game. Almost all Lansdorp protégés developed huge forehands. He teaches a fairly flat, clean, economical stroke, and he was especially good with girls, including Tracy Austin, Lindsay Davenport, Melissa Gurney, and Stephanie Rehe, all of whom were junior sensations and, to varying degrees, successful pros. Robert's best male player, until he started to work with me, was Eliot Teltscher. Ironically, Eliot became better known for his powerful backhand, and that's what I meant when I said that every player has natural tendencies that prefigure how he would turn out, stylewise.

Robert and Pete Fischer didn't get along—Robert flat-out thought Pete was a quack. And that meant something, because Robert was a good guy who already had great credentials when we met. Robert comes across as very tough; he's certainly outspoken and brutally honest. If he didn't care for you, he didn't hide it. Those qualities hurt him, but he was kind of a loner who always insisted on doing his own thing his own way. I don't know if he intimidated Fischer, but they more or less worked around each other.

I was a hard worker as a kid, and I respected Robert. He intimidated me. He's a big guy with huge hands and a very gruff manner. My lessons were on Thursdays, and I remember being in school and feeling kind of nervous, looking at the clock, because I had Robert from 3 P.M. until 4, and as much as I liked taking lessons from Lansdorp, I also couldn't wait until they were over.

When I started playing, it was still the wooden-racket era, and

Robert taught me to hit properly. A few years later, technology would transform the basic tennis racket, and eventually it would be easier for everyone to develop a weapon. But I shaped mine the hard way. Some of the things we did were very basic. Robert would open his racket cover—back then, it was just a soft, zippered vinyl case that covered the racket head down to the throat—put his keys inside of it, and close it back up on the head of the racket. (Robert always had about forty keys, so his key ring was heavy as an anvil.) Then I would practice the forehand stroke with the weighted racket. For a little kid, that was tough, but it taught me to drive through the ball. With Robert, it was all about the sweet spot and driving through the ball.

There was no secret technique in Lansdorp's repertoire. His big thing was repetition, which had a critical side effect: it taught extreme stroking discipline. Robert had this big, supermarket-size shopping cart filled with balls, and whatever we were working on—preparation, taking the short midcourt ball, the running forehand that became my trademark shot—we would do it for an hour, or my half of the hour that I shared with Stella. We did drill after drill after drill.

Eliot Teltscher thinks that Robert has a genius for feeding balls— a job you wouldn't think is that difficult. But Eliot is right; Robert put the ball in exactly the right place, time after time. And we're talking about hundreds of balls an hour, day after day. I hit a million balls and that was important—I had to get that muscle memory, burn it in so it was a natural thing.

One of Robert's favorite tricks was hitting these big topspin shots right at me, jamming me. And remember, this is a very big man who weighed two hundred plus, hitting with a skinny twelve-year-old. Fending off those shots taught me to stand in and go toe-to-toe with him, trading shots. That toughened me up. Robert would stand in a position favoring one leg so that he could get balls out of the cart in a hurry with one hand and feed with the other for hours. He ultimately had hip surgery, and I swear it was because of that leaned-over feeding position. He would take up that post right around the middle of the center service stripe and bang big forehands cross-court for fifteen-minute stretches at a time. It was exhausting.

My running forehand is all Robert, and so is my version of the forehand approach shot from the midcourt—one of the trickiest if least flashy of shots in tennis. This shot can be a putaway, an approach shot, or a rally shot. It's a tough one because it's much easier to hit running side to side than forward and back. When you're moving into the court, you've got to get enough lift on that shot to clear the net, but cover it enough to get good pace and depth (and not drive it long).

I changed my forehand a little as time went on in the pros, using a little more topspin to increase my margin of error. But it's changed very little over the years, and if one of my kids decides he wants to play tennis, and Robert is still on the court, he'd be the man I would ask to teach it. A few years ago, I was at the Riviera Club, where Robert was teaching at the time, and he asked me to hit with this twelve-year-old he was developing. I helped him out and thought nothing of it until a few years later I recognized the girl on television; it was Maria Sharapova. Robert had a sharp eye for talent. He was also good at intuitively understanding who "had it"—who had the potential and grit to be great, psychologically. He figured out your personality and heart. But God, was he tough!

Fischer became a daily presence in our family's life as time went on, and we soon had a comfortable pattern going. I would work with Del Little on Tuesdays, take from Lansdorp on Thursdays, and work with Fischer at the end of his workweek, on Friday. Between lessons and on weekends I played practice matches with other juniors, or went to tournaments.

Little was very close to the Austin family, who were like royalty in Southern California tennis, having produced Tracy, Pam, John, and Jeff—all of whom played on the pro tour, with Tracy leading the way as maybe the most celebrated prodigy in the history of the game. Little taught at the Kramer Club, but he took a lot of kids from there up to his place, near Lomita. The setup there was far from fancy; in fact, the two courts he used were in some kind of trailer park. Little was a great teacher; he would stand in the corner and just run me around, hitting balls to all the different areas of the court, always emphasizing footwork. We did a lot of drills involving the split step and things like that. He was very big on always being in balance.

Fischer's tennis time was limited, because he was much in demand as an endrocrinologist and pediatric growth specialist with health-care provider Kaiser Permanente. But while he wasn't around much to work with me on weekdays, he was always in and out of our house, having dinner with us and talking with Dad. Fischer had a good grasp of tennis style and strategy, and he tried to impart that knowledge to Dad and me. Pete was a pretty good feeder, and I got a lot out of working with him, especially on the serve, which is where things get a little weird.

Pete and Del Little had this thing they called "the Chong." God, it still makes me laugh just to think about it. It sounds mysterious, like something out of martial arts. The Chong had something to do with the way you took your service stance and how you brought your heels together to create a certain angle. I never did understand it, but it was wild to hear Fischer say, "That's right, Chong!"

One of my signature mannerisms is the start of my service motion (some players, including Sharapova, have incorporated this move). I have my left foot up at the baseline, more or less pointing toward the court I'm serving into. Then I slightly shift my weight back, and lift my left toe well off the ground, signaling the true start of my service motion. Pete and Del started me doing that, because it had something to do with bringing my feet together to Chong.

But Chong or not, I did end up with a pretty clean, simple service motion, and that would be a great plus. The more glitches and ticks you have, the more things can go wrong. In later years, Pete often said I was very "coachable." I was just a kid, of course, and I did what all kids do—I soaked things up like a little sponge.

Fischer made another big contribution that I can explain more easily. He taught me to disguise my serve. During lessons, he would have me toss the ball in the air, and then he would call out where he wanted me to hit it, and with which spin, if any. Later, players would say they had trouble reading where my serve was going, or what kind of ball movement it had, and that was all Pete's doing.

Over time, I learned to use my wrist and I had a talent for "pronating," or bending my wrist in a way that enabled me to use the same basic motion to hit different kinds of serves. The kick serve was the only one that was a little different, because you have to toss the ball farther back and to the left to get that big kick, and it's impossible to disguise. But even then, I didn't telegraph my intention as much as most players.

Larry Easley came into play when I abandoned my two-handed backhand and started serving and volleying. Easley, who was terrific with the volley, helped me out. We had moments of serious doubt and struggle during that transition, as I discuss later, and people at the Kramer Club thought I was crazy to change my backhand—especially when my rival Michael Chang gained valuable ground on me as a result. So much for short-term rewards.

I didn't really have heroes, tennis or otherwise, when I was a kid. I didn't have posters in my room, I wasn't a fanatic, obsessed with collecting autographs or anything like that, but tennis became a family affair because of my involvement. We would watch all of the Grand Slam finals at home together. At one point our television was out for a long time. I think it broke and my dad, who thought maybe we were watching too much, decided to take his sweet old time fixing it. That year we went down to the Jack Kramer Club at 6 A.M. to watch the Wimbledon final. I remember that vividly; it was like this big family adventure.

Pete Fischer would sometimes come to the house after dinner with Del Little, who had a lot of old tennis films. My father would set up the old 16 mm film projector, and Del would train it on a white wall in our dining room. And then all of us—my dad, Pete, Del, Stella, and me—would sit there and watch some final between guys like Rod Laver, Ken Rosewall, and Lew Hoad. Pete had this Rod Laver fixation, and I remember watching Laver traipse around the court on the wall of our dining room. I was deeply impressed by how smoothly Laver played—even on grainy, black-and-white 16 mm film.

In the morning, I would go to Vista Grande Elementary at eight and stay until noon. Then mom would pick us all up and take us home. I would eat lunch, change, and head over to the Kramer Club at three, where I would play a set or two with whoever was scheduled that day. There were enough fast-track kids—there's that California tennis advantage—that partners were always in abundance. I played with Melissa Gurney, Joey Ladam, Pete Fitzpatrick, Tom Blackmore, Eric Amend, and others. Some of them, like Gurney and Amend, went on to have pro careers. Others were merely outstanding juniors. Two days a week there was tennis camp at the club, and some days—more often, as time went on—I had a lesson. My day ended around 7 P.M., when I would have dinner back at home, do homework, go to sleep, and wake up—only to do the whole thing again.

It was as regimented as it sounds—and it only became more so as I got older. But in order to be great at something, it really needs to be the focus of your life. In that sense I don't think you can have your cake and eat it, too. You can't have this great social life, a big academic load, and athletic ambitions, and be able to focus on all of them. It takes a lot of time and work to get good at tennis, and those childhood years are pivotal.

It wasn't like I neglected school, either. I was a solid student, maybe in the A– or B+ category. I worked pretty hard, was pretty organized, and was always in the advanced math section of class, as I was very good with formulas. Although I wasn't very verbal or expressive even then, I've always been a good reader. I get bored quickly, though. I've only read a handful of books in my life. The one I really liked and remember best is J. D. Salinger's classic *The Catcher in the Rye*. I read *Catcher* during sophomore year of high school and was very curious about what was going to happen to the protagonist, Holden Caulfield—a kid about as different from me as you could get.

I had no "best friend" at school, or time for the kids I did call my buddies. What I had of a social life was based at the Kramer Club. We tennis kids played together, went to some of the same tournaments together, and all fit in at the club as well—or better— than we did in school. That remained true right up through high school.

The club was overwhelmingly about tennis, although there was the occasional social event, a barbecue or something. I didn't really feel pressured to play, and I had already made this naive and, in some ways, groundless assumption that I was going to make it. I was going to win tournaments and have a lot of money and fast cars and all those trappings that ended up not meaning very much to me at all. I never felt like I had anything to worry about on that score.

I eventually moved along from Vista Grande to Ridgecrest Inter- mediate School. My tennis education and training continued, and when it came time to move on to high school, something pretty dra- matic happened to shape my future. Most of the kids from Ridge- crest moved on to Rolling Hills High School. But for some reason, Gus and I were assigned to Palos Verdes High School. If I had gone to Rolling Hills, I would have been among all my school friends. But at PV, I knew nobody. At the same time, my tennis development was becoming more time-consuming, and that denied me the chance to make new friends.

At 11:30 A.M. every day, I would go home from school. I had nobody to hang out with, because my friends were in Rolling Hills. My life revolved around home and the Kramer Club. I was shy to begin with, but as I got deeper into adolescence, I grew even more introverted. When other kids were thinking about going out or going on dates, I was in an awkward phase. I wasn't interested in girls, I was just thinking about tennis. Stella led a much more active social life; she went on dates, she attended her prom. But that was all okay, because I had no aspirations to be class president; I knew what I was, and what I would be in the future: a tennis player. Around school I became known as "the tennis kid."

Tennis wasn't a big sport in my school the way football was, despite all the tennis talent in the area. I played for the PV team and didn't lose a match for two years. I was a bit of a loner, by circumstance if not choice. Part of it was that I didn't have time for other people. But I wasn't all that interested in what other kids were doing, either. I didn't feel competitive with them, or judge myself against them. I never got in a fight and I didn't envy the football team quarterback, who was the big man on campus. I just lived in a parallel reality that sometimes intersected with the life of an average high school kid.

Palos Verdes has some pretty well-to-do people, and some of the kids embraced that "teenage wasteland" mentality. They were unfocused and bored, but wealthy enough to have no material concerns. They were a little out of touch with the realities of everyday life, except as it pertained to the school social order, or the alternative one that existed among the kids who rebelled. Some of the kids smoked weed on lunch break, there was a little bit of that "secret life of suburbia" going on, but it meant nothing to me. Tennis was great for me in that way; it kept me clear of trouble and blunted whatever teen angst I carried around.

Knowing what my life was like, and how withdrawn I was, you could easily cast me as some kind of tennis robot. I don't think that's accurate, because I truly loved what I was doing. There were days when I rebelled and didn't want to practice. When I just wasn't into hitting balls for a couple of hours yet again. But largely, I stuck with it. A lot of that had to do with Pete Fischer, kind of by default. I mean, it wasn't my dad telling me I had to go and play, it was Fischer encouraging me to keep at it. Dad took a more hands-off approach. He let Pete run the show. I can't remember a single occasion when my father came down on me for not wanting to practice.

There definitely was a part of me that wanted to have fun, that wanted to live like the other kids did, but it never got to the point where I struggled with it. I was motivated, and I had all the support I needed, tenniswise. I was pushed a little bit, sure, but I never felt pressured to do anything; what pressure I did feel was self-imposed. I knew we were putting a lot of money into my development. I knew from our family dynamics that I was getting the lion's share of attention. The entire family was there for me, doing things like driving for six hours so I could play the Fiesta Bowl junior tournament. I saw my father, who never uttered a word of complaint, playing that ATM like it was a slot machine, day after day, to finance my training. *Cha-ching, cha-ching* . . . That was real money, and I knew it. I loved playing, but I also felt responsible for making sure that all that sacrifice and effort—by my dad, my siblings, and my coaches—paid off. I felt it deep inside.

Most of my peers and even teachers had no idea of where I was going with my life. When I started traveling to play tournaments, I sometimes had to take a letter to my teachers, explaining why I would be away for a few days. One math teacher—a Mr. Eberhard—reading of my need to go to South Africa for ten days, rolled his eyes. I could tell exactly what he was thinking: *Who the hell do you think you are, leaving school for ten days? The chances of you making it as a big tennis star are slim to none.* . . . And you know what? I would have done the same thing in his shoes—the chances really are slim to none.

I can see where being "the tennis kid" might seem kind of depressing—a pretty grim, regimented life. I had no dates, no prom. I had endless lessons and practice sessions, year-round. But it was my choice, and I was happy at the time. I have an actor buddy, Luke Wilson, who's had a pretty robust social life. I've often told him, "If I had met you when I was twenty-five, I'd have six majors, max."

As a junior player between the ages of ten and fourteen, I was both a happy-go-lucky kid and an intense little dude who could lose it with the best of them in the heat of combat. I was a racket hurler, if you can believe that, and a baseline grinder with a two-handed backhand. I was always yelling, but it was more from sheer joy and effort than frustration. I remember playing my junior archrival, Michael Chang, and hitting these two-handed backhands and yelling—like, really loud. I showed a lot more of what I was feeling then than I would as a pro.

Dad was pretty strict. I've heard that Björn Borg's legendary self-control and calm and dispassionate focus began soon after his father took his racket away for a few weeks because Björn had been such a bratty junior. Dad never took away my racket but I could feel his disapproval, and Pete Fischer's, when I acted out, and when I sensed that from men who inspired so much respect, the message came through loud and clear.

The pivotal moment in my development probably occurred when I was fourteen, and Pete Fischer persuaded my dad that I ought to switch to a one-handed backhand. I remember that took a lot of persuading on Fischer's part, because I was doing pretty well with the two-hander. But Fischer was a man of convictions that way—he had a big ego and a definite vision of me as the next Rod Laver. That meant winning Wimbledon, and that meant playing well on fast grass courts—something that, up to that point in tennis history, meant playing a one-handed backhand.

In order to appreciate what a difficult and risky gambit that was, you have to look through the prism of junior tennis. The competition at that level is fierce, and unregulated by social approval or media scrutiny. It's dog-eat-dog, or puppy-eat-puppy, out there. Ambitious parents, wild-eyed coaches; they're all jockeying desperately for the upper hand, using every trick in the book to move their kid up in the rankings and gain attention and notoriety. To some degree, the strategy pays off; you can bully, intimidate, and mesmerize your competition in the juniors, although it doesn't work in the pros. Everyone who makes it to the top level has already become immune to most mind games.

Going to the one-handed backhand had obvious drawbacks—I would struggle (in my case, the transition lasted for two years). No junior player in his right mind, and none that I know of, was willing to take a risk of that magnitude. When you're that young, your ego and spirit are that much more tender. If you suddenly end a winning tradition and slip back, everyone starts whispering. You hear the whispers—you *always* hear the whispers. And that isn't even getting into how your parents, if they're the hands-on type, are going to react.

Before I switched to the one-hander, I had a very competitive rivalry with Michael Chang. Michael's parents, Betty and Joe, were very intense, but when it came to Joe Chang vs. Sam Sampras, everything was cool. They got along fine, despite the quality and intensity of our rivalry. I remember the very first time I played Michael, I won in three sets and my dad wasn't happy that I'd lost one. He wasn't happy about that at all. I don't remember all he said, or exactly how he put it, but I distinctly remember that he used a word I've hated ever since: *lousy*. He said I played *lousy* in that set I lost. It's a tough word. But he used to say it when I deserved it: "You played *lousy*."

After I switched to the one-hander, I started losing to all kind of players, everywhere, including Michael—and that was the worst. When you're fourteen, it's hard to take the long view. The facts were simple: Michael and I were pretty even; in fact, I probably had a head-to-head advantage in our rivalry—until I switched to the one-hander. Then he started to hammer me. It was terrible.

What's worse, Michael was the same age as me, and played his age division, while I "played up." That means that when he was playing in the fourteen-and-unders, I was playing in the sixteen-and-unders. And a lot of people looked down on me for doing that: *Pete's doing that because he doesn't want to deal with the pressure. He's playing older kids so he's not expected to win and he can rationalize losing. He went to the one-handed backhand, and he's struggling, so he's ducking the guys he needs to beat. It's a cop-out.*

You can argue the playing-up issue either way. There's a lot to be said for taking on the pressure of beating the people you're expected to beat day in, day out. I know, because that's what I eventually did during my entire pro career. For me as a junior, though, the dynamic at work was Fischer's conviction that I needn't worry about how I fared against my peers; I had to think long term, and where the game I played would take me in the long run. Fischer was very stubborn about that, and my dad trusted him.

To us, it was always about playing the *right* way, trying to develop a game that would hold up throughout my career. It was a calculated risk. If it didn't pay off, it would have shown that I was either not good enough or delusional. On the other hand, some of those juniors were like starving guys, eating everything on the table while the eating was good. They didn't think long term, they lived and died by their daily results, ignoring the fact that what worked in the juniors (like endless soft, arcing rally shots) wouldn't necessarily be useful on the pro tour.

There's another factor in this discussion. The great challenge in junior tennis is avoiding pressure, because it can be huge, just huge—especially at the nationals level (the most important of the junior events, open to kids from every different USTA geographic section). By putting pressure on myself to develop a great game, I had less pressure to win. These days, I tell kids that the way I grew up, it wasn't about winning. It was about playing well, about playing the "right" way. That approach helped me enjoy the game and develop mine to its maximum potential.

As I kept playing through that transition, I saw how much pressure to win some kids had placed on them, and what it did to their ability to compete. I can honestly say I never felt that pressure, not from my dad and not from Pete. It was never like, "Okay, you have to go out there and win this match."

Another very valuable side effect of playing up and making a radical change in my technique was that I learned to lose. A champion is supposed to hate to lose, and it wasn't like I was ever crazy about the idea. But I learned to deal with losing without having my spirit or confidence broken, which would help me immensely over time, not just in the big picture but even in specific matches when I found myself in a jam. Fear of losing is a terrible thing.

That may explain why I developed a trait that served me well through my entire career, although few people ever made note of it (probably because it had a lot to do with something I *didn't* do, instead of something I did). I didn't choke. Not as far as I can ever remember. Don't get me wrong: I had bad days, matches in which I froze up because I felt overwhelmed, or in which I never got my game together. There were days when I lacked determination, and lost. But choking is different. Choking is being in a position to win, and then experiencing some critical failure of nerve or spirit. That never happened to me. And I can't help but think it was because I was never afraid to lose.

It didn't hurt my cause that as competitive and wound up as I could get in the heat of the moment, I was basically easygoing and had no trouble letting go of a loss. In fact, around the Kramer Club my nickname was "Smiley." Martin Blackman, a former Stanford player who had a solid pro career, remembers playing me in the finals of the consolation round in the same tournament two years running. The first year, when I was still using the two-handed backhand, I beat him. The second year, when I was already in transition to the one-hander, he creamed me. But both of those years, he remembered, I came loping up to the net to shake hands after the match with the same goofy grin plastered on my face. I wouldn't say that the result didn't matter to me; I just trusted my mentors and took the losses in stride.

It's an easy thing to overlook, but always remember that everyone is different. There is no one-size-fits-all formula for development; if there was, a dozen or more players would all stand atop the record book, with exactly two Grand Slam titles each. I wouldn't suggest that, say, Michael Chang would have benefited from going to a one-handed backhand, or that he would have won Wimbledon if he had made the change. A lot of other factors would also have to have fallen in place for that to happen.

What I am saying is that it's wise to look at your game and take the long view—where can your natural athletic inclinations take you in five, ten, fifteen years? Given Michael's size and the pace he generated, it would have been silly to try to create a power-based serve-and-volley game for him. It was clear in a dozen ways that he would be most effective as a counterpunching baseliner.

Everyone is different emotionally and mentally, too. Are you malleable, or rigid? Are you patient, or attracted to risk? Do you seek attention and approval, or are you content to work hard, keep your head down, and just win? Do you have the emotional strength to handle losing, or do you need the shot of confidence winning on a daily basis can provide? Do you have all the qualities—some of which have nothing to do with how you strike the ball, or what grip you use—that potentially add up to a Hall of Fame career?

In spite of the struggle I had making the transition from two-handed grinder to all-purpose player, the junior experience was big fun. I loved the traveling and staying in hotels. I thought that room service was the coolest thing on earth. Dad was a big Denny's guy, so when we were on the road we always found a Denny's, and the simple act of going out to eat—sitting in one of those Naugahyde-covered booths, with a laminated menu in hand—was a real treat. Plus, I had Stella with me. She was going through some of the same things as I was, even though she was two years older. She was really good, too, so she was a role model and a source of comfort to me.

My Southern California section had some great players in it. In addition to Michael Chang, we had Jeff Tarango and a few others who formed a team when we traveled to national tournaments like the Easter Bowl. But when I played our big SoCal event in Whittier, Chang, Tarango, and others of their ilk were my big rivals.

My dad got along with just about everybody. There are no crazy stories about Sam Sampras the way there are about some of the other parents. My dad never got into a shouting match with another parent, much less a fistfight. He always took the high road. And I was a compliant kid.

I never knew what was going to happen next, in terms of my development. I knew I was destined to be a tennis player, but at fifteen, sixteen years of age, I was just trying to figure out my game. Pete Fischer was busy teaching me how to play a serve-and-volley game, and even though I wasn't on a fast-track junior career, Glenn Bassett, the coach at UCLA, was already coming around, trying to pre-recruit me for the Bruins. That was flattering, but the bottom line was that I wasn't winning national titles; I was pretty good in my USTA section—admittedly, one of the toughest sections—but that was about it. All the while, I was concentrating on getting better, not winning. I implicitly trusted Pete Fischer and what he was doing with my game.

My father was, in many ways, the most potent, if unobtrusive, force in my evolution. His words and opinions carried great power in my life. I remember playing David Wheaton when I was twelve and he was just a little older. I beat David, who later had a good pro career, in the second round of the clay-court nationals when he was the number two seed. It was a really big win for me, and afterward a local reporter sought me out for an interview. That was great; I felt like the king of the world.

The next day, on the very same court, I lost something like 6–1, 6–0, to Mal Washington. I mean, he really schooled me. So after that match, the same reporter went over to Mal and got an interview from him. My dad pulled me aside and said, "You see that guy who talked to you yesterday? Now he's talking to Mal, because it's all about how good you are every day, not one day."

That's how Dad was; he just cut to the chase. And that's how I turned out to be, later in life. Call it being a realist, call it being hard-nosed. It's all the same. I felt bad about losing to Washington that day, and my dad had to add a little fuel to the fire to make sure I didn't forget the lesson. I had played lousy. What I did yesterday no longer mattered. It's always about today and tomorrow.

1986–1990

KEY MATCHES . . .

March 1988, Indian Wells, second round

P. SAMPRAS	7	6
E. TELTSCHER	5	3

August 1989, U.S. Open, second round

P. SAMPRAS	5	6	1	6	6
M. WILANDER	7	3	6	1	4

September 1990, U.S. Open, final

P. SAMPRAS	6	6	6
A. AGASSI	4	3	2

YEAR–END RANKING . . . 1988: No. 97

1989: No. 81

1990: No. 5

A Fairy Tale in New York

My journey to tennis stardom was a pretty straight path that I traveled quickly, thanks to my great developmental environment. But there were uphills and downhills, and my toughest challenge was changing my mind-set from grinder to attacker. I had to learn to start thinking differently, and more.

A grinder can lay back, waiting for a mistake, or tempt you to end points too quickly. An attacker has to think a little more: Flat serve or kicker? Charge the net, or set up a groundstroke winner? Is my opponent reading my serving pattern or shot selection? As a serve-and-volleyer, you attack; as a grinder you counterattack. The basic difference between attacking and defending is that the former requires a plan of attack and the latter calls for reaction and good defense. In both cases, execution is paramount.

Early on, I had to play attacking tennis with a so-so serve; the shot would not jell for me until around the latter half of 1989. Have you ever seen a bowler in cricket throw the ball with that stiff, roundhouse motion? It's an exaggeration, but my serve was a little like that. I got the ball to the right place, with decent power and spin, but the loose, whiplash swing, the explosive snap—those were yet to develop.

But the upside as I grew into my attacking game was that my emerging talents and personality were well suited to the style. As I became an attacker, my athleticism began to emerge; as a result, my entire game and attitude changed. But I made one big mistake. As I began to rely more and more on my natural athleticism, I worked less diligently. Some of that had to do with the normal rite of passage to manhood. As I approached sixteen, seventeen years of age, I became more introverted. I started to experience feelings of insecurity. I had a lot going on internally, and in some ways my tennis suffered. My maturation was a drawn-out process, and I more or less marked time, tenniswise. But I did reasonably well—well enough to begin testing the waters at pro events. I had a breakout in 1988 at sixteen, at the U.S. Pro Indoor tournament in Philadelphia.

It was a fitting place to pop onto the scene. The Pro Indoor was an established event with a great tradition, run by a couple of old-school tennis types who were part of the game's establishment, Ed and Marilyn Fernberger. The Fernbergers ran a classy event; the U.S. Pro Indoor was a fixture on Philadelphia's winter athletic calendar, and it had always been at the forefront of the tennis boom. The event was played in February in the cavernous Spectrum arena (capacity seventeen thousand), then the home of the NHL Flyers and NBA 76ers.

The Fernbergers had been dedicated tennis aficionados since forever; they wooed and consistently got the support of the best players, including Aussie icons Rod Laver and Ken Rosewall. The Fernbergers flew in former champions as their guests. On any given night, the hospitality suite at the official tournament was open until three or four A.M., and players, officials, and even press mingled freely and sat around talking tennis with tournament guests like Don Budge, Vic Seixas, and John Newcombe. The Ferbergers routinely flew in a planeload of British reporters to give the event added prestige.

I went to Philly to play in the qualifying draw in February of 1988. The main draw at an event has a few places reserved for the survivors of the qualifying tournament, which can be a pretty grim experience. It's often played at a local club or in a big gym, and it generally attracts few or no spectators. The players are journeymen, declining veterans, and still-developing talents fighting it out, hoping to make the big show.

I battled my way through the qualifying, and was most impressed when I went to the Spectrum to practice as a main-draw player. The painted cinder-block hallways under the stadium were lined with posters of Bruce Springsteen, Rod Laver, Elton John, and others. The tournament picked up my expenses—hotel, meals, transportation—and that seemed like a really big deal. But my euphoria was short-lived: in the main draw, I lost to Sammy Giammalva in the first round. However, I'd gotten a taste of the big time.

A few weeks later, Gus and I went to Indian Wells together, and we stayed in this really crappy motel. It was a run-down joint where you parked your car right in front of your door and you could hear people walking by at all hours. I ended up making it through the qualifying tournament there as well. Therefore, as a main-draw player, I got a free room at the posh Hyatt Grand Champions hotel. Gus and I were like two guys who had just won the jackpot in Las Vegas. We walked into that room and our jaws dropped at the sight of the welcome-gift fruit basket. The towels were thick and fluffy. We flopped onto the bed and watched cable and on-demand movies, and they had pistachio nuts—free pistachio nuts, just laying there! I was never so happy in my life.

At Indian Wells, I beat Eliot Teltscher and Ramesh Krishnan, who were top-twenty players. Things were really starting to click, and people were taking notice. Tournaments began offering me wild cards, which are slots in the main draw set aside for use at the discretion of the tournament director, who might give it to a former star, a player coming back from injury, or a local hotshot junior. He could even give it to a bum off the street. Grand Slam tournaments hold open 8 places for wild-card entrants out of the 128 places in the draw. Smaller events dole out fewer wild cards. If you get a wild card, you don't have to face the stress and pressure of qualifying; you're guaranteed first-round-loser prize money, which easily covered whatever portion of your trip you've paid out of pocket.

In my era, wild cards became a tool used by tournament directors to establish relationships with budding stars. When you took a wild card—and they were like gold, especially for aspiring pros—you got all the perks of the main-draw players, like free luxury hotel stays and meals, a courtesy car and driver, and a lavish goody bag. Sometimes the tournament director wined and dined you and your parents, working hard to make an impression so that you might develop loyalty to the event and keep coming back.

By the time I beat Teltscher—a big name at the time—at Indian Wells, the agents were coming around to check me out. Pete Fischer had come down to the desert to bask in the glory, too. By then, I knew that Glenn Bassett, the UCLA men's tennis coach, was going to be disappointed—there was no way I was going to UCLA, or any other college. The die had been cast, and now it was just a matter of exactly when I would turn pro. We decided to make the leap right then, after I beat Krishnan, even though it meant setting up a whole new lifestyle for me. Who would travel with me? What contracts would I sign? Where would I play next—and then after that? We had no idea. It was like, *Okay, now I'm a pro, what happens next?*

My dad and Pete Fischer began dealing with all of the action, and the action was moving fast. In those early days of my pro career, I would often tell myself, *Hey, it's all a learning experience. . . .* It was a hedge against feeling pressure, because I had been thrown off the deep end. One minute, it seemed, I was just a decent amateur, slowly making progress, and the next I was a blooded pro, with a couple of gaudy scalps hanging from my belt and expectations hanging over my head. I was pretty good, but not *that* good. I didn't pop onto the pro tour with a seamless game. I still had lots of holes, and I would kind of fill those in as I went along, reciting my mantra: *It's all a learning experience.*

In the summer of 1988, I finished my junior year in high school and then traveled the tour. I have no strong memories of where I played, but I remember hooking up with Jim Courier to play doubles, and we enjoyed some success. I first met Jim when we were both on the Junior Davis Cup squad, as sixteen-year-olds, and we picked the same agency to represent us, the International Management Group (IMG). Gavin Forbes, whose own dad, Gordon, had been a player (he also wrote the classic book about amateur-era tennis bums, *A Handful of Summers*), was a young guy and he represented both of us.

Gavin saw that Jim and I could benefit from a friendship I was too shy to pursue on my own. So he arranged for me to go and train with Jim in Florida. Compared to me, Jim was worldly and experienced. He had fought his way through the pack at the prestigious Nick Bollettieri Tennis Academy—even as Andre Agassi stole a lot of his early thunder—and, most important, he was talented, ambitious, and blessed with a huge appetite for work.

Jim and I hit it off right away, and he showed me how hard you needed to work to keep your game and fitness at an acceptable level. We would hit balls for three or four hours a day, go to the track to work on our legs and speed, go to the weight room to develop our strength. That was all new to me, and Jim and I became close. We lived together at the NBTA, and through him I met the teaching pro and coach Joe Brandi. I began working with Joe informally, because Pete Fischer still had his day job as a doctor.

Over the next two transitional years, I would get help from various people. By that time, I was high on the radar of our national tennis association, the United States Tennis Association (USTA). Part of their mandate is to develop junior talent, so they hooked me up with a series of coaches on a one-off basis. I went out to see the clay-court expert Jose Higueras in Palm Springs. (Jose would become Jim Courier's coach and guide him to his great French Open wins.) I also spent time in Jacksonville, Florida, with a guy whose game was more similar to mine, Brian Gottfried. He was an old-school-type serve-and-volley player who worked with me on various aspects of the attacking game. We would drill for ninety minutes in the morning, and play matches in the afternoon.

We would do this full day of workouts, and then at 4 P.M. he would drop me back at the condo where I was staying. I did that for a three-week stretch. This was different from the Kramer Club—that had been pretty easy stuff. It was also more lonely.

I broke into the top one hundred pretty quickly in 1989. The first really big win of my pro career was a second-round upset of Mats Wilander at the U.S. Open, where he was the defending champ. Mats was the proverbial "regular guy" and a consummate team player; as I write this, he's still the captain of the Swedish Davis Cup team. But beneath that friendly, laid-back, humble Swedish persona was one of the toughest, most focused, and gritty of Open-era competitors. He proved that in 1988, when he became the first player since Jimmy Connors (in 1974) to win three of the four majors in one year (only Wimbledon eluded him). Mats won with his brains and heart as much as with his steady, adaptable, baseline game.

When Mats and I met in the second round, it was my first appearance on the Louis Armstrong Stadium court at the original USTA National Tennis Center. It was a night match, which made me nervous. I knew we would have a standing-room-only crowd of about eighteen thousand, and that New York fans had a reputation for rowdiness. I was a little apprehensive and still green—emotionally, mentally, and even technically. My forehand—my best shot—was a little shaky, and in the big picture I had no backhand worth the name. But the one thing I suddenly *did* have was a serve. In 1989, I suddenly started serving up aces. Don't ask how, because I can't give you a good answer.

Pete Fischer and Gavin Forbes were both there for my match with Wilander. Serving well, I won it in a barn burner, 6–4 in the fifth. It was a huge win, and a harbinger of sorts because, as crafty and tough as he was, Mats couldn't do enough to offset my advantage in power. Some circumstances also took a little away from the upset. At the time, Mats's father was struggling with a terminal illness, and Mats himself was feeling the aftereffects of his great 1988 season. He was a bit fried, mentally, and soon after the U.S. Open he began a dramatic downward slide in the rankings.

As my small team rode back into Manhattan on the Grand Central Parkway after the match, Gavin said, "You know, you're going to be all over the papers tomorrow." I thought, *Well, this is cool, what's going to happen now?*

What happened was that I won another round and then lost to Jay Berger, winning just eight games in three sets. But I'd made a statement: Mats was a top-five player and the defending champion in New York. I was an American upstart, a total underdog, and the media and fans both at the match and afterward were really into my story.

These rapid changes tied to my sudden success threatened the status quo I had established. There was no way Pete Fischer was going to give up his career in medicine to travel with me. But Pete loved publicity, and he enjoyed taking credit for shaping my game. As I started to become the player he had predicted right before his eyes, it made him a little crazy and greedy. Also, while he was back home in California, I was in Florida training with various coaches whose credentials were far more impressive than Fischer's. He was probably afraid he was going to be cut out of the action, so he tried to retain control even if he couldn't—make that wouldn't—be my regular coach. And he wanted to be compensated for his trouble.

Even before my big upset of Wilander, Pete had started making some huge demands—astronomical demands. Pete wanted something like 25 percent of my Grand Slam earnings, 50 percent of something else. He basically wanted a cut of everything. One night Fischer showed up at our home in California and wrote down his demands on a paper plate: If I achieved a Grand Slam, winning all four majors in the same calendar year, he wanted a bundle of rewards—including a Ferrari Testarossa. That was written on the plate. In fact, I remember that in one story Pete did with *Tennis* magazine there was a picture of him sitting in an umpire's chair, wearing a hat with the logo of . . . Ferrari.

The night Pete waved that plate around was surreal; I remember it in detail to this day. He and my dad had a huge fight. It got very uncomfortable, because Fischer was like family and nobody was trying to screw him out of anything. We knew what he'd done for us, we were grateful, but the long-distance coaching arrangement he proposed was untenable, and his demands seemed outrageous. As he was losing it, emotionally, he seemed bent on blowing up the whole relationship. On another level, it was just funny. I remember thinking: *I'm just a seventeen-year-old kid, I can barely keep two balls in the court, and Pete is talking about me winning a Grand Slam (something only two men in the entire history of the game have accomplished) and getting a Testarossa out of the deal?*

The craziest thing is that it wasn't like Fischer needed the money. He was a wealthy doctor with a great practice, and he lived on a five-acre estate. Our relationship effectively ended the night of the paper plate. My dad quietly decided to cut him off, and he had an even more powerful reason for that than the demands Fischer was making. Dad was worried that I relied too much on Pete, and that my development was being arrested. I needed to get out in the world and learn to deal with it, firsthand.

As the rift with Fischer grew wider, I was resolved to hire a coach. I settled on Joe Brandi. It was a good fit; I was living at the Nick Bollettieri Tennis Academy, and Joe was coaching there. He was tight with Jim and his coach, Sergio Cruz, so the four of us spent a lot of time together on the road. By then, I had a solid idea of how he operated. Joe was an older guy, in his fifties or thereabouts, when he started traveling with me. It was a sweet arrangement: Jim and I practiced and played doubles together (we won the Italian Open in 1989). After workouts or matches, the four of us went out to dinner. I can't exactly say Joe and I really bonded, because he was so much older. Maybe it was better that way, too, because I needed to come into my own as a man, and Jim was there as a buddy and brother-like figure to ease the transition.

My results opened doors for me. Ivan Lendl called late in 1989 and invited me to stay with him and his family at his home in Green-wich, Connecticut (he always pronounced it "Connect-E-coot"). He was the top player in the world at the time, and he lived in this huge mansion. After I stowed my stuff in a guest room, he introduced me to his wife, Samantha, showed me his dogs (Lendl bred German shepherds), and gave me a tour of his grounds and facilities. When I next spoke with my dad, I eagerly told him all I had seen, and he just said that if I worked as hard as Lendl had, I could create that kind of a life for myself, too.

Ivan had that iron man reputation and image, and he definitely could be intimidating, with that clipped Czech accent and hard-assed attitude. But he welcomed me into his home and made me feel comfortable. He was courteous, and curious about me. One thing that struck me right away was that he had our entire week planned out in advance, in terms of when we got up, when we prac-ticed, when we trained, ate, or slept. He was up at six every morning himself; he was very regimented and focused. You could call it ro-botic, I guess; many people did. But he had it pulled together. He knew exactly what he wanted and how he was going to pursue it.

That week, I helped Ivan prepare for the year-end Masters tour-nament (which ultimately morphed into the ATP Finals and later, the ATP World Championships) for the top players of the year. We talked quite a bit that week about working hard. At that stage I was just kind of floating along, and maybe Ivan sensed or saw that, and just wanted to clue me in on what it took to be great. He asked me a lot of questions about my tennis, and about what I wanted to achieve in life.

I got a strong taste of Ivan's own work ethic. Within a day or two, he had me going on these bike rides of thirty miles or so, through the cold and sleet, following a car driven by one of his trainers, who was all snug and warm inside. At the time, Ivan was number one in the world and I wondered what he wanted with me. I don't think he wanted to be my mentor; he had plenty of other things to worry about. I don't think he was trying to get some kind of advantage over me, either, by having me in his shadow. I don't think he was manipulative that way. I think he just wanted to get a feel for me, get a sense of what made me tick because he saw that I was going to be a top player. Also, I think Ivan might have been looking to get into sports management. He had an entrepreneurial spirit and already owned a few indoor tennis clubs. Maybe he was checking me out as a potential client.

A few months later, at the start of 1990, I made the fourth round of the Australian Open. And just weeks after that, I played Ivan in the semifinals of the big indoor event in Milan. I won the first set pretty easily but then Ivan simply overpowered me. This was not the same Lendl with whom I had trained. In competition he was a different animal. One thing he did, after I got off to a fast start, was slow down the pace. It was partly a way to get into my head, because young, impatient players would rather hit and play than think and maneuver.

Up to then, I hadn't run into many guys who could really intimidate me with their game. But Ivan seemed to be on another level. He had that sledgehammer forehand and a tough serve. He could rifle a flat-to-topspin one-handed backhand with the best of them, or use the slice to set up a forehand. He generated so much pace, and moved the ball around so well, that I always felt rushed, like I didn't have enough time to settle into my game, plant my feet, and trade shots with him. The encounter left me shell-shocked. This was one of the big cats of the game, and as kind as he had been to me earlier, he just mauled me.

Philadelphia was friendly to me again in 1990. This time, I won the whole shooting match. After getting into a war with Andre Agassi in the round of 16 (he retired because of a stomach bug after we'd split 7–5 sets), I convincingly took out Andres Gomez, who was on an upward arc that would end up carrying him to a Grand Slam title—his first and only one—in Paris later that spring. My ranking had been climbing steadily, and it took another uptick.

In the months that followed, I kept going deep in tournaments. But I wasn't ready to compete on the clay-court circuit that culminates with the French Open, or Roland Garros. I played just one of the European spring clay tournaments, Munich, where I got waxed by one of the legion of Swedish Dirt Devils, Jonas Svensson. I moved on to the summer grass circuit and, despite having very mixed feelings about grass courts, won a small event in Manchester. At Wimbledon, I lost in straights to Christo van Rensburg—a very effective grass-court player.

I treaded water until the U.S. summer hard-court circuit. At the Canadian Open in Toronto, I met John McEnroe in the quarters. There was one important similarity between Wilander and McEnroe; different as they were, neither could overpower me the way Lendl had done. Oh, John could slice me up and jerk me around, use that can-opener lefty serve to make my returning life miserable, but I always felt like I had the one thing I most needed—time to hit my shots.

When I played McEnroe in Toronto, he was in the waning years of his career. I was comfortable. I also knew him a little bit. It's funny how quickly you get over your awe of a top player when you come onto the tour, especially if he's your countryman and you have the inevitable string of experiences and contacts with him. I can totally understand why Jimmy Connors was always such a loner—so stand-offish and aloof. He wanted his peers—all of them—to *stay* in awe. John had always been nice to me, and so had Lendl. But where Lendl's game still gave me pause, I was in a comfort zone with John, physically and psychologically. At Toronto, I beat him 6–3 in the third, but I lost a heartbreaker to Michael Chang in the semifinals, 7–5 in the third.

When Joe Brandi and I rolled into New York for the U.S. Open in late August of 1990, we bunked together at the Parker Meridien. I wasn't really a city guy; I was a shy nineteen-year-old going about his business from the player hotel. I don't remember if Brandi snored, but I know I slept very well in our shared room, and it was because I had nothing to lose. There was no pressure. About the only other person I spent time with during the tournament was my friend Jim Courier.

I started my quest at Flushing Meadows as a dark horse, although I was definitely on the radar of my rivals, the pundits, and knowl-edgeable fans. Through 1990, I was slowly becoming a better mover and all-around athlete, and my serve—already vastly improved—just kept getting better. There was no magic bullet, coaching or techniquewise. Suddenly the big serve was just *there*, and getting bigger as the months passed.

In the early rounds at the Open, I beat Dan Goldie, Peter Lund-gren, and Jakob Hlasek. Those were solid wins, and each one seemed to increase my momentum. I got hot and stayed hot, playing almost the entire event in the proverbial zone—that tranquil state of mind and body in which nothing can go wrong, you seem to have all the time in the world, the ball looks big as a grapefruit, and nothing can disturb or stop you. If ever there was a "good" time for me to go up against Lendl again, it was then—in the quarterfinals at Flushing Meadows. But the assignment was a tough one. Lendl was a multiple Grand Slam champ with more big titles than McEnroe, and he was gunning to make an unprecedented *nine* consecutive U.S. Open finals. He was at or very close to the peak of his powers and still driven to add to his résumé. This would be different from the Wilander match in '89.

I had reason to hope that I wouldn't be blitzed like I had been in Milan. I had seen Ivan's A game, so there would be no surprises. And my improved serve gave me more offense; it made me a little more dangerous, and that had psychological as well as physical implications. In the six months since I had last met Ivan, I'd grown stronger and sharper. I felt that, and I knew that I could give as good as I got. I was confident that I could put Ivan under as much pressure when I was serving as he put me under when I was returning. But it didn't exactly make me comfortable knowing that the match might be decided by our ground strokes because, in that department, Lendl still had me beat—hands down. My job was to make it a service brawl.

I won the first two sets 6–4, 7–6, and the tennis was high-quality stuff. I was serving big, and my basic strategy was to hold easily and slap a few forehand winners here and there—just enough to take advantage of any momentary lapse or weakness in Ivan's game or resolve. After the second set, though, I made the classic rookie mistake. Finding myself in control, I thought I had it won—ignoring the fact that I was up against a lethal opponent who had found his back against the wall on plenty of other occasions, only to extricate himself. And that's exactly when Lendl's experience and determination kicked into high gear.

Lendl came storming back, with the leverage of eight straight U.S. Open finals and eight Grand Slam titles giving him emotional and physical fuel. He took the next two sets 6–3, 6–4. In the fifth set, though, it seemed that my serve was getting stronger and more dialed-in than it had been earlier in the battle. I began spewing out the aces; I could see he was having an increasingly hard time trying to catch up with the serve. And it was helpful to my cause that even as he was making a furious comeback, I felt no panic. No fear.

When you let a guy off the hook, like I had Ivan, you might hear this little voice: *You had him, you're in trouble now. . . . Don't panic, but this is kind of scary. . . . Play safe . . . play aggressive . . . forget your game, listen to me; we've got to do something!* Listening to that voice is the downfall of a competitor, and if I'd paid attention to it, I would've lost that match. No doubt in my mind. And if I had lost that match, chances are I would pick up that dialogue again in similar circumstances in the future. It's true what they say about winning being a habit. Once you open that Pandora's box of doubt, all kinds of nasty things come flying out. I can't stress how important it is to train yourself to seek clarity at moments of doubt. You have to stay calm and have complete faith in your abilities. It takes a strong mind.

I was able to do that, and it helped me establish a career precedent. With aces pouring off my racket, I won the fifth set going away, 6–2. In the end, it was my game that got me through that situation, not my heart or my mind. But neither of those two organs intervened to screw things up, either. When it was all over, I found myself on a higher plateau as a competitor. It was the match that launched the *Sports Illustrated* headline A STAR IS BORN.

At the time, though, I was oblivious. I just focused on getting ready for a semifinal rematch with McEnroe. I had a day off to prepare, during which I did a few interviews. But I still felt no pressure. It was ironic—as a kid I had been wide-eyed about the prospect of playing on a stage like the U.S. Open, but when I got there, it didn't really feel much different to me than Cincinnati or Toronto. It's a measure of how off the radar I was that McEnroe, on the eve of the match, said, "I can't ask any more than to be playing Pete Sampras in the semis." He didn't mean it as an insult, and I didn't take it as one. Lendl owned Flushing Meadows, and he was now out of the way for McEnroe. I was a stripling, happy with anything the tournament gave me.

It was a godsend that at some level I really didn't know what I was doing. I was simply focused on the job at hand, and unaware of the ramifications my success might have. I didn't have any desperate hunger to be a celebrity or the toast of the town. I liked playing tennis, I felt comfortable playing tennis, and I saw no reason why you shouldn't, or couldn't, play the same way on one court as you did on another. I just thought, *Well, here I am, doing what I've always wanted to do. . . . I'm just going to throw the ball up, serve as hard as I can, and hope I hit the line.* Sports psychologists make a living trying to teach athletes to adopt that attitude, but to me it came naturally. I doubt whether it can be taught, or learned.

I played Mac in the third and final match of Super Saturday, and picked up right where I had left off with Lendl. In the McEnroe match, I hit a few of those jump-shot overheads, which would become a trademark of sorts. But overall, I was popping aces, serving and volleying effectively, and hitting my backhand return really well—and that's always a key to success against a lefty, especially one like McEnroe, who had that vicious southpaw slice that curves away from a righty in the advantage court. I won the first two sets comfortably, he started coming back a little in the third and won it 6–3, but I didn't feel he was getting to my game at all. I still felt in complete control and rolled through him 6–3 in the fourth.

The only good thing about Super Saturday, which for most of my career consisted of the two men's semifinals sandwiched around the women's final, was that it didn't leave you time to overthink the final. Sometimes you had to play that final less than twenty-four hours after the end of your semi, but I was lucky in '90. I wasn't exhausted by the McEnroe match. I did my press chores after that match and ended up staying up pretty late. When I woke up the next day, it was almost time to go out there and play the last match of the tournament.

The guy on the other side of the net the late afternoon of September 9, 1990, was Andre Agassi—a kid, just like me. And he was easy to find over there in his wild, fluorescent, lime green outfit, and big hair.

I couldn't know it at the time, but Andre and I would have a historic rivalry and both wind up in the International Tennis Hall of Fame. In fact, up to that point in our young lives, Andre and I had met on a court just four previous times. We were unfamiliar with each other's games because Andre had played most of his tennis in Florida, while I was a California guy.

The first time we played was on a hard court in a twelve-and-under junior tournament in Northridge, California. Neither of us can remember who won that match, but I still have a strong visual memory of Andre. He rolled up with his dad, Mike, in a huge green Cadillac worthy of a mobster. It was fitting, because the Agassis lived in Las Vegas and Mike worked as a pit boss in Caesar's Palace. Way back then, Andre already had this junior rock star thing going. He was skinny as a rail, but so was I. He already had that big forehand and those quick, happy feet.

Andre and I were supposed to meet at another junior event. In juniors, you often have to play two matches on the same day, and both of us had won our morning match. But for some reason, Andre and Mike disappeared—just up and left the site, enabling me to advance by default. In our first meeting as pros, on the red clay of Rome in 1989, Andre had waxed me, losing just three games. But I had played him even-up in that Philadelphia match I mentioned earlier.

Andre was the clear favorite in the U.S. final. He had shot up to number three in the world, and he had beaten Boris Becker to get to the final. He was an over-the-top showman, but pundits were questioning his ability to win big matches and suggesting that he was more image than substance. That was odd, because nothing was more clear-cut and substantial than scores and results. And by that measure, Andre was the real deal, even though he had been upset in the French Open final by first-time Grand Slam finalist Andres Gomez. The critics, ever ready to heap scorn on Andre in those days, went to town on him after that one. But I wasn't really aware of all that Andre was going through at the time because I had my own fish to fry.

Our two previous pro meetings were not a good preview of the Open final, because my game had grown by leaps and bounds in the summer of 1990. Andre couldn't have had a handle on it, which had to be a little spooky for him—if he was aware of it at all. I didn't put much thought into such things—I was in the U.S. Open final and felt like I had nothing to lose. A great deal of what was going on was way over my head, and any payback that my blissful ignorance would demand—and it definitely would ask a price—was not even on my horizon.

The stadium was packed for our match, but I felt relaxed and comfortable. After the wins over Lendl and McEnroe, I was utterly at ease with the situation and with my game. I had lived a fairy-tale U.S. Open—the kind of tournament, really, that a kid would only invent in a fantasy. It was a saga that deserved a thrilling ending—an incredible see-saw battle, moments of realization, twists and turns in the flow of the match. But it wasn't like that at all.

The match, at my end, was played in a fog of inevitability and invincibility. With my ground strokes working well, the final piece had fallen into place. I was in contact with the Gift. From the start, I was making Andre move around a lot, and he was missing quite a bit. Once again, I was serving huge—it was like I could hit an ace any time I wanted. To this day, I have a visceral memory of that feeling and rhythm. I could feel the ace coming before I hit it: *All right, I'm gonna pop an ace, here it comes—boom! Ace!*

And there it was.

I reached match point with Andre serving at 2–5 down in the third set and stood at the threshold of becoming the youngest U.S. Open winner in history. I looked across at him and he looked very small, very far away. Yet the balls I was swinging at looked as big as grapefruits, and I felt I had all the time in the world to make my shots. Things get a little bent and distorted in the zone.

Andre was bouncing the ball, getting ready to serve. His hair was a little stringy from perspiration and he was almost glowing in that loud, lime green outfit. I got into my receiving crouch. Being up at least one service break and having a match point with the other guy serving is the ideal way to finish a match. There's not a lot of pressure. You're in position to hold one or two more times and end the match. On a medium to fast court, you love your chances as long as you have a solid serve—and don't choke. You're playing with house money; you can take a big cut on the return, risking nothing. Meanwhile, the guy serving to stay alive in the match is feeling the noose tighten.

Throughout his career, Andre generally played fast. He was all business. But at big moments, everything slows down a little—and if it doesn't, you have to make it slow down. That's one of the first and most important things you need to know if you want to close out matches. You need to be deliberate, because it takes great self-control to close matches.

Andre bounced the ball, looking at his shoes, no doubt wondering whether he should go for an aggressive serve to win the point or play it safe and make me win it with a good shot. It's easy in that situation to get overcautious, or overeager. That is one of the oldest dilemmas in the book, but it's still a dilemma I'll take at any time. I want to be the one to control the last point, for better or worse.

Andre bounced the ball one last time and went into that quick service motion of his. I was ready. Some six thousand miles away, at a mall near my family's home in Palos Verdes, a slight man of Greek descent was walking around in a shopping mall with his wife. That was my mom and dad; they were too nervous to watch the match, so they decided to go shopping instead.

Andre hit a good serve, and I returned with the backhand. It was a defensive, fend-off return that fell kind of short. He moved in to take a relatively easy forehand and he flubbed it, driving the ball into the net.

I put my arms in the air, and looked over at the player guest box. It was full of cheering people, but the only guy I knew in there was Joe Brandi. Across the continent, in that mall, my dad and mom were still wandering around, not knowing what had happened. It was some time before they strolled by an electronics store and saw that the televisions were all tuned to the U.S. Open trophy presentation ceremony.

The kid on camera accepting the U.S. Open men's singles trophy was me. I had arrived, at blinding speed. But now I found myself in territory that was unfamiliar, and for which I was unprepared. There would be payback, because nobody gets a free ride.

Chapter 3

1990–1991

KEY MATCHES . . .

September 1991, U.S. Open, quarterfinal

P. SAMPRAS	2	6	6
J. COURIER	6	7(4)	7(5)

November 1991, ATP World Championships, final

P. SAMPRAS	3	7(5)	6	6
J. COURIER	6	6	3	4

November–December 1991, U.S.A. vs. France, Davis Cup, final (Lyon, France)

P. SAMPRAS	4	5	4
H. LECONTE	6	7	6

P. SAMPRAS	6	6	3	4
G. FORGET	7(6)	3	6	6

YEAR–END RANKING . . . 1991: No. 6

That Ton of Bricks

When I won the 1990 U.S. Open, I found myself the youngest American champion since the beginning of the twentieth century. You might think that savoring a huge win is part of the deal, but you don't have time to do that, because the real chaos begins the moment the last ball is called. You've earned the right to take a deep breath, sit back, and savor the moment. But it doesn't happen that way. The only time you have is those few moments between the handshake with your opponent and the trophy presentation and speeches. Everything that follows, for hours, is a kind of dog and pony show as you make all the appointed rounds of the media and accept congratulations from anyone whose credential gets him near you.

Of course, in '90 I wouldn't have known what to savor; I was too young to appreciate what I'd done. After the match, I kind of floated through it all in a happy daze. I was shell-shocked, and so were a lot of other people. I had been in the zone. None of the weaknesses or green elements in my game came into play. Pressure? What did I know from pressure? I was a kid who just threw up the ball, hit it, and watched as it hit lines, one after another, time after time. And if you hit lines, nobody is going to beat you, period.

My family back at home was stunned, too. It took me forever to get back to the Parker Meridien hotel in Manhattan after the final, and the first thing I did was call home. When Stella got on the line, she was crying and I grew alarmed. "What's the matter," I asked. "Why are you crying?"

She was crying because she was so happy; everyone else at home was feeling pretty good, too. Dad was in a great mood. I knew that on this occasion, there was no way he could use that dreaded word, "lousy." It was satisfying to know that all that money he had poured into my development, the endless hours various members of my family had spent ferrying me around to lessons and tournaments, all the sacrifices the entire family had endured to enable this to happen— all that was now justified.

That evening I clearly remember Joe Brandi saying, "Well, Pete, this is where your work *really* begins." At that moment, I didn't know what he was talking about. Winning the Open was something that just kind of happened and it was definitely cool. I'd had a blast in New York. But the big question left in the wake of my win was one of which I was blissfully ignorant: how would I handle the new-found fame and the expectations that came with it?

I'd be crazy to look back at winning that first Open title with regret, but I honestly wish I had been a little older. I wish I had been a little better developed, both as a player and a person, a little wiser to the ways of the world and what it expects of you and how it judges you. I didn't know it then, but that win was a one-way portal; once I went through it, there would be no turning back. Maintaining a high position was a big responsibility and it called for a lot of work and a certain kind of maturity and toughness that I lacked. There were tricky times ahead.

In the hours after the match, my agent at the time, Ivan Blumberg, was going crazy. He was giving me minute-by-minute updates: "Okay, we've got *CBS Morning News* lined up." "*Good Morning America* wants you." "Do you want to do *Larry King Live*?" I was just like, "Okay, okay, great. . . sure!" But I had no idea what he was talking about. I was a shy, introverted kid, and I had not undergone the kind of media training that is routine for up-and-coming players today.

It's a pity that in today's game, going to college is no longer an option for a gifted player. At one time, right up to the early years of the Open era, when the United States still dominated tennis and set the tone and values of the game, most of the more promising players went to school—powerhouse, traditional tennis universities like UCLA, USC, Stanford, Pepperdine, and Trinity (the one in San Antonio, Texas). The kids had a "normal" late adolescence, and in the summers between semesters they played the major tournaments. That all changed as the big money came into the game and forced people to focus exclusively on tennis at ever-younger ages.

The rewards and opportunities that came my way for winning a Grand Slam were mind-boggling. Phil Knight, the founder of Nike, was in the stands the day I won the U.S. Open, presumably watching his star client, Andre. He was so impressed by my performance, he wanted to sign me up. But I would later learn that he never got the chance; Blumberg had jumped the gun before Knight could get into the bidding war. Besieged by shoe and clothing guys as I became more and more of a force at the tournament, Blumberg watched the numbers grow and when Italian sportswear company Sergio Tacchini guaranteed me a million dollars a year for the next five years, Blumberg decided he couldn't let that offer pass. He signed me with Tacchini before I played my quarterfinal. By the time I beat Andre, I probably could have named my number for Nike, but I was already locked down by Tacchini.

People bombarded Blumberg after my first Open win; they wanted me for exhibition matches (usually one-night stands against a fellow pro, with the result having no bearing on your official ranking). I was offered product endorsements, one-off appearances, charity events. . . . I had walked into the USTA National Tennis Center a few weeks earlier very much in the red, careerwise, with memories of my dad playing that ATM like a slot machine. At the end of two weeks, I was well into the black and a made man. I was a nineteen-year-old millionaire, but I didn't really think about that, either. Nothing about what I had accomplished sank in, except that I had won my national title.

I returned to Los Angeles the following day via a connecting flight. When I got off to change planes, a CNN crew ambushed me at the airport. Another television crew had gone to Palos Verdes High School, stalking my sister Marion. All of that struck me as weird. Johnny Carson called, too, and it finally hit me: this was a big, big deal. It might've started as just another tennis match to me, and an occasion on which I had nothing to lose, but it became a life-altering event. Soon I would have to deal with something I had not known in my entire life: pressure. The pressure to defend my position, the pressure to carry myself like a man and champion, the pressure to meet demands and obligations that came with my new station and wealth, the pressure to take on the obligations that come with being a "professional" anything, and, most demanding of all, the pressure to win, day after day, round after round, to hold my new position and potentially improve on it.

It might have been easier if, like a football player, I had the support of teammates and could play just once a week. But my game is played by individuals on at least four major surfaces (grass, hard court, clay, indoor carpet), almost year-round. At most tournaments, you have to beat four to seven guys to win. Those guys all play different styles and have different qualities. Just compiling a book on the guys I would run into, roughly the top hundred players in the world, would be a massive, two-year job. And while you could count on meeting the top players in later rounds, there was no telling whom you might encounter in the first few rounds. In that way, tennis is, more than any other sport, a crapshoot.

One thing was for certain: I now had a huge bull's-eye permanently tattooed on my back.

• • •

My next event was Stockholm in late October, and I struggled through three three-set matches (including one that I won by a third-set tiebreaker over the flashy Czech shotmaker Petr Korda), and was happy to reach the semifinals, where I lost to a guy who would be one of my career rivals, Boris Becker. He handled me, four and four, with a rough, physical game that was similar to Ivan Lendl's.

I won just three matches in my next three events on the traditional fall European indoor circuit, even though the fast indoor carpet used at most of the indoor circuit events suited my emerging game. There were two giant events on the winter European circuit: the Paris Indoors (later the Paris Masters), and the season-ending ATP finals. The ATP (Association of Tennis Professionals), which started as the players' union, is like the PGA. At the end of every year, the top eight players compete in the ATP Finals, or World Championships (lately, the event has been called the ATP Masters Cup). The players are divided into two groups of four; each group plays a round-robin, and the two men in each group with the best record in that portion go on to the four-man-knockout semifinals and final.

The round-robin was a disaster for me in 1990. I got just six games off of Andre, and I lost to Stefan Edberg in straight sets, so I failed to make the semifinals. But I soothed the pain of that performance with a huge payday at a brand new and somewhat controversial event, the $6 million Grand Slam Cup.

That tournament was created by the International Tennis Federation, which is the parent group of the various national federations (like our United States Tennis Association). Those affiliates of the ITF control the respective national championships, which over time evolved into the most important tournaments on the calendar. The Grand Slams, or majors, are basically the "open" (meaning open to anyone who qualifies, based on rankings) national championships of Australia, France, England, and the United States. In order to push back against the growing power of the ATP, the ITF decided that they would stage the Grand Slam Cup as a rival event to the ATP Finals. The GS Cup would bring together the top performers in the four majors for a big year-end event. It's a legitimate idea, but we already had the ATP Finals, so all the GS Cup did was confuse people—and dump tons of money on the players.

The Grand Slam Cup was based on a points system that measured the top sixteen performers in the majors, so there were always a few guys in the event who just had a good run at a major or two, and thereby qualified for the event. The prize money was insane; John McEnroe publicly criticized the event, calling the payday "obscene." Even first-round losers were lavishly compensated, taking home six-figure paychecks, while the winner earned a mind-blowing $2 million (losing semifinalists took home a mere $450,000). Unlike the round-robin of the ATP Finals, the GS Cup was a knockout event with a sixteen-man draw from the start. This meant that a guy who had played over his head at one or two majors and qualified for the Grand Slam Cup was looking at a payday he was unlikely ever to see again.

The surface at the GS Cup was fast carpet, but I got mired down in three-set battles that I was lucky to win. I took out one guy who was lucky to be there (Russia's Andrei Cherkasov), one who would emerge as my chief Wimbledon rival (Goran Ivanisevic), and my childhood rival—and the only guy from my Golden Generation to have won a Grand Slam title at that stage—Michael Chang. That brought me to the final against Brad Gilbert.

Gilbert, who went on to become more famous as Andre Agassi's coach and a television commentator than he had been as a player, was renowned for, as the title of his own book put it, winning ugly. Unlike McEnroe, Brad found nothing obscene about the money and played his heart out to get to the final. But I never had much trouble with guys who played ugly and won in straights.

• • •

That year ended okay, and it prefigured the roller-coaster ride I would take in 1991. There were two reasons for my fluctuating results, and I could control one but not the other. My game was still developing. My serve-and-volley game was reliable, but I had great and not-so-great days with my return game (especially on fast surfaces), and with my ground strokes. That was the part I couldn't control. The part that I could've controlled had to do with commitment—the desire to play my best and leave it all out there, win or lose, every time I stepped on the court.

Winning the Open had dramatically improved my lifestyle. I could eat in the best restaurants and play golf wherever I wanted, and was catered to by people, including complete strangers, in whatever I wanted. Materially I was comfortable, but I was also uneasy in my own skin. At the same time, the pressure that came along with being a U.S. Open champ—the guy who suddenly had a bull's-eye on his back—was very quietly and slowly wearing on me. I became a little sullen and withdrawn. I resented the expectations that people had of me.

Although I missed the Australian Open, I started 1991 on a pretty good note at my old standby tournament, the Pro Indoor in Philly. I made it to the final, notching up another win over McEnroe, but Lendl, perhaps still stung by my win over him at Flushing Meadows, wore me down and beat me in five sets in the final. I made it out of the second round in just one tournament between the end of Philadelphia and Wimbledon, and that was a relatively minor event in Orlando. Even there, I lost in the semis to Derrick Rostagno, one of those guys who was occasionally a giant-killer but never played consistently well against his peers.

I stank the joint out at the big warm-up for Wimbledon, the tournament at London's Queen's Club. I lost to barely known Mark Keil in straights in the first round. Although I bagged a semi at Manchester I was beaten by Goran Ivanisevic. At Wimbledon, I crashed in the second round, and by then I just wanted to get off the grass and away from London as fast as I could. The truth was that grass baffled and frustrated me, even though I was theoretically groomed to be a guy who would play like four-time Wimbledon champ and grass-court wizard Rod Laver.

The cure for my grass-court blues was right on the horizon, though, because the American hard-court season starts right after Wimbledon. I always liked the laid-back atmosphere at those events, and I was first and foremost a hard-court player. I tore it up in the summer, getting a little revenge for a spring that you didn't have to be Sam Sampras to call "lousy." In the three big summer events I entered—all of them basically tune-ups for the U.S. Open—I made three finals and won two. I beat Brad Gilbert in Los Angeles and Boris Becker at Indianapolis. At Cincinnati, the biggest of those three events, though, I lost to the tricky southpaw Guy Forget. But I was in good shape for the Open.

I got off to a great start at Flushing Meadows, with Joe Brandi by my side. I gave up just five games to a good fast-court player, Cristo van Rensburg. I was clubbing Wayne Ferreira into submission in the second round when he retired with an injury. I dropped a tiebreaker set in my next match, and a poorly played first set in the fourth round to a talented but overshadowed American of my own generation, David Wheaton. All the while, though, the pressure was mounting. I was the defending champion, and I was coming to understand something: the greatest challenge in my sport is defending a major championship. Period. Everyone is gunning for you.

All the pressure was quietly building, and I carried it into my quarterfinal match with Jim Courier; it was on my back like a ton of bricks. When we met that day, the friendship between Jim and me was already cooling down. Our gifted generation was emerging, and we were becoming rivals. Michael Chang had, surprisingly, set the bar for all of us when he became the first to win a Grand Slam (the

French Open in 1989; Michael was just seventeen). I was next, in 1990. Andre made the third final of his career at Roland Garros in 1991, and that's where Jim made his move, inflicting another bitter and unexpected loss on Andre. So Jim, Michael, and I each had a major, Andre had been to three finals, and from then on it would be every man for himself. Each of us was trying to carve out his niche, and looking to separate from the pack. Trying to sustain a friendship under those intensely competitive circumstances would have been a sham, and we all knew it.

I felt anxious about my match with Jim, even though I had tagged him in straights in two of the three big hard-court events that summer. I was a little shaky and tight in the early going; my nerves were getting the better of me. I also chose to play Jim from the baseline, which was a mistake necessitated by my poor serving. By contrast, Jim was highly focused and on top of his ground game. I won just two games in the first set. I lost the next two in tiebreakers, 7–4 and 7–5, respectively. As I said in the interview afterward, "I felt like I was on my back foot and he was on his front foot. I certainly wasn't going out there to try and lose, but today, not serving well, I had to stay back a little too much, and he was wearing me down from the backcourt."

Still, it's not like I folded up in those tiebreakers. I was struggling with my serve, and I made more than two dozen backhand errors. In a larger way, I was just confused and writhing from the pressure. Another comment I made in that fateful press conference shows just how lost I was: ". . . There was a lot of pressure involved. I don't even know how to explain it. It's not exactly like a release, but now I won't have to be that thing that everyone was talking about and looking at and criticizing. It's over, it's done with, and now I can just go back to being myself."

Even I am surprised today at how bitter and defensive that sounded. What's worse, another sentence I uttered during the press conference would haunt me for a long time to come. At one point, I admitted, "I feel like a ton of bricks has been lifted off my shoulders." Jim followed me into the interview room, and when my comment was related to him, he carefully replied in that low-key way of his: "There are a lot of guys out there wishing they had that load of bricks on their shoulders."

That was all the press needed; they were off and running, and I was embroiled in the first real controversy of my career. I was able to avoid the blowback from my comments the day after I made them because, since I wasn't entered in the doubles, I just left town as soon as possible after my loss. But in New York over the next few days, reporters sought out player after player, looking for analyses of my comments as they worked on stories about my character.

One guy who called me out was Jimmy Connors, who was still in New York because he was in the midst of that great late-career run that captured the imagination of the entire nation. That was both good and bad luck for me. Jimmy's heroics had become the main story of the Open, so that took the heat off me. On the other hand, Jimmy's own reaction to my words was broadcast from a huge bully pulpit. In a good example of standard-issue Connors self-promotion, he said, "Here I am almost forty years old and busting my hump and these young guys are happy to be losing. I don't know about these young kids anymore. . . ."

When the comment reached me, it stung. I was always sensitive to what Jimmy said about me and my whole generation. As much as we—meaning the "stars"—say we don't care about what people say, we do. And one way or another, we hear everything. Jimmy had been reasonably friendly toward me, but I always felt that he didn't go out of his way to give anyone in my generation credit. We were stealing his thunder. He would just say things like, "I brought the ball to the five-yard line, it's up to them to take it in. . . ." I understood, even then. Jimmy was never close to his peers; he saw everyone on the planet as his competitor, and he was on his way out of the game, clinging to the last rays of glory. I was fine with that; his clinging didn't bother me.

Jimmy's comment added fuel to the fire, and the incident took on a life of its own. The story was no longer just about what happened at the Open and what I said about it, it was about what Jimmy Connors had said, and then it became about how I felt about what Connors had said, and so forth. . . . That's the media snowball effect.

It's not easy being called out by a great player, but there are ways you can rationalize anything. So in my own mind, I had a problem—or I didn't have a problem. My loss to Courier was symptomatic of something—or it was just a tough loss. I had exposed a deep fault line in my competitive makeup—or I was just a little out of sorts and had bad luck in the tiebreakers. . . . I wasn't certain what was going on.

But the controversy touched on some realities that, one way or the other, would have to be faced, and how I responded would have a shaping influence on my career. At the time, though, I kind of hid from the significances. Many years later, Jimmy and I happened to be sitting a few rows apart at a Los Angeles Lakers game, and I decided to reach out to him. I got his attention, and we exchanged pleasantries. I asked for his telephone number and called him a few days later. We scheduled a round of golf, played it, and that was the end of our communication. It may be surprising, but Ivan Lendl, who many people thought was a cold fish, was a stronger rival as well as a better, warmer friend and role model than Jimmy.

One odd thing about the "ton of bricks" incident is that all I had really done was tell the truth about how I felt, but you all know that line Jack Nicholson famously said in *A Few Good Men*, "You want the truth? You can't handle the truth!" I felt it was a little like that in New York in 1991. I gave the press a sincere, open statement about what I was going through, and I got hammered for it.

I know what the problem was: theoretically, I came across as sounding happy rather than bummed out about having lost my title. But I say "theoretically" because anyone in that interview room that day knew darned well that I wasn't happy, even if I did feel relieved. I learned a lesson that day: some things are better left unsaid. I should have phoned in some trite, stock answer about how devastated I was, and how I was going to focus "110 percent" on my next tournament.

The "ton of bricks" episode ended a Grand Slam year in which I ran into a lot of bumpy air. I was struggling, and after the U.S. Open everyone knew it. My character became an issue. But I don't think people understood that I was very much a work in progress. I've never been very interested in gossip, or analyzing other people intensely, especially those whom I don't know. I've always been a live-and-let-live kind of guy. So seeing how people focused on my character, and picked apart the things I said and did, made me uncomfortable. I was feeling a bit of heat, but I wasn't the only one. Andre Agassi, 0–3 in Grand Slam finals, was also dealing with "character" issues and getting beaten up pretty badly by the press.

Things were simmering under the surface on a few fronts as I took off for the post–U.S. Open indoor swing. And one of the most turbulent issues was my coaching situation. Joe and I both freaked out, in different ways, after I won my first U.S. title. I was so young that it was hard for us to have an easy, mature relationship. We both knew my game wasn't as developed as it might have looked, and now we were looking at defending a reputation. How were we going to cope with the pressure?

Unfortunately, Joe had never played the pro tour, so there was a dimension of my life that was unfamiliar territory for him. That put Joe, who wanted to do the right thing, under a lot of strain. During the 1991 Open, while I was progressing toward the "ton of bricks" episode, Joe was often in the hotel bar, having a few glasses of wine. It's a lonely life on the tour for a coach who hasn't bonded fully with a player. He has to be there all the time—even when he doesn't have a lot to do.

But while I was struggling, I was deeply entrenched in the top ten. I was callow in many ways, but I could tell Joe was getting nothing out of his job. I've always had pretty good radar for what I need, coachingwise, so I decided to tell Joe that, for everyone's benefit, I needed to make a change. I wanted to do it when we were back in secure surroundings at the Nick Bollettieri Tennis Academy.

It was pretty weird—there I was, at nineteen, about to "fire" a guy more than twice my age. I just told Joe that I appreciated all he had done but that I felt our relationship had run its course. Basically, that was it. And he got it. Not just that, I actually think he felt relieved. For the rest of my career, I always did the unpleasant job of firing someone instead of leaving it to an agent, my dad, or some other third party. I owed the people who worked hard for me a face-to-face explanation, I believed. Thankfully, I didn't fire a lot of people.

Ivan Blumberg, my agent at the time, then suggested that I get together with Tim Gullikson. But the Gullikson who first came to see me at my home near the Bollettieri academy in late 1991 was Tim's twin brother, Tom. The Gulliksons were interesting guys— they had a well-deserved reputation as blue-collar tennis pros. They were teaching pros from Wisconsin—not exactly a tennis hotbed— who decided to take a crack at the tour. The unusual part is that they actually made it to the top level.

These two quintessential "regular guys" also formed one of the best doubles teams of their time and used their earnings from doubles to finance their singles ambitions. Tim was the more successful singles player—over the years, he'd notched up impressive wins over a lot of top players, including John McEnroe at Wimbledon.

When Tom came to see me in the fall of '91, we talked and hit some balls. At the end of his visit, he told me that he had a commitment to coach Jennifer Capriati for something like thirty weeks a year, but that his twin, Tim, would be interested in working with me full time. I don't know if this was a preplanned bait-and-switch move or not, but I agreed to meet with Tim.

We met in Florida, hit some balls, and talked. Tim, it turned out, was more easygoing than Tom, which suited me. He was also gregarious—a natural communicator, which would be a good quality in the coach of a reticent, reserved kid like me. While never a great player himself, Tim was a student of greatness and loved being around it. By nature, Tim was an attacker with a superb volley, so he had an affinity for my style. And he was still a young man—just about forty when we met—so he had energy, passion, and commitment. I decided to hire him, effective January 1992.

The unsettled coaching situation contributed to my inconsistency during the fall of '91. I took a loss to Brad Gilbert in Sydney, but won Lyon. I had back-to-back losses to Boris Becker and Guy Forget in Stockholm and at the Paris Indoors. I put a little balm on my wounds at the year-end ATP Finals, where I beat Agassi in the round-robin and Lendl and Courier, back-to-back, to win the fifth most important tournament of the year.

My last event of the year was my Davis Cup debut, against France, back in Lyon. Those who love Davis Cup, like John McEnroe or Andy Roddick, make it a top priority and consider it the ultimate honor. Playing with the name of your country on the back of your shirt and on the scoreboard is a unique experience. On that I'll agree. It creates a special kind of pressure that you just don't feel when you're playing for yourself, even at places like Wimbledon or Flushing Meadows.

Davis Cup is a team effort, which is also different and interesting, and the nationalistic nature of the competition ensures that you play under some conditions you just don't have to face on the tour. Everything gets magnified or skewed in Davis Cup, and you can throw the records, the rankings, and the form chart out the window. That makes Davis Cup a tough assignment for a rookie.

The Davis Cup format is a single-elimination tournament featuring sixteen nations that have qualified for the elite World Group, and each match (in Davis Cup it's called a "tie") consists of five matches—four singles and a doubles—that are played over three days (Friday through Sunday). The teams usually devote the entire week leading into the weekend tie to on-site practice, so Davis Cup can eat up as much as four weeks of a player or team's time.

The four Davis Cup weeks take place over the course of the year; the big final is played in late November or early December. The home-field advantage (every tie is either a home or an away match) is determined by previous history on a simple basis: the teams take turns hosting ties. So if the last time France played the United States the tie was played in France, the United States is automatically the host for the next meeting—even if it doesn't happen for four or eight to twelve years. Hosting is a huge advantage. You get to fill the stadium with your home crowd (and Davis Cup fans are the rowdiest and most vocal in tennis), but even more important, you get to choose where you play (indoors or out, at a small club or in a huge arena) and on what surface.

Davis Cup didn't mean much to me when I was growing up. I don't remember watching it on television (and it isn't like Davis Cup was all over the tube back in the pre-cable days). So I had no preexisting reverence for the event. This made it tough to commit to Davis Cup because, like most top players, I put the ability to perform at my peak in Grand Slams at the top of my priorities. And Davis Cup asked for a lot, timewise.

In 1991, France put together a magical run under captain Yannick Noah, a very popular former player and French Open champion. Guy Forget and Henri Leconte, two flashy lefties, carried the French squad to its first final in the Open era. And the French also had the home-court advantage over their final-round rivals—the United States. They chose to play the tie on fast carpet in an indoor stadium in Lyon.

When France announced the surface, U.S. captain Tom Gorman had a stroke of genius—at least theoretically. Although I had lost my U.S. Open title in the "ton of bricks" match, I was the best fast-court player in the nation. I was the ideal guy to have on the squad alongside Andre Agassi. But Gorman seemed to completely forget that I was a rookie on the tour, and he discounted the unique pressure for which Davis Cup is renowned. For some reason, playing for your country on a team can really get to you. Some players are inspired and react heroically; others get cold feet and feel intimidated by nationalistic pressure. Throwing a green player into the cauldron in an away final before a wildly partisan crowd was an enormous gamble.

When I arrived in Lyon, I found the anxiety and stress surprisingly high. I guess that's partly because all these USTA officials were around, like they always are at Davis Cup, looking over the team's shoulder. It also had something to do with the fact that this Davis Cup final was a huge, huge deal in France—it seemed like the entire French national press corps had descended on the venue (the Gerland Sports Palace) for the final, hoping to record how France won its first Davis Cup since the days of yore when the famed "Four Musketeers"—Jean Borotra, Jacques Brugnon, Henri Cochet, and René Lacoste—reigned over international tennis.

We had a team Thanksgiving dinner at the hotel in Lyon the day before the start of the tie. It was prepared by a famous chef, but even that event was slightly strained, because we were together with a bunch of tennis officials, and we all had to wear a coat and tie. I've got nothing against appropriate dress, but it seemed that everything was ceremonial, forced, difficult . . . when what we really needed as a team was to relax. All these things bore down on me extra hard, because I had been nominated as the number one singles player for the United States. It was like an NFL rookie quarterback getting his first start in the Super Bowl.

Gorman was also uptight; that became evident to me. We were always having these team meetings, and to me that didn't make sense. They just magnified everything and added to the stress. All my life, I preferred to operate with a low profile—I'd rather be understated than dramatic, cool and aloof rather than confrontational and all gung ho. I just don't believe in making things bigger than they need to be, even some things that may seem awfully big, like winning the Davis Cup. At the end of the day, it's easier to take the attitude that they're just tennis matches; you go out, do your best, let the chips fall where they may.

I was happy to talk tennis with Gore, our veteran captain and a former Davis Cup star himself. I was glad to hear what Andre Agassi thought. But these meetings—everyone was just sitting around talking about the next day's practice or the upcoming pairings. Ken Flach, one of the doubles players (partnered with Robbie Seguso), looked at me in one of these meetings and asked, "You going to serve and volley on both serves, Pete?" I just looked at him, thinking, *I'm one of the top players in the world, and you're a doubles specialist who can't even make it in singles. Where do you get off, asking how I'm going to play?*

It sounds arrogant, but I was just feeling prickly and uptight. At the same time, though, I never went into a match with a cut-and-dried game plan. I knew my own strengths and the kind of game I felt most comfortable playing, and I tried to be aware of what my opponents did well or badly, and how to get to their games. But I always liked to "feel" my way into a match, fine-tune what I would do based on my level of play and the feedback I was getting from across the net.

The quality of my serve on any given day often dictated how aggressively I played. My feeling for how I moved on a given surface (or on a given day), combined with the quality of my opponent's return game, determined how often I followed my serve to the net. I operated by instinct, figuring things out as I went along. Flach's question put me on the spot, seeking a commitment I wasn't prepared to make. It was innocent enough, I guess; my reaction spoke volumes about how defensive and tense I was feeling.

On top of everything else, the French singles players were veterans capable of playing lights-out tennis. There were no question marks about the team; if anyone could handle the pressure of playing at home, it was these guys. The adulation of the home crowd would inspire them. If the fast carpet suited my game, it suited theirs just as well.

A Davis Cup squad has two singles players, a number one and a number two, and a doubles team. The three-day tie begins on Friday, with two singles (pitting the number one from one nation against the number two from the other). Saturday is doubles-only day. And on Sunday, the "reverse" singles pits the number one and number two guys from each nation against each other. A draw determines who plays the first match (or "rubber") of a tie, and from there on a formula takes care of the rest.

I was our number one singles player, but the draw determined that France's number one (Forget) would open the proceedings against our number two, Andre. I watched from the bench, cheering Andre on as he took care of business to put us up 1–0. I was impressed and slightly intimidated by the crowd. The place held just over seven thousand, but it was sold out, so the overall effect was of a huge, deafening crowd. My moment of reckoning was rapidly approaching; I was up next, the U.S. number one against France's number two, Leconte.

What happened was, I froze. It was that bad. It was deer-in-the-headlights-grade paralysis. Notice that I didn't say I "choked." As I wrote before, there is a big difference. Freezing is worse. It prevents you from getting to that critical point where you can choke (or not).

The score just seemed to fly by, like so many of Leconte's winners. When I was serving, I'd stand up at the line and wait, while the crowd was going nuts. I just stood there, absorbing all the karmic energy, waiting for them to quiet down. That was a big mistake—I should have asserted greater control over the situation by walking away from the service notch to wait until they calmed down. That would have represented control, and playing at my pace. It was something I learned in Lyon that would come in handy in many later matches.

I lost to Leconte in straight sets and left the court shell-shocked. On Saturday, the French won the doubles to take a 2–1 lead. On the decisive final day, I faced Forget in the first singles match to keep the U.S. hopes alive. I hadn't had enough time to process what happened on Friday, or to identify the lessons from my awful first-day experience. I gave Forget only token resistance as he clinched the Cup for France in four sets.

I felt terrible afterward. I'd been overwhelmed. For all the talk about Davis Cup being a team thing, I'd felt very lonely out there—as alone as I would ever feel on a tennis court. Sure, the other guys were right there on the bench, encouraging me. And you have your captain sitting on court with you so you can talk and get advice on changeovers. But people make too much of that. It's not like you can hand your racket off to a teammate and say, "Hey, I'm struggling with this, how about picking up the slack?"

It was a tense and miserable week. Gus, who was my roommate on the trip, tells me that the night we lost, we went to sleep pretty early. I woke some hours later, clearly in the throes of some night-mare, and screamed—at the top of my lungs—*Go USA!* Then I went back to sleep. I think it was a reaction to the crowd noise during the tie. I had never been exposed to anything like that, and maybe I just needed to fight back or assert myself, even if it was just in a dream and too late to matter.

The explanation for this disaster seems simple. I was the wrong man for the job. And to this day, whenever anyone brings up that tie in Lyon, I just shrug, grin, and tell them "Wrong man for the job." I don't want to blame Gorman, or anyone else, but the one thing that was painfully clear by the end of the final against France was that Pete Sampras, a raw youth, was completely unprepared for the de-mands of Davis Cup play. He was the wrong man for the job.

There was, however, a personal silver lining. Tim Gullikson, wait-ing in the wings to take over as my coach, saw how much I struggled against the French lefties. He felt that I stood too far to my right when I was receiving serve, exposing too much of my backhand. He wanted me to stand farther to the left to send the signal that I was looking to touch off a big forehand return. It was a cagey move, be-cause lefties just love attacking a righty's backhand, especially in the ad court. The results were remarkable; I think I won my next thirty-two matches against left-handers after he passed on that tip.

I shudder to think how different my rivalry with Goran Ivanisevic, another lefty, might have turned out had I not changed my receiving stance.

1992

KEY MATCHES . . .

July 1992, Wimbledon, semifinal

| P. SAMPRAS | 7(4) | 6 | 4 | 2 |
| G. IVANISEVIC | 6 | 7(5) | 6 | 6 |

September 1992, U.S. Open, final

| P. SAMPRAS | 6 | 4 | 6 | 2 |
| S. EDBERG | 3 | 6 | 7(5) | 6 |

December 1992, U.S.A. vs. Switzerland, Davis Cup, final (Fort Worth, Texas)

| P. SAMPRAS
J. McENROE | 6 | 6 | 7 | 6 | 6 |
| J. HLASEK
M. ROSSET | 7(5) | 7(7) | 5 | 1 | 2 |

YEAR-END RANKING . . . 1992: No. 3

My Conversation with
Commitment

J ust weeks after the debacle of my Davis Cup debut, I began working in earnest with Tim Gullikson. Joe Brandi had been good to have around to organize things and crack the whip. He had worked me hard, getting me out early to run, forcing me to take part in two-on-one drills. And while he knew the fundamentals well, I can't think of a single thing he taught me that became part of my secret knowledge as a top pro. It would be very different with Tim.

It took just a few days for my relationship with Tim to jell. It usually takes time to break the ice with me, but Tim got the job done quickly because he was such a social, good-natured guy. We had separate rooms at hotels, but it was more like I had a college roommate. Tim always wanted us to hang out in my room or his. One time I wanted to get a little time by myself, so when Tim followed me back to my room, I tried to give him a hint. I said, "Tim, I have to make a phone call, it's kind of private."

"No problem," he said.

I retreated to my room, and Tim stopped to talk for a moment with the concierge (we were staying in one of those fancy hotels where we had a concierge of our own, right on the floor). Tim was talking with the lady, and when I poked my head out of my room two hours later, he was still talking with her—he hadn't even left the floor.

When we first went to Australia together, in 1992, Tim would come to my room every night and we would order room service, talk, watch television. I guess he liked the company because he had a twin brother and was accustomed to having him around all the time—even when they played on the tour. And Tim was a family man. His wife, Rosemary, was acknowledged as one of the nicest of spouses on a tour on which even the girlfriends and wives could be competitive. He was really in his element when there were a lot of people around.

Tim was curious about everything in a way I wasn't, and had opinions about everything in a way that I didn't. The way he expressed his feeling so freely seemed unusual to me; it was good for me to see that you could do that. But even though Tim was opinionated, he was open-minded and decent—he would give you the shirt off his back. From the very beginning of our relationship, he was full of questions—questions about my tennis, my life, my family. I didn't realize it until later, but he was opening and loosening me up. From the start, it was me—the insecure, unsophisticated kid—who needed his "space."

A relationship with a coach is a tricky thing to manage, especially for a young player. When you hire a coach, you're to some degree hiring a new best friend—someone in whom you choose to invest your trust. But I was always wary of getting too involved emotionally. I'm naturally aware of boundaries, and always thought you played by certain rules—mutual respect being the chief one, and not unloading all your problems on someone else being another. At times, my way must have been hard for Tim (and later, Paul Annacone), because a coach is supposed to be a confidant, and usually wants to be your confidant.

Tim and I sometimes had a little tug-of-war going—he would probe and pry, and I would resist revealing how I really felt or what I thought. That even happened in tennis terms. I was trying to figure out my game, yet I was reluctant to reveal my concerns, even to a coach. In fact, I confessed weakness and confided in a coach that way only once in my career, and it was much later (as you'll learn).

I never wanted to come across as vulnerable or insecure about my *tennis*—not even to my coach, no matter how much I was struggling. I always had my guard up about that, even as Tim became a close friend and something of a big-brother figure. Maybe I was too cautious, too closed off. Coaching me demanded a lot of reading between the lines, and Tim, like almost all great coaches, was good at that. I've been told that artists are often very reluctant to discuss their own work, as if the magic would somehow go out of the process if they did. I can understand that, even though I wasn't making art. And if my reticence asked Tim to read between the lines, my stoic nature probably made some parts of his life easier. It wasn't like we didn't talk about tennis—we talked a lot about tennis, and we watched the game and played a lot. What we didn't do was obsess about *my* tennis, and I never used Tim as a therapist.

By nature I'm not emotionally needy, so I tended not to take many people deeply into my life. That kept them from having undue influence or controlling me—and saved me having to rebel against their control, something that happens pretty often in coaching relationships. I was more self-reliant than that. I wanted help with and support for my game on an as-needed basis, and beyond that I always kept a healthy emotional distance. I internalized my emotions, even when it was just Tim and me working out or preparing for a tournament. I gave Tim his space, too, instead of demanding that everything be all about me all the time. It's got to be exhausting, always dealing with a needy player.

The best coaches out there develop tricks for getting their jobs done, and some of the ploys are strategies you might use on a kid. For example, a common technique for getting a great player to make some change in his game is to plant the idea in a conversation, and then manipulate the discussion in a way that allows the player to take ownership of the idea—like it was his, not yours. It seems transparent, but it works. Tim never had to resort to that kind of stuff with me, but he did need to know what to say, when to say it, and how to say it. That part is critical, probably for any coach, because top players aren't like journeymen, willing to do anything to get better. They already have great games and great pride. Often sensitivity is part of the package.

Over the next year or two, I would come to know all of Tim's war stories—how he and his twin, Tom, had made the big time starting from the least likely of tennis outposts, Onalaska, Wisconsin. They taught the game for a while in clubs in the Midwest, raising seed money for their crack at the tour. I knew all of Tim's big matches as a pro by heart, I swear. I could practically recite point by point Tim's biggest win, his upset of John McEnroe, on Wimbledon's famous Graveyard Court (Number 2). If we were out to dinner with other people, I could bust his chops and make him squirm by feigning ignorance and innocently asking him about matches that he knew darned well he had told me about a few hundred times before. Then I would sit back and grin.

But Tim wasn't blowing his own horn with all that tennis chatter— he was a real student of the game, that rare combination of a guy who played at a high level (he won three tour singles titles and fifteen in doubles, and was ranked as high as number fifteen in singles), but also loved it with the purity and the wide-eyed enthusiasm of a fan.

When it came to the x's and o's, one of the first things Tim did was get me to shorten my practice sessions. This was something Tim learned from Jimmy Connors, who may have practiced less—in terms of minutes spent—than any other top player. Jimmy was legendary for his short, intense practices. He sometimes practiced for as few as forty-five minutes, but *always* with total focus and purpose. He ran for every ball, hit his best shots, and kept up the pressure all the way. He could wear out a guy accustomed to two-hour practices in less than half that time. With Jimmy, you didn't play two points and then stop, drink some Gatorade, and chitchat.

Tim made a few technical adjustments to my game. Some of them were simple, but critical—like his theory that I ought to overplay to protect my backhand in order to make opponents think I was looking to hit the big forehand. That made many of them try to squeeze the ball into a very small backhand window. It seems so simple, but just moving over a few feet when you return can make a huge difference in how your opponent is going to approach and play points—if you have the return to back it up.

That tactic seemed to work throughout my career, especially in matches against Andre; he maybe pressed a little on his first serve, cutting it too fine as he tried to sneak it to my backhand, or to blow it by the forehand down the T in the ad court. That left me looking at more second serves, which were then easier to take with the forehand. The strategy also worked against Michael Chang big time, because Michael's serve was relatively weak and easy to attack with a big forehand return.

At the start of our relationship, Tim thought I was getting a little "handsy"—inclined to use my hands loosely to compensate for a lack of technical discipline. In other words, I was a little lazy. Hands and wrists play a role in almost all of your shots, but they shouldn't be doing work intended for your arms, feet, and torso when it comes to hitting a firm, penetrating shot. It's especially tempting for players with good touch to get handsy, and they always pay a price in the way of less weight and penetration on their shots.

Tim firmed up my backhand volley and slice, or underspin, shot. He had me shorten up my backhand slice motion to get a little more weight behind the shot even if it meant less spin—à la Ken Rosewall, whose famous slice was surprisingly firm and heavy. Soon my backhand produced fewer "floaters." It penetrated better and went through the court more quickly. That made it harder to attack.

On the backhand volley, we focused on getting my entire body down lower to meet the ball. Dropping the racket head always robs a shot of pace; it's one of those things handsy people do. But the firmest volleys are hit more decisively, with more weight behind the racket. That calls for a little positioning, which is a little more work, but it paid off. These tunings all helped, and shortening up my back-swings on all my returns was of critical importance in my transformation into a good grass-court player.

But the biggest area of concern for Tim was my attitude on court. I tended to slump and slouch, especially when things weren't going my way. Anyone can play great tennis when he's firing on all cylinders. The challenge is to play well enough to win when you're not at your best. There's a sneering inner judge in all of us, and a big part of being successful is tuning him out. And sometimes you have to fight through the indifference and fatigue you sometimes feel, even at big events. Instead of listening to that judge when he says you're lousy, or should pack it in because you're tired and there's always next week—that's when you need to suck it up and act like a man—hang on, fight on, show the pride of a champion.

Tim understood that I wasn't fully evolved as a competitor. I was a little soft. He kept telling me never to worry about what happened on the last point, or the one before. He wanted me to intimidate opponents with my bearing as well as my game, and it drove him nuts when I slouched. But I'm a lanky guy, with pretty wide shoulders, so the slouch was deceptive. People described my "hangdog" look a million times in print, but there was a big difference between "young hangdog" and "old hangdog." Early in my career, I slouched and wore a grim expression that advertised my discouragement. Later, the grim look denoted absolute focus, and the slouch hinted of a gathering storm. Some people even suggested that I was a sand-bagger—looking one way but playing another.

As a blue-collar-type guy, Tim was all about the work, all about wringing every bit of potential out of my game. That's what he and his twin brother, Tom, had done to make it on the pro tour. Tim tried to turn me into a rough-and-tumble, confident, take-it-as-it-comes guy. It was a tough task, and the results were definitely mixed, because in the end I was built differently from Tim, and a leopard doesn't change its spots.

The Davis Cup debacle was still fresh in my mind in early 1992, and as an old-school, Davis Cup–loving kind of guy, Tim put priority on helping wipe the bitter taste of that Lyon final out of my mouth. As it turned out, the opportunity came up the following January, shortly after the Australian Open. (After an exhausting 1991, I chose to work with Tim instead of making the trip to Melbourne.) In the first round of the '92 competition, the United States had been drawn to play Argentina, and we were the hosts. The USTA decided to play in Hawaii on hard courts, knowing that the location would appeal to our top players, who were likely to be traveling homeward after going deep in the draw in Australia.

The tie worked out exactly as planned—and hoped—for me. Tom Gorman was very upbeat and he really wanted me to do well. We still had all those team meetings, but I didn't mind them as much the second time around. I played the first rubber, and, after losing the first set, I played with authority and confidence to beat Martin Jaite. My teammates did their share and we swept, 3–0. That put us in the March quarterfinal against what was then still Czechoslovakia. By luck, we again had the home-court advantage. The USTA decided to hold the tie at Sonesta Sanibel Resort in Fort Myers, Florida.

I was returning to the place where I'd made my debut as a Davis Cup hitting partner in 1989—on a team that featured Andre Agassi and Michael Chang, playing against Paraguay. On that occasion, the $2,500 Dan Goldie and I got as hitting partners was a welcome paycheck. Now I was back at Sanibel and sharing the singles duties with Andre. I was starting to take more pride in Davis Cup, and I was certainly more comfortable with the nature of the challenge. In fact, I began to invest a lot of emotion in it.

Andre was a big Davis Cup guy, but the team still belonged to the ultimate U.S. Davis Cup warrior, John McEnroe. He was winding down his career and mostly playing doubles, but he was still the glue that held the squad together. Todd Martin, who would become a good friend over the years, was a hitting partner on that 1992 squad. During one practice before the tie, McEnroe finished a point, looked at Todd sitting on the sideline, and barked, "Towel." Not "Towel, please" or "Can you get me a towel?" Just, "Towel." I happened to make eye contact with Todd at that moment, and saw that he was surprised by McEnroe's gruff manner. He took a towel and sort of halfheartedly threw it toward John.

I suppressed my urge to laugh, because I understood exactly what Todd was thinking: *Who the hell do you think you are?* But, being a lowly hitting partner, he could say nothing. We talked about the little incident that night, and I knew that Todd was pissed. To this day, when I see Todd in a hallway or a locker room, I glance at him, wink, and bark, "Towel." And he knows exactly what I'm talking about.

I split my singles matches in Fort Myers; I beat Karel Novacek but lost to Petr Korda. Andre emerged the hero, pulling our 3–2 win by taking the fifth and decisive match over Novacek.

My tournament results early in 1992 were so-so; Tim and I were just getting rolling. I would go deep in one event and struggle in another, and failed to win a title until late April. But then I had perhaps my most consistent season on European clay, reaching the semifinals in Nice and the quarters at the Italian and French Open.

The next stop was the Wimbledon tune-up at London's Queen's Club, where I lost to Brad Gilbert for the second time that year. At

Wimbledon, I lost to Goran Ivanisevic in the semis, still hating the grass all the way. The tennis was lightning fast; the balls were hard and they flew like bullets. Goran served me off the court, but that wasn't just because of his superior firepower—it was partly because I was a flawed competitor.

I got down on myself in that match, which is very easy to do on grass when the other guy is firing aces left and right, and you see your chances of breaking serve degenerating from slim to none with each passing bomb. Grass demands more patience and a higher threshold for frustration than any other surface. Although I was happy to reach the semis, the experience harkened back in some ways to my loss to Jim in the previous U.S. Open. I didn't really dig deep enough into myself against Goran. No one had to tell me that. I'm not even sure anyone noticed. I knew.

I left Wimbledon looking forward to my comfort zone, the U.S. hard-court season. First, though, I won a big clay-court event in Kitzbühel, Austria, beating some very solid players (including Alberto Mancini, who at the time was one of the three or four best players on red dirt). It's probably my second-best win on clay. I was in good shape for the Olympic Games in Barcelona, where I had a good run, given the slow red clay surface. I lost in the third round to the Russian clay expert Andrei Cherkasov, 6–3 in the fifth.

My game seemed to be coming together again and, returning to the States, I went on a rampage. I won Cincinnati and Indianapolis back-to-back, with wins over Edberg, Lendl, Becker, and Courier. I rolled into New York riding a wave of confidence. I felt no pressure at all, like I had the previous year. I was comfortable being, on any given day, one of the top three players in the world. I carried a winning streak of ten matches that I improved to twelve with no trouble in the first two rounds at Flushing Meadows.

In the third round, I had an epic battle with my pal Todd Martin. I outlasted him, 6–4 in the fifth, and then beat an old nemesis,

Guy Forget. In the quarterfinals, Alexander Volkov of Russia played like he had a plane to catch. I'm not sure anyone ever packed it in as quickly or obviously as he did, even though this was a Grand Slam quarterfinal. I'd like to think it was because he saw no chance against me, but I know better. Some of these guys are like finely tuned race cars; they're fast, but prone to spinning off the track without warning the moment they lose a little confidence or face a challenge that makes them uncomfortable.

In the semis, I handled Jim Courier in four fast sets and found myself in my second U.S. Open final. This time, though, I wasn't going up against a fellow prodigy and peer. I was facing a seasoned, extremely cool competitor who had battled his way to the final, Sweden's Stefan Edberg.

Edberg and I had a few things in common. We were both reserved, shy, old-school sportsmen. Although Stefan grew up in Sweden, he went against the grain in that clay-court haven and switched to a one-handed backhand, much like I had, because he wanted to play attacking tennis. Edberg was a prodigy, too, but in a slightly different way. He'd won a junior (eighteen-and-under) Grand Slam. As a pro, he'd been through something similar to the struggle I was unconsciously dealing with in 1992—the battle to become a great competitor as well as a great talent. In Stefan's case, the catchphrase that haunted him wasn't "ton of bricks" but "fire in the belly." Early in his career, Stefan was accused of lacking a gut-level, burning desire to win.

In a good example of bad timing, I was catching Edberg just as he was proving the critics wrong. The previous year, he had taken over my U.S. Open title with a flawless, artful, straight-sets deconstruction of Courier's straightforward game. The breakthrough put to rest the "fire in the belly" issue, because nobody without that kind of motivation won the U.S. Open—it was simply too tough and grueling an event. This was doubly true for European players at the

U.S. Open. Many of them just never got comfortable with the conditions, which usually included suffocating humidity and heat, sizzling-hot hard courts, and the chaotic, egalitarian New York vibe.

Any remaining doubters were convinced by the epic way Edberg went about defending his U.S. title at Flushing Meadows in 1992. In his last *three* matches before the final, he was down a break in the fifth and final set against high-quality opponents: Richard Krajicek, Ivan Lendl, and Michael Chang. The semi against Michael remains one of the all-time great matches, in terms of the struggle if not the quality of play. At five hours and twenty-six minutes, it set a new record as the longest match in recorded U.S. Open history.

Lanky and tall, Edberg was a great mover. He lived and died by his kick serve, which he liked to follow to the net, where he could use his superb volley to cut off all but the sharpest of returns. Stefan's game plan was straightforward: get to the net. He wasn't afraid to surprise you by employing the chip-and-charge tactic—returning the serve with a sharp slice or dink, and charging forward to take the net and challenge the server to make a great passing shot. Closing—that was his game in a nutshell.

The matchup was simple; we both wanted to attack. I thought I had an edge in power, especially on service, and on defense I gave away less than he did with his weaker wing, the forehand. I went into the match knowing I had to keep the service returns low; I practiced getting up and over the kick serve to rip back low, flat returns. With a guy like Stefan, I couldn't afford to think too much about exactly where to put the return. If he was on his game, I would have enough trouble just getting the return low enough to make him lift and float his volley over the net, thereby giving me a look at a passing shot. Also, I wanted to attack Stefan's forehand and serve well enough to stay out of those pressure situations that would invite him to chip and charge. I would wait for the inevitable, small opportunities that, if converted, could turn the match around.

When I woke up on the morning of the final, I felt great. I had accomplished a lot, getting to the U.S. Open final. I felt pretty content, and that probably explains why I didn't feel nervous at all. I was happy to have gotten to the final. It was a blustery day, with the wind swirling around even more than usual in the bowl of Armstrong stadium. There was one mitigating factor when the match got under way: I was suffering from cramps and dehydration owing to a case of food poisoning. It was something I downplayed because I believe in the Aussie rule: If you're fit enough to start the match, you're fit enough not to make excuses about why you lost. And ultimately, my performance in the match had much less to do with any physical issue than mental, emotional ones that were coming to a head.

I came out pretty strong and won the first set. But it was a terrible struggle from there. The "new" Stefan Edberg was on full display. He was full of emotion, pumping his fists, yelling, doing everything to show that he had fire in his belly. He won the second set. At the critical juncture of the match—a third-set tiebreaker— I threw in an ill-timed double fault to give Edberg a 6–4 lead and double set point. Stefan capitalized to go up two sets to one, and then I double-faulted away the first game of the fourth set. In a blink, it was 3–0 to Edberg. I went through the motions the rest of the way; I packed it in. Afterward, I told the press: "As the match wore on, I was running out of gas. I was very, very tired, maybe more mentally than physically. Mentally, I was telling myself that my body just couldn't do it, and as a result, it didn't."

Once again, I was talking from the heart, but what I said was a curious combination of truth and cop-out. For instance, my physical problems were fatigue and dehydration, yet I admitted that I was more tired "mentally." That's not even logical, but nobody picked up on it. I admitted that my mind was telling me that my body couldn't do it, when my mind should have been telling my sore body that I could. In short, I was explaining away my inability and unwillingness to dig deep. It wasn't just that I had played "lousy," I also played without heart, which is a greater sin.

In the aftermath, I was stunned and confused. Over the next few weeks, while I recovered from the long hard-court summer, a few painful truths would slowly crystallize in my mind.

S hortly after the U.S. Open, we played our Davis Cup semifinal against Sweden on indoor clay at the Target Center in Minneapolis. Because clay was not my best surface, I played only doubles—with McEnroe. We toughed out a real war with one of the best doubles squads of the era, Stefan Edberg and Anders Jarryd.

This was my first Davis Cup experience as a "doubles specialist," and I was surprised by how much I enjoyed the assignment. Doubles is an enjoyable sideshow at most tournaments, but it has a starring role in Davis Cup because of the format. As the third and only match on Saturday, doubles is the kingmaker in Cup play. Most Davis Cup teams that enjoyed long-term success were anchored by a great doubles team. When a tie is 1–1, which is often the case after the Friday opening singles matches, getting to that 2–1 lead can be huge. It also didn't hurt my own enthusiasm level, or results, that my partner on some key occasions was McEnroe. Remember, it was McEnroe's own longtime partner, Peter Fleming, who famously quipped, when asked to name the best doubles team of all time, "John McEnroe and anyone."

We went on to meet the Swiss team in the 1992 final, on an indoor hard court in Forth Worth, Texas. Gorman, perhaps still mindful of Lyon, decided to play it safe. He named Courier and Andre, who were both playing very well, to the singles slots, and put me down for doubles, again partnered with Johnny Mac.

That was fine with me—Andre had proven himself a great Davis Cup singles player. He's an emotional guy who really gets into all the hoopla. Jim was right there with Andre as a Davis Cup warrior. He gave his all, he was gritty and very cool under pressure. We had, arguably, the greatest Davis Cup team of all time—and a pretty stubborn bunch. In the opening ceremony, the promoter wanted us to wear these ten-gallon hats and it kind of freaked Jim out. He snapped, "I'm not wearing that stupid hat!" So there were no cowboy hats.

The Swiss had a very tough two-man team consisting of Jakob Hlasek and Marc Rosset. Both guys were very good on fast courts, which is unusual because most Europeans prefer the slower clay. So much for our home-court/fast-court advantage. Hlasek was in the midst of his career year in singles, and Rosset was a guy with a game as tricky as it was big. He could play serve and volley, even though his career moment of glory occurred on slow clay a few months earlier, when he won the singles gold medal at the Barcelona Olympic Games.

Andre won the opening rubber, but then Rosset showed his mettle with an upset of Jim. McEnroe and I would be playing Hlasek and Rosset in what suddenly looked like a critical doubles match. And when we lost the first two sets, both in tiebreakers, it looked like tiny Switzerland might pull off one of the most shocking of Davis Cup upsets—and on U.S. soil, no less.

John was in one of his McEnroe moods. Throughout the match, he trash-talked Hlasek, a very quiet but cool guy who minded his own business and got along with everyone. John was suffering, and coming dangerously close to losing control. But then he was unlike anyone else in that he often played better after going nuts. Some of the line calls in the first two sets seemed dodgy, and in the third set John finally lost it over another apparent bad call. He started in on the umpire, and he just kept going on. He yelled at the official, and he yelled at our own captain, Gorman (for not making more of a fuss and "standing up for us"). He was just going ballistic in general, in any direction he wanted, long after the point in question was over.

Finally, I just lost it myself. I turned on John and snapped, "John, it's over. Done with. Let's not harp on what happened three games ago, it's time to move on, man." For some reason, my own little outburst had two welcome results. It calmed John down (emotionally, if not verbally) and it fired me up. We won the third set and adjourned for what was then still the required ten-minute break before the start of the fourth set. John and I came off the break with wild eyes and fire in our bellies. It was one of those rare occasions when I got into the emotion of it all. I was pumping my fist and yelling. McEnroe must have said, "Come on, let's kick ass" a thousand times. We clawed and fist-pumped and yelled our way to a not very pretty but extremely relieving win, 6–2 in the fifth.

Although I became very emotional in that match, in general John and I were like a Jekyll and Hyde pairing; I tended to be cool and forward-looking, he was hot-tempered and all wrapped up in the moment, always ready for an altercation. He thrived on that, and I understood it. We were good for each other. He pumped me up with his emotional outbursts, even if I didn't show it, and I calmed him down with my self-control, even if he was, externally, still the same contentious, fiery player.

The next day, after Jim beat Hlasek to clinch the tie, I became a Davis Cup champ. It mattered not at all that I had played only doubles in the final; I had done my share all year and felt as proud and entitled as if I had played every singles match for the United States in our drive to win the Cup.

But throughout the fall, I kept harkening back to the loss at the Open to Edberg. It was eating away at my guts. I occasionally thought about what Dad had said a lifetime earlier in Shreveport. I had been a U.S. Open finalist, sure, but who cared? The guy whom the press—and everybody else—was interested in was Edberg.

The real giveaway, I came to realize, was that I hadn't been nervous before the match. There are two kinds of nervous in tennis: bad nervous, which can make you freeze up, play an inhibited game, or choke, and good nervous, which is a sign that the match you are about to play really means a lot to you—a sign that you can't wait to get out there to mix it up with your opponent, even if you're not guaranteed the win. It's the kind of nervous that makes some great football players throw up before a big game.

I also thought about how the final hadn't been a well-played match. Sure, the wind might have had something to do with it. My food poisoning may have been a factor. Stefan's own fatigue, after his death march to the final, was in the mix, too. But this is what I kept thinking: *If he didn't play that well, and I didn't play that well, why did he win?* And the answer dawned on me, slowly, over a matter of weeks. For the first time, I understood and could articulate the truth: *I lost because I had packed it in. And it was part of a pattern.*

Coming face-to-face with that reality enabled me to admit that on two critical occasions in 1992—the Wimbledon semi with Goran and the Open final with Edberg—I had more or less quit while I still had some reserves to call on. The Edberg match was the straw that broke the camel's back. If I didn't care, who would? I had wasted two big moments, and there was no guarantee that I would experience those moments again.

My future was no longer a matter of how good I could get in order to put myself in a position to win big events. I was there; I was plenty good. I wasn't developing anymore in any significant technical or physical way, I was developed (except in my grass-court game). The real question was, Did I want to win majors? The Edberg match forced me to confront that. I slowly came to a realization about myself that wasn't very pretty. I didn't tell anyone, not even Dad. It would have been easy enough to do; all I would've had to say was, "Listen, I have a confession to make: I packed it in on some big occasions." But I internalized it, and got no forgiveness from the harshest judge of them all—myself.

My inner dialogue went on for about two months: *Why make this thing more complicated than it needs to be? If you see the other guy struggling, why follow suit?* True, I'd been feeling a little overwhelmed by my swift climb to the top of the game, but I was also a little too content with what I was achieving. *Why,* I finally asked myself, *are you being such a pussy?*

It took me some years to come up with the answer, and here it is in its most simple form: Everybody has a place in this world, and spends a good part of his mature life carving out his niche—the zone where he is comfortable. Some guys, they get to number one and they think, *I don't really like it up here, it's too lonely. Too stressful. Too demanding.* So they settle back a little. They find a comfort zone at number three, or five, or whatever. I could have done that; a part of me *was* doing that early in my career. The truth is that when you're *anywhere* but at number one, you can hide. You can get to the second week of majors regularly, win one now and then, earn a lot of respect and money, and lead a great, stress-free life.

I honestly can't tell you why my conversation with commitment took this tack, but it did: I decided that I had this great talent and I wasn't taking care of it. I had the Gift, and I was turning away from it, at least on some of the very occasions when it was maybe the only thing that could pull me through. It wasn't going to be good enough for me to just be in the mix; it would nag and wear at me. I realized that the game was not about getting somewhere, but staying somewhere. Some of us, we get there and we don't want to let it go. We don't want to see some other guy take it. And that's ultimately what makes you a warrior—a fully formed, mature competitor.

You can't really teach someone determination, although you can nurture it. It's something that is either in you or not, and you have to figure it out as an individual. And if you decide you need to be number one, you have to realize you can't hide. You have to get fitted for the bull's-eye on your back and get used to living with it.

I was ready. That 1992 Edberg match was my Rubicon, my version of that famous Muhammad Ali moment when he threw his Olympic gold medal into the Ohio River one night. At the end of 1992, I was determined to have a huge 1993.

Chapter 5

1993–1994

July 1993, Wimbledon, final

P. SAMPRAS	7(3)	7(6)	3	6
J. COURIER	6	6	6	3

September 1993, U.S. Open, final

P. SAMPRAS	6	6	6
C. PIOLINE	4	4	3

January 1994, Australian Open, final

P. SAMPRAS	7(4)	6	6
T. MARTIN	6	4	4

July 1994, Wimbledon, final

P. SAMPRAS	7(2)	7(5)	6
G. IVANISEVIC	6	6	0

August 1994, U.S. Open, fourth round

P. SAMPRAS	6	3	6	6	5
J. YZAGA	3	6	4	7(4)	7

YEAR–END RANKING . . . 1993, 1994: No. 1

Grace Under Fire

I went into 1993 determined never to give up in a match again. Whatever happened, I would never lose another battle—especially a Grand Slam final or similar big opportunity—because I didn't have the heart to fight to the finish and walk off the court spent. I'd had my conversation with commitment; now it was just a matter of backing up my promise on the court.

As the year developed, I felt I was right in the mix of top players, and enjoying the game more than ever. I lost to Edberg in the semis at the Australian Open, where he always played well and I did not. I won Philadelphia, Miami, Tokyo, and Hong Kong, and claimed the number one ranking on the computer for the first time in my career. It was a controversial ascent because I became number one by winning everything *but* slams. Still, I was hardly to blame for the way the ATP computer allocated points, and I was clearly the most consistent player in the early part of the year.

It rankled me that I had yet to win my second major, while Jim Courier by then had a whopping four (two at Roland Garros, two from the Australian Open). He'd taken command in our generation (Michael, Andre, and I had just one major apiece), and I was determined to regain my place at the top of our pecking order. It was more important to me than the computer rankings.

I turned in a good clay-court season, putting up wins over Alex Corretja, Andrei Cherkasov, Guillermo Perez-Roldan, and some other clay-court experts. At Roland Garros, I lost in the quarters to the eventual champ, Sergi Bruguera. Then it was on to the grass: I went on to

Queen's Club and lost in the first round to one of those accomplished South African grass-court players, Grant Stafford. But that wasn't so bad, because I never did well at Queen's in the years when I was in the hunt at the French Open. This had less to do with having to make the transition from clay to grass than the letdown I always felt after missing a chance to win a Grand Slam. I needed time to recuperate, emotionally and mentally, from a major campaign—especially one that was unsuccessful.

I was one of the clear favorites going into Wimbledon in 1993, and not just among the pundits and London bookmakers. This time I was comfortable with the expectations, and I wanted to win. One of my major goals when I hired Tim was figuring out the grass-court game, and we worked on that, in various ways, from the onset of our relationship. We felt that the early loss at Queen's Club could be helpful, because it meant we had almost two full weeks of valuable extra time to iron out what we both hoped were the final kinks in my redesigned Wimbledon game.

When my brother, Gus, and I first arrived at Wimbledon in 1989, we'd gone straight to Centre Court and just sat there, taking it all in. Centre Court—it had such a huge impact on me as a child that years later, as a young pro, I was almost shocked to see that the place really, truly did exist. And it was much smaller than Gus and I had imagined. We just sat there for ten minutes, drinking in the sight of the empty, quiet stadium and gazing at that cool, inviting, emerald green grass. This was the place where, as we'd watched, John McEnroe had won; this was the place where Laver had played all those matches—on our living-room wall.

But there was this little problem of actually having to play on that grass, instead of merely watching others do it. And that problem was relatively simple: I could hold serve easily and still lose matches 7–6, 7–6, 7–6. Despite the hype, grass-court tennis isn't about the serve; it's all about the return. My game was developed on hard courts, where you have a pretty good look at serves, especially second serves. You didn't get that on most grass courts in the early 1990s, especially against great grass-court players who knew how to keep their service games safe with serve-and-volley tennis.

Tennis on grass was all about holding serve and finding ways to eke out those one or two breaks of serve that determine the outcome of a match. If a guy got lucky and framed back a return winner or two and you made an error . . . good-bye set. It seemed like a crapshoot; it was unfair. Another thing that bothered me more than it should have, early on, was the erratic bounces you invariably get on grass. This problem was more pronounced in the events leading up to Wimbledon and in the late stages of the main event, when heavy use really beat up the courts.

A related issue was the different movement you needed to use on grass. You had to play from more of a crouch, sorely testing your hamstrings and lower back. That's because the bounce on grass is relatively low, as well as unpredictable. That called for plenty of adjustments, but that part I could deal with—I was limber enough to make those last-second changes. Also, on grass you needed to hit a ton of passing shots against any opponent who had a big to huge serve. That was unfamiliar to me, because on other courts my return and ground games were good enough to make it tough for guys to attack me.

That's about it for the laundry list of complaints. Suffice it to say I was so negative about grass by the time I started working with Tim that even John McEnroe, who struggled with the British crowd but never with the grass, got on my case about it. We were practicing side by side on the Aorangi Park practice courts one day in 1992, and I was having a frustrating time of it, and letting Tim know. I heard John say out of the side of his mouth, "You've got to get rid of that negative attitude." I still remember that—something about the way he said it made something click inside me.

In the two weeks leading up to Wimbledon in 1993, I had the growing feeling that I had finally figured out the grass-court technique. It all hinged on my return game. Tim had shortened up my swings, especially on my backhand return. He wanted me always to keep the racket in front of me, because there was rarely enough time for a backswing, never mind a big roundhouse one. He also wanted me to use an opponent's pace to block the ball back. When an opponent was attacking on grass, you were fine just slipping the ball by on either side, or hitting such short, soft returns that the guy would have a lot of trouble doing anything threatening with his volley.

During the calm before the Wimbledon storm, we weren't doing drills or anything too intense. We just focused on sharpening up my returns. And Tim kept telling me that I ought to be extremely hard to beat. Tim was doing all he could to make me a more confident, assertive player. It was pretty straightforward stuff on grass, and Tim sensed that my biggest challenge would be having the confidence and courage to play the way he knew I could.

The Wimbledon draw gave me a pretty tough row to hoe. My half was loaded with guys who weren't necessarily big stars but who knew how to play on grass. In the first three rounds, I had to beat two Aussies (Neil Borwick and Jamie Morgan) and a Zimbabwean (Byron Black), although the payoff was a round-of-16 meeting with Andrew Foster, a low-ranked British player who had somehow snuck through. This was dangerous, though, because the British are perpetually starving for a British male Wimbledon champ—something they hadn't produced since Fred Perry in the 1930s.

Even a British optimist couldn't envision Foster winning Wimbledon, but upsetting world number one Pete Sampras, who had always been vulnerable at Wimbledon, wasn't a bad start. So Foster was being carried on a wave of adulation and hope, and he was having the run of his life at the only tournament that really matters to the vast majority of his countrymen. To make matters worse for me, we were assigned to the most remote court on the grounds, Court 13.

Technically, 13 was one of the main or "show" courts, because it had a towering stand of portable aluminum bleachers on one side of the court. (In contrast, the "field" courts, where they usually put obscure players, have very little seating room.) But it was first-come, first-served seating at 13, and anyone who had a ticket or pass that got him onto the Wimbledon grounds could stake out a place there. That meant the most passionate and enthusiastic fans would be there, but also the rowdiest, most partisan—and most inebriated.

The matches scheduled before ours went long, so it was early evening by the time Foster and I took the court. That gave fans plenty of time to lube their pipes with British lagers or the traditional fruity Pimm's cups. I was determined not to get into a war out there, because that's just the kind of situation that could spin out of control. I played nearly flawless tennis to win the first two sets, losing just three games.

But Foster, stoked out of his gourd by the occasion and the vocal fans, hung tough in the third set. We stayed on serve through six, eight, ten games—by which time the crowd, sensing life in Foster, was really getting into it. It was also getting toward twilight. All the elements that a favorite dreads were falling into place: lousy conditions, unruly fans, a lead that could slip away.

Still, I figured that in the worst case I could just extend the match until it was called because of darkness, and regroup to put the guy away the following day. But something inside me didn't want to do that. Something in me really wanted to bear down, dig deep, and put the guy out. This was part of wiping away that bitter aftertaste that had lingered in my mouth after the last U.S. Open final. Foster was no Edberg, and Court 16 was not Louis Armstrong Stadium, but in its own way this was a pivotal moment for me.

I hung in there and got to the tiebreaker, where I took care of my serve and greased out a few returns to stop Foster's run. As soon as I won match point, I flung my arms in the air, turned to the crowd, and yelled, "Take that, you motherf#$@&%rs!"

The photographers courtside heard exactly what I said and, in England, where the tabloid press is a real force, that spelled trouble. The "Fleet Street boys" (and girls) who write the tabs are exceptionally good at digging up information and blowing up routine incidents into front-page news. One of their favorite tricks at Wimbledon is working hand-in-hand with the photographers, who are positioned much closer to the action than the writers. In fact, they can hear and see just about everything a player says or does during a match. And they definitely heard my taunt, even if most of the fans it was meant for did not.

When I went to my press conference, I felt relaxed and proud. The front row was filled with guys who were very well dressed, for reporters. It's one of those crazy ironies that the people who write the most tacky and irresponsible stories in the British tabloids always dress impeccably, right down to wearing pocket handkerchiefs or flowers pinned to their lapels. And so this one perfectly attired guy says, in his perfect British accent, "Is it true that you called the British crowd a group of 'motherf#$@&%rs'?"

I froze up. It hadn't even occurred to me that this could be a big deal. I'll never forget the discomfort I felt at that moment—or that I wussed out. I flat-out denied having said what I did. It maybe wasn't the right thing to do; I felt funny about it. But the last thing I needed was to get in a big fight over a thoughtless remark tossed out in the heat of combat. Not that my denial mattered—the incident was all over the papers the next day anyway, and suddenly it seemed that all of England hated me. Put it down to a thoughtless comment—and the power of the tabloids.

Of course, the toughest part of my 1993 Wimbledon still lay ahead of me: a quarterfinal pairing with the defending champ and my emerging rival, Andre Agassi. We had a tense, high-quality struggle, with multiple service breaks. The match went down to the wire, see-sawing right into and through most of the fifth set. To my advantage, Andre looked like he was feeling the pressure of defending his first Grand Slam title, and the surface was playing fast. I knew I could take care of my serve; it was just a matter of finding a way to break. It was a very high quality match, but the air totally went out of it when I finally got a break late in the fifth set and then served it out.

I played Boris Becker in the semifinals; he was already a multiple Wimbledon champion and an established icon. We had a tug-of-war for the first set, and I won it in a tiebreaker that seemed to break his will. I capitalized on single service breaks in the next two sets to wrap up a satisfying straight-setter. Ours was the later match, so I got to watch portions of the earlier semi between Jim Courier and Stefan Edberg. Like most everyone else, I was expecting an Edberg win, because he was such a good grass-court player. But Courier was a battler on any surface, and he found ways to win. In one of his finest moments, given the circumstances, he punched through to the final.

I would play my first Wimbledon final against a guy I'd more or less grown up with, a calm, steady, worldly guy who—unlike me—never lost matches because he got discouraged. Although we were no longer close friends, we didn't have a problem with each other, either. We would say hi in the hallways or locker rooms, and if we found ourselves sitting side by side in the training room, or a hotel restaurant, we would chitchat.

Many people felt it was unfair that I had taken the top ranking from Jim, who clearly was performing better than me on the Grand Slam stages. But I was undeterred, and determined to hold on to the number one ranking. More to the point, while Jim had played very well on some big occasions, I had beaten him in the four finals we'd played and enjoyed a 3–0 edge on him in Grand Slam battles.

I was nervous from the moment I woke up on the day of the final—it was the opposite of how I'd felt before playing Eberg in the 1992 U.S. Open final. I'd slept horribly and, although I didn't throw up, my stomach was so jumpy I had trouble eating. I was haunted by memories of the '92 Open. This was my first major final since then, and I experienced something new—the fear of losing. I felt it would be devastating if this chance, too, slipped away. It felt less like I was going to play a tennis match than to stand trial, and I had no idea what the outcome would be. Although I had played a few dozen tournament finals by then, this was a Grand Slam and it was going to be more like my first time.

As much as I'd been through since September of 1990, this was still just my third major final. I was 1–1, and had been badly shaken up by the one I lost. I didn't know what lay in store, and there was no longer any place to hide. Whatever happened, it wasn't going to be a joyride with nothing to lose. I was the favorite—there's pressure right there—because of the advantage my serve-and-volley game provided on the grass.

Tim wanted me to impose my game on Jim—smother him with a serve-and-volley display. Jim used pretty extreme grips and fired his forehand with rifle-like power and accuracy, but if I could keep the ball low and keep him from setting up to unload the way he did on clay, I might keep him off balance. But Tim also knew I was capable of getting down on myself, and even wilting in the heat.

My prefinal warm-up with Tim was brief; I was distracted and, instead of taking a leisurely hit to get the blood flowing and find my game, I kind of raced through it. I just wanted it to be 2 P.M. so I could face my moment of reckoning. All the while the knowledge pressed in on me: the job doesn't end when you get to the final; in some ways, that's just the beginning. Your tournament is like a sand castle. You lose the final and it's like the big wave came and, in seconds, washed away all that you had built. The reality is that nobody remembers the guy who loses the final. I remembered my dad and that acid comment he made in Louisiana: *Look, that reporter is talking to Mal now.*

The tension was excruciating. It was the Fourth of July, and hotter than hell. But as soon as Jim and I started the warm-up on Centre Court, everything went away—and I mean *everything.* All the anxiety, nerves, and pressure. To fall back on a familiar phrase, I felt like a ton of bricks had been lifted off my shoulders. Thirty-six hours of intense pressure just went out the window. I had this acute realization that I could finally breathe, and it felt great. I'll never forget that feeling. The weight of my shoes was the only thing that kept me from floating away.

I'd hit with Jim so often through our young careers that I almost felt his ball coming off the strings, and that familiarity made me even more comfortable. And it also hit me that this wasn't just a major final—it was the Wimbledon final. The end match at a tournament I grew up watching on TV. I was aware of the Royal Box, that dark green enclosure where the spectators had a lot more room than the ordinary schmoes, and sat in wicker armchairs with tan-and-green cushions. The ball echoes on Centre Court in a deeply satisfying way, because it's small, close, and partially covered.

From the start, I played well—very well. But it was never easy against Jim, and I had to take care of my serve and look for my opportunities to break him, which didn't materialize in the first two sets until the tiebreakers. In a way, this was the dangerous aspect of grass-court tennis personified. I dominated with my serve (I had twenty-two aces in the match), and backed it with precise volleys. But solving Jim's serve was a far tougher assignment. As we arrived at each tiebreaker, I was well aware that an errant shot by me here, or a great or lucky shot by him there, would win him the set.

My serve and volley carried me through the first-set tiebreaker. The decisive point of the match probably was a set point Jim had in the second-set tiebreaker, at 6–5. At that point, I kind of mishit a volley. It was a strange floater that looked like it was going to sail long and give Jim the set, but it died in the air and nicked the baseline to tie it up in the breaker, 6–6. Jim was discouraged and I leaped on my chance, ending the set two points later with a running crosscourt forehand. Later Jim would hit the nail on the head when he contemplated his missed set-point chance: "It's just grass-court tennis—roll the dice."

But even with two sets in hand, the job wasn't nearly done. In fact, the enormous relief I felt when I won the second set led to a huge letdown on my part. Serving the second game of the third set, I double-faulted on break point and that put a new puff of wind into Jim's sails. I managed to get the break back, but I was still drained from all the nervous energy I had expended, and although I was still playing hard and playing well, I was starting to feel fatigued.

I knew better than to show my fatigue. I needed to keep my shoulders up and squared away. This was something Tim had worked hard to impress on me in the eighteen months that we'd been working together, so I pushed myself. I told myself not to dig too deep a hole. But Jim broke me again in the eighth game, and then he served out the set with an ace.

We battled on serve for five games in the fourth set, and I sensed that I was in trouble. And that's when my newfound determination kicked in. A year earlier, I might have wilted in the sun and let the fourth set slip away and then—who knows? I felt the truth and reality of that possibility in my gut, but I didn't think about it. I was always good at shutting out the doubt. I forced myself to fight harder—harder than I ever had before. I pulled my game together and I broke Jim in the sixth game of the fourth set with another running forehand pass.

Suddenly I had room to breathe, and I was just two games from the title. Those games went by in a flurry of aces and winning volleys. And when I converted match point, I felt this surge of joy mixed with relief. I finally understood what it meant to be a worthy Grand Slam champ. It didn't matter what anyone else thought or said, I knew in my own mind that this was the moment when I truly arrived. Up to then, I had known I could play great matches and win tournaments, even the odd major when everything else fell into place. But this match wasn't about merely playing well, it was about legitimizing my character as a champion.

I'd emerged from the crucible of anxiety and proved my worth. The big difference between this final and the ones that came before it was that on this occasion, I was fully aware of what was at stake. I set a pattern that day. In the future, I would take that feeling—that sense of acute anxiety melting away into total focus and a great sense of liberation when a match finally started—into every critical match I would play.

My win at Wimbledon in 1993 was really the beginning of my career as a dominant champion, although an incident in the press conference underscored how green I still was, emotionally. The late Princess Diana had watched me beat Jim, and she had clearly been in my corner as a fan. When the British tabloids pointed this out and asked for my reaction, I flippantly replied, "Maybe she has a crush on me." Some of the people there laughed—somewhat nervously. The incident is better forgotten.

There is no one way to greatness, I've always realized that. Take my rival in history, Roger Federer. He went sixteen Grand Slams without reaching a quarterfinal, a mind-blowing statistic given what he has since accomplished. But in my case, I shudder to think what it might have meant for my future to lose that match to Jim. It was the final piece of my champion's puzzle. I had come to grips with the Gift, and had learned to deal with the expectations and challenges created by having it. In Tim Gullikson, I had a coach who truly understood my game and personality, who knew what I needed, and could be a friend. He had been holding his breath, hoping I could close out my inner battle. Did I really want to be a champion? Did I really have a champion's heart, and mind, and will?

After Wimbledon, Tim exhaled.

My tennis mission was redefined by that Wimbledon title. The new mandate called for me to win a boatload of matches to prove I was a dominant champion. The challenge would be staying in close touch with the Gift. I would lose plenty of tennis matches in the future, I knew that. How could you not, playing one-hundred-plus matches a year against a staggering array of individuals and styles of game?

I would lose matches for a variety of reasons, including injury, low energy, poor execution—and the most acceptable of reasons, because I just got my butt kicked by a guy who did everything better on a given day. Sometimes a very big day. It happens, but trust me—that's the least of your worries. I learned early in life how to lose matches, but in 1993 I finally learned how to win matches when I was tired, or discouraged and tempted to call it a day and move on. Once I learned how to tap into my pride and inner reserves of determination, I felt much more comfortable being the guy with the bull's-eye on his back. I was getting over the typical insecurities of youth, and feeling focused and ready to lay claim to every Grand Slam title that came my way. It looked like clear sailing, too, but things rarely work out exactly as you expect.

After Wimbledon, I lost in four straight tournaments on my surface of choice, outdoor hard courts. But I went deep in three of those events (Los Angeles, Cincinnati, and Indianapolis). I made two semis and a quarterfinal, and I lost to a Grand Slam champion (or future Grand Slam champion) each of those times (Richard Krajicek, Stefan Edberg, and Patrick Rafter, respectively).

I felt fine going into the U.S. Open, and it was one of those years when the draw simply opens up like the vault of a bank, leaving the gold there for the taking. The toughest guy I faced during the Open was Michael Chang in the quarters, and by then I had too much game for my childhood rival. I simply overpowered him, playing out the most basic story line in men's tennis.

I faced a surprise finalist at Flushing Meadows, the Frenchman Cédric Pioline. This was a guy with a tricky game; he was a good mover, and he had a stroking repertoire that he used to good effect to keep opponents guessing. But it was also his first Grand Slam final, and that's a pretty daunting assignment for a guy well along in his career, unaccustomed to the thin air at the peak of the game.

One of the curveballs thrown at guys who get one or two chances at the golden ring of a Grand Slam title is the conditions that greet you on the big day. Nobody daydreams about playing a Grand Slam final under difficult conditions that make it tough to play your best or most attractive tennis. In the finals of your dreams, the sun is shining, the air is still, the crowd is poised and hanging on every forehand and backhand with *ooo*hs and *aaa*hs.

But it rarely works out that way. It was windy on the day of the Open final—it seems like it was always windy in Louis Armstrong Stadium—and that probably bothered Pioline. I went into the match thinking, *How do I win this match with the least amount of drama and trouble?* I played within myself, and he seemed nervous and not entirely comfortable on the big stage.

I won 6–4, 6–4, 6–3, and the match marked the beginning of the period when I dominated the game. Jim Courier briefly snatched back the world number one ranking in August of 1993, benefiting from the points-based computer ranking system just like I had back in April. But by September, I had the top spot back again, and this time I would hold it for more than a year and a half. I felt that I was the man in command and, with Tim encouraging me to show it, I made an effort to cultivate an aura of invincibility. I became more and more averse to demonstrating any kind of weakness.

For the rest of 1993, I was always in the hunt. I lost a few big matches: Goran Ivanisevic, my Wimbledon rival, tagged me on the fast carpet at the Paris Indoors in the quarters. I got my revenge a few weeks later in the ATP year-end championships, although I lost the final to Michael Stich. That surprised many pundits, but Stich was the player whose arsenal scared me the most. He had a great second serve, he could do anything, including serve and volley, and he moved easily and naturally. Those qualities, combined with the fact that he was playing before his countrymen in Germany, proved too much for me to handle.

In my last event of the year, the Grand Slam Cup, I lost a whale of a final to the emerging Czech player Petr Korda. The match went to 13–11 in the fifth (the tournament had no fifth-set tiebreaker), and Korda picked up the whopping $2 million check.

D own in Australia for the start of 1994, I played my first two matches and then came up against a newcomer from Russia, Yevgeny Kafelnikov. People had warned me about this tall, rangy kid with straw-blond hair, a jack-o'-lantern grin, and a high-quality two-handed backhand. His forehand was one of the all-time ugly shots in tennis; he hit it with a bent arm and it looked really ungainly, especially in comparison to his smooth, sweet backhand.

But that forehand was a better shot than it looked, and the guy had plenty of talent—enough to push me, hard. What's worse, I never did very well with guys I hadn't played before. What advantage I had in terms of my reputation was offset by the fact that it usually took me a match or two to figure a guy out, and get into a comfort zone against his unique game.

But I survived Kafelnikov, then beat Ivan Lendl and got my old friends Jim Courier and Todd Martin, back to back, in the semis and finals. I rolled through Todd in straight sets to win my third major in a row. I was on fire. Next I won the two big U.S. winter hard-court events, Indian Wells and Key Biscayne. I began to sense that people were a little in awe of me, a little fearful, and I liked that feeling.

From Miami, I went to the Far East to play the mini–hard court circuit that had grown up around Osaka and Tokyo. Tennis may be booming in Asia now, but at that time it was tough for promoters in that part of the world. In order to attract top players, they had to offer appearance fees in addition to whatever prize money was at stake that sometimes went into mid-to-high six figures if the player agreed to play at least two events.

I never did anything just for the money. Part of it was that I was lucky—I didn't need to. But part of it was also that bad things can happen if you just chase the dough in exhibitions or tournaments that you wouldn't bother playing if it weren't for those appearance fees. Those bad things include burnout, injury, mental fatigue—all of which can affect your performance later in tournaments that really count, and as the year grinds on. At times I pulled out of events where I was getting an appearance fee because I didn't feel I could give my best effort (usually for physical reasons).

In my case, playing in Asia was appealing because I was in no hurry to get to Europe to play on the red clay. From the get-go, clay was a crapshoot for me, and my results showed little correlation between the time I spent playing clay events and my results in the red-dirt tournaments that most counted. In Europe that spring of 1994, I put up the best clay-court result of my career, winning the Italian Open on the golden clay courts of the Foro Italico in Rome. At the time, the Italian featured the fastest clay courts you could find, which helps explain how I came to play the Wimbledon icon Boris Becker in the final. But along the way I also took out solid clay-court players like Alex Corretja and Andrei Chesnokov, losing just one set in the entire tournament.

That win satisfied the popular former pro and television commentator Vitas Gerulaitis. We'd been friends ever since Vitas, seeing how I struggled on clay, sought me out to encourage and advise me. He had credibility because even though he played serve-and-volley tennis, he'd won the Italian Open twice. He told me that if he could do it, I could, too. I really respected what Vitas had achieved with his daring chip-and-charge game, and he was just a great guy to be around because of his energy, big personality, and obvious zest for life.

Vitas, Tim, and I spent a fair amount of time together in Tampa, where I lived for training purposes for most of my career. Vitas would come by frequently; he was a golf nut after he quit tennis and he liked to play with Tim. Our friendship surprised many people, because we were so different. Vitas, in his heyday, was the ultimate glam tennis player—a habitué of Studio 54 who had the charisma, big hair, and habits of a rock star. He was a favorite of Andy Warhol's, and a regular in the New York gossip pages. But Vitas had been ranked as high as number three, and he'd won the Australian Open and reached two other Grand Slam finals. The 1977 Wimbledon semifinals, in which he played his great pal Bjorn Borg, is still considered one of the greatest matches in Open-era history.

Vitas was probably most famous in tennis circles for the great quip he delivered when, after losing to Jimmy Connors in their first sixteen meetings, he finally chalked up a win over Jimbo. He strolled into the pressroom after the match, leveled a stare at the assembled scribes, and, utterly deadpan, declared: "Nobody beats Vitas Gerulaitis seventeen times in a row."

I was in great shape moving on to Paris and Roland Garros. Although clay wasn't my favorite surface, at times I felt very comfortable on it and I assumed that sooner or later, my window of opportunity in Paris would open. One of the guys I beat at the French Open was a newcomer, Marcelo Rios. He was very young at the time, but already "discovered." In fact, we shared an agent in Jeff Schwartz. But Jim Courier, working very hard to push me and continue challenging for the top ranking, took me out at Roland Garros in a four-set quarterfinal. He was still in his golden age in Paris; he had been to the final the preceding three years, winning twice.

During the grass-court season, Todd Martin won two tiebreakers to beat me in the final at Queen's Club, and I moved on to Wimbledon to defend my hard-earned title. I lost just one set, to Todd, as I served and volleyed my way to the final opposite Goran Ivanisevic.

I had my hands full with Goran, as I would on grass during my entire career. A great deal of Goran's juice at Wimbledon came from being a left-hander. That natural edge made his first serve even better and more effective than mine; I really believe it was. When Goran's serve was on, it was pretty much unreturnable on grass. He was the only guy I played regularly who made me feel like I was at his mercy. I never felt that way against that other Wimbledon icon, Boris Becker.

But my second serve was better than Goran's, and the key to beating him for me always was getting hold of and punishing his second serve. Goran put tremendous pressure on my service games, because he usually held so easily. I felt that if I played one shaky service game against him and was broken, the set was gone. Very few people were able to make me feel that way, once I'd figured out the grass game. That was very tough, mentally. Goran's serve also gave him a huge advantage as a returner—he could afford to take huge, wild cuts with his return. If he happened to tag two of those in a row, I was down love–30—and from there anything could happen.

The final was incredibly fast tennis, played on a hot day, with balls flying all over the place at warp speed. It was a gunfight, both of us dodging bullets we could barely see, hoping to connect with a semilucky return here, or tease out an error there. That kind of tennis calls for a firm hand and intense focus. I proved slightly more steady in the crapshoot tiebreakers, and after I won two of them, Goran folded up. I won, 7–6, 7–6, 6–0.

The match marked the high point in the growing debate about grass-court tennis. A growing chorus of critics charged that Wimbledon tennis had degenerated into a serving contest between two giants who almost couldn't lose serve, but couldn't break each other, either. Goran and I personified the trend, never mind that neither of us was the biggest guy around. Our big serves and our desire to end points quickly added up to a perfect storm of Wimbledon controversy.

Tennis at Wimbledon, some pundits said, was in danger of becoming irrelevant, because ongoing technologies had produced more powerful rackets that buried the needle on the power meter deep in the red. Even the tabloids got into it, running pictures of prominent politicians and others in the Royal Box sleeping soundly. Ostensibly, that had something to do with the way the game was being played.

Ironically, though, I never did take advantage of the evolving racket technologies. My earliest racket as a junior player was the wooden Wilson Jack Kramer Pro Staff. I also played with a Kneissel, briefly, and a Donnay that was essentially the same as the racket I would come to use for my entire career—a Wilson Pro Staff 85

Graphite with an 85-square-inch head (the smallest available). It was a racket that probably lost whatever "cutting edge" appeal it had long before I posted my best results with it.

Every one of my frames was customized for me by Nate Ferguson, who worked for the guy who pretty much invented the high-end customization trade, Warren Bosworth. All of my rackets were weighted with lead tape and balanced. I also had grip work done. I played with a big grip—somewhere between 4⅝ and 4¾, and I liked a fairly big butt cap; I always wrapped my grips with Tourna Grip. I admit I could get pretty neurotic about racket tuning. I would go to these events early in my career, and the stringing machines were different and the stringers were different guys, so I would have to get four, five rackets done before they got it right—*if* they got it right. I was always worried that poor or inconsistent stringing might cost me matches, so as I began to win big, I decided to spend a little money. I hired Nate.

Nate basically traveled with me as my racket guy; he also did all of my stringing. I was very particular about my tension, and used the thinnest strings available, 17-gauge gut. On clay, I strung 32 to 33 kilos (70.4 to 72.6 pounds); on grass, 32 kilos; on some fast hard courts, I went to 34 kilos (74.8 pounds). Because of the thin string and high tension, the gut sometimes snapped at crazy times—like in the middle of the night, when the pop would wake me up. One year, I went through more than seven hundred sets of gut (gut sells for about $35.00 a set, retail). I wanted my rackets strung for every match, which means that if I won a major, I went through at least fifty-six sets of gut over the two-week period. At the French Open, if I had my rackets strung after a match and it happened to rain on the off day, I had the frames torn apart and restrung before I played again.

Over the years, I was offered money—sometimes a lot of money—to switch rackets. I went as far as trying a few demos. But they never felt the same, and I'm the first to admit that a lot of this probably was in my head. By the same token, you hear a lot of war stories about tennis players and golfers who changed rackets or clubs and ended up miserable. Wilson was all too aware of my feelings, and had me captive to that Pro Staff 85. I was so fastidious about this issue that for a few years I played with the racket even though Wilson and I had not come to terms on a contract and I was basically getting paid nothing.

Looking back on it now, I think changing to a larger-headed racket in the latter years of my career would have helped me. My racket was great for grass—it was very precise, with that small head and narrow string at high tension. But on clay, you can benefit from having a greater margin of error. The sweet spot on my racket was just three or four inches. With a larger head and different strings, I might have generated a lot more power and spin from back in the court. I would have played more like guys play today.

It's hard to know just what would have happened, but in any case I'm certain that my small-headed racket was an ideal tool on grass. I admit that the critics had a point when they claimed that we were in danger of turning tennis into a schoolyard rock fight. In terms of artistry, my final with Goran was a bust—although I still believe that it was less because of the styles we played than the specific way Goran and I matched up. Against a lot of my other grass-court opponents, it was a different story.

Here's another thing to consider: I'm not sure that long points automatically increase interest in the game—not by a long shot. People have complained for ages about the boredom of watching endless, sometimes seemingly aimless, rallies on clay. I think the mix of court speeds and styles of play are great assets to tennis, and one hidden cost of that tradition is that you occasionally get matchups that produce one-dimensional tennis on a given surface.

Note that nobody complained about the game being too "fast"

or "boring" when Andre Agassi was playing, say, a Pat Rafter. And nobody rhapsodized about the glories of red clay when two grinders were having five-hour rallying contests. Goran and I were not the ideal matchup at Wimbledon, although we often played each other. In the wake of our 1994 match, Wimbledon went to softer, slower balls, and they began to develop a new grass mixture that ultimately slowed down the courts and made grass-court play more rally-friendly.

The "Wimbledon is boring" theme spun off another story line: "Sampras is boring—and a menace to the game with his domination." I stood accused of playing brilliant tennis that won minds, but not hearts. After one of my matches, a tabloid ran the simple headline SAMPRAZZZZZZZZ. . . . I had been raised to believe that winning matches is what counted, and that you didn't make a fuss or draw attention to yourself as you went about that job. Now being good was boring, and a threat to tennis.

It wasn't easy to read that stuff, and it was the last thing I wanted to talk about in my press conferences. Whatever I said was bound to come off as defensive, self-justifying, or both. Some people took it upon themselves to interpret my extraordinary self-control as evidence of a lack of emotion. This struck me as pretty arrogant. I had emotions, all right, trust me on that; I just knew how to master them, and that was true on and off the court. That's no mean feat in a sport known for producing hotheads and emotional powder kegs.

Players like John McEnroe, Jimmy Connors, and Boris Becker won legions of fans because they so freely vented their emotions. I understood that they needed to do that to play—or feel like they were playing—their best tennis. And, of course, it always made good copy, and added an extra layer of interest to the personalities of those guys. I never begrudged or envied that. But I also felt that the media could have done more to appreciate that I was the yin to their yang.

In tennis, you always have two opponents out there—the other guy and yourself. You can't worry too much about the other guy, other than dealing with the shots he sends your way. The most important guy you have to beat is yourself—the part of you that's prone to doubt, fear, hesitation, and the impulse to give up. If you're too busy struggling with yourself, like some players, you can hardly be expected to beat your opponent.

If you want to be great, get your own issues out of the way and play with a clear mind—then it's just a constant struggle for mastery of your opponent. The John McEnroes of this world are the exception rather than the rule. Like most players, I always took emotional outbursts by my opponents as opportunities. When a guy started losing it out there, I knew I'd gotten to his game or his mind.

I also was less interested in being appreciated or understood than in being a champion, and I didn't mind being an exemplary one. I wanted to wring every ounce of potential out of the Gift, and the only way I could see doing that was through self-control. I also believed that if I just lived up to my potential, appreciation and even understanding would follow. That was my blueprint for success, and it created a backlash once it began to pay off. It didn't help that guys like McEnroe and Jimmy Connors were running around bemoaning the lack of "personality" in tennis.

In fact, I had a bizarre locker-room encounter with McEnroe over that issue. John, who at the time had recently retired and was working as a television commentator, wrote this little column in the London *Times*. In one of his Wimbledon pieces he went after me; he more or less trashed me for being boring, and gave me some paternalistic advice about showing "more personality." Basically, he was berating me for being what I am, instead of what he thought I should be. Besides, who said a tennis player was obliged to show personality (if that's what you want to call it)? I wasn't in tennis to win popularity contests, to show how interesting a person I was, or to be an entertainer. I was in the game to play tennis at the highest level within my reach, and to win titles. Tennis was my first love and also my professional business. And I never confused that with show business. If I wasn't going to be remembered for my game, I wanted to be remembered for the way I carried myself. If I wasn't going to be remembered for that—I didn't want to be remembered.

I was pissed about this issue, and word got back to John. So he came into the Wimbledon locker room, put his arm on me, and brought his head real close. He was saying something like, "Pete, no offense meant, man . . . I just want you to do this, I want you to show a little more of this, do a little more of that . . ." And all the while I was thinking, *This is weird. The guy has basically been saying that I should be more like him, that I was boring and not great for the sport, and now he's not just my great buddy, he's got even more advice. It's like he thinks it's no big deal.* I could forgive John quite a bit; he'd said some pretty out-there things over the years, and we'd been Davis Cup partners who'd shared some great times. So this was extra-awkward, but I had to stand up for myself. We got into it a little bit and I told John exactly where to get off, but without losing it or getting all agitated. To this day I don't know what John was thinking but I can't really explain some of the other things he did, either— I'm not sure anyone can.

Over the years, I would get more emotional on the court. I showed that in different ways, including some of which I'm sure John McEnroe approved. But overall, I remained pretty self-controlled. My version of the tantrum or savage fist pump and primal scream was that trademark, leaping overhead smash. That was all the message I felt compelled to send.

There was no downside to my cool approach as there had been

to my lackadaisical attitude. But the cost ultimately manifested itself as a health issue that cropped up about six months after my win over Goran.

Right before the 1994 Wimbledon, I got out of my Sergio Tacchini contract and signed a new clothing and shoe deal, with Nike. Wimbledon was my first official tournament for my new brand, and I was pretty fired up about being with the U.S.-based giant. The color of the money might have been the same in Italy as Oregon, but having your big endorsement deals with companies in your native land is always preferable; it's just a much more natural connection that can be exploited more effectively for everyone's benefit.

Nike had developed a nice, classic clothing line for me, along with a shoe that was part of the massive new "Air" campaign that would prove to be such an enormous hit. Unfortunately, the shoe didn't agree with my foot, and by the time I left Wimbledon my right foot was hurting and swollen. I went to a doctor and had an MRI, and was subsequently diagnosed with posterior tibial tendonitis.

I was scheduled to play Washington, D.C., but had to withdraw. I also pulled out of Montreal and Cincinnati; my summer preparation for the U.S. Open was shot and Nike was scrambling around to find me a shoe I could wear for the American Grand Slam. I survived three matches at the Open, but my fourth-round opponent was the crafty, slightly built Peruvian Jaime Yzaga. A player with nice touch and nimble feet, Yzaga moved me around, made shots when he most needed them. He found a way to break me enough times on a hot, humid afternoon to drag me into a fifth set.

I was in poor condition and had very little left in the tank but, remembering the pact I'd made with myself, I fought like mad. The New York crowd was firmly behind me, and they really appreciated the lengths to which I went to try and stay in the match. But woozy and clearly on my last legs, I lost, 7–5 in the fifth. The struggle was of such high quality that it captivated many, and by the time it was over, chaos more or less reigned. Jaime and I had turned in the most riveting match of the tournament, providing many with an unforgettable moment.

As soon as the match ended, tournament officials hustled me into the referee's office, which was alongside the short tunnel through which players entered Louis Armstrong Stadium. Attendants there stripped me and hooked up the IV bags. If you've never had an IV, it's a really weird experience. The IV bag contains water loaded with various minerals that alleviate dehydration. Since they hook you up intravenously, the effect is instantaneous. Seconds after the fluids enter your bloodstream, you go from being a near zombie to bright-eyed and bushy-tailed. When the IV kicked in for me, the first thing I saw was the familiar face of Vitas Gerulaitis.

Seeing the kind of shape I was in, Vitas had rushed down from the commentary booth as soon as the last ball was hit. He volunteered to go over to the locker rooms to get my clothes and incidentals (back then, the locker rooms were a long walk from Louis Armstrong Stadium). When he returned, Vitas waited until I was sufficiently recovered to dress, and then he helped me out of the place, carrying my racket bag. The minute we stepped out of the office, the flashbulbs went off and I realized that a long line of reporters had formed along the wall in the bowels of the stadium, waiting for me.

I declined to do any interviews, claiming I just needed to rest. But Vitas exchanged a few words with some of the writers whom we both knew. Later, the New York *Daily News*'s ace sports columnist Mike Lupica had a great piece that really nailed the spirit of the moment. It was mostly a tribute to the bond between Vitas and me. Other writers described the match in riveting detail, and everyone seemed to agree that it was an epic.

I didn't know it at the time, but that was the last I would see of my friend Vitas. He died in a tragic accident just weeks later, succumbing to carbon monoxide poisoning while sleeping in the pool house on a friend's estate in the glitzy Hamptons on New York's Long Island. When I got the news, I immediately called Vitas's mom. Like everyone else, I just called her "Mrs. G." She was much loved by Vitas's friends (and they were legion), and she was always happy to cook for Vitas and whichever of his friends happened to be around on any given day or weekend. When I got her on the line, she was still so distraught she could barely speak. It was terribly sad. I joined countless people in and out of tennis in mourning the loss of a great friend.

I couldn't know it then, but there was more devastating news to come.

1994-1995

Chapter 6

KEY MATCHES . . .

January 1995, Australian Open, quarterfinal

| P. SAMPRAS | 6 | 6 | 6 | 6 | 6 |
| J. COURIER | 7(4) | 7(3) | 3 | 4 | 3 |

July 1995, Wimbledon, final

| P. SAMPRAS | 6 | 6 | 6 | 6 |
| B. BECKER | 7(5) | 2 | 4 | 2 |

September 1995, U.S. Open, final

| P. SAMPRAS | 6 | 6 | 4 | 7 |
| A. AGASSI | 4 | 3 | 6 | 5 |

December 1995, U.S.A. vs. Russia,
Davis Cup, final (Moscow)

| P. SAMPRAS | 3 | 6 | 6 | 6 | 6 |
| A. CHESNOKOV | 6 | 4 | 3 | 7(5) | 4 |

| P. SAMPRAS T. MARTIN | 7 | 6 | 6 |

| Y. KAFELNIKOV A. OLHOVSKIY | 5 | 4 | 3 |

| P. SAMPRAS | 6 | 6 | 7(4) |
| Y. KAFELNIKOV | 2 | 4 | 6 |

YEAR-END RANKING . . . 1995: No. 1

The Floodgates of Glory

The new shoe episode in 1994 set me back a good deal at a time when I was really starting to roll. In addition to having my momentum broken, I lost out on prize money as well as a $1.6 million bonus I would have earned from the ATP Tour for finishing as the top player *and* meeting all my tournament commitments (meaning if I showed up at all the important events I had signed up to play; the tour was always trying to induce players to play as often as they could). But I was clearly unable to make my commitments because of the foot injury.

Endorsement deals are not especially complicated or risky (rackets can be an exception), but sometimes you have conflicts. Nike was confident that it made a great shoe, and believed that the problem had more to do with my foot than their product. It was tricky, as I was just entering into what I hoped might be a long-term relationship with Nike (I always preferred long, stable relationships, in every aspect of my life), and coming into the golden age of my career. The last thing I needed was to get into a tiff with Nike, which had already launched a major ad campaign (you may remember it as that "King of Swing" series of commercials). I accepted the shoe problem as an unfortunate start-up glitch, and before six months were out we came up with a good shoe that I wore for the rest of my career, the Air Oscillate.

I started my 1994 fall European tour in Stockholm. One night while I was at the practice courts, Tim fainted, landed on a glass coffee table, and cut his face all up. At the time, Tim was on a crazy diet and he was running a lot. He was a bit of a health nut, and he never met a fad diet that he didn't try out. When they found me at the courts and told me my coach was at the hospital, I was stunned. But they said he had just fainted and cut himself up, so I played and won my match, and then went to see Tim. It looked like he'd gotten his ass kicked in a bar fight. The doctors suspected that the fainting spell or blackout had something to do with his heart.

I went on to have a solid fall, winning Antwerp and the year-end ATP Finals, where my last two matches were wins over, respectively, Andre and Boris Becker. In my last event of the year, I was upset in the final of the Grand Slam Cup by Magnus Larsson, who walked off with the biggest—by far—payday of his career: $2 million. But the memorable thing about that tournament was Tim Gullikson having another fainting episode—the second in the span of just a few weeks. It occurred one morning while I was busy doing some promotional things with local Nike guys; Tim passed out back at the hotel and ended up in the hospital again. This time, his wife, Rosemary, flew over to Germany. Again, the doctors looked at his heart—they thought they found some congenital deficiency, but nobody was convinced of anything. Everyone just carried on, with growing concern.

The fainting incidents did nothing to dampen our enthusiasm at the end of the year. I had won two majors, plus the ATP Finals. The foot injury may have cost me a U.S. Open title, but despite missing all those summer events I still finished the year at number one for the second year in a row. I felt confident enough to take a brief rest for the holidays and go into the 1995 Australian Open without playing any official tournaments to tune up my game. Tim was all fired up, too. He loved the game of tennis and enjoyed the laid-back atmosphere in Melbourne. Many of his pals from his days on the tour would be there, coaching or working in various tennis-related businesses. And his twin brother, Tom, would be there, too.

I won my first two matches down under with a total loss of just eight games, and was due to play Lars Jonsson in the third round. Tim warmed me up and returned to the locker room, where he suddenly and inexplicably collapsed. By then Tim was already on medication for what was supposed to have been a congenital heart condition; doctors said that he had suffered ministrokes the previous times he collapsed, and traced the blackouts to a heart-valve malfunction. Tom rushed Tim to the hospital while I went out and played—and won—my match. I went to the hospital later, just to see what was going on, and I was told that Tim was going to be "okay." The press was waiting for me after the visit, and I repeated the information.

My next match was against Sweden's Magnus Larsson, the same guy who had tagged me in the Grand Slam Cup barely a month earlier. I started terribly, although I can't say Tim's collapse was a factor. At the time, there was still no real cause for alarm because nothing was determined.

Soon I was down two sets to none and in a third-set dogfight. In my entire Grand Slam career, I had only come back from a two-sets-to-none deficit to win once before, at the French Open, against Tomas Muster. But I fought my way back into it, winning the last three sets 7–5, 6–4, 6–4. When the smoke cleared, Larsson had fired one more ace (nineteen) than me. He told the press he simply couldn't play any better than he had on that day.

After the Larsson match, I went to the hospital again. When I walked into Tim's room the mood was very subdued. Tim and Tom both made an effort to remain calm, but they couldn't really hold it together. They both tried to make small talk but soon broke down in tears and wept. Tim had gone through a barrage of tests at a private clinic, they told me, and had been advised to return home to Chicago for further tests.

Up to that point, the Gulliksons had been vague about Tim's

problem, and didn't know themselves what might be wrong. They were also trying to shield me from distraction by downplaying things. They continued to take that tack, and I didn't press them for answers they either couldn't or didn't feel right about providing. I figured they would tell me what they wanted me to know when the time came. My own job, I felt, was to stay strong and focused. I needed to go out and play well, because the last thing Tim needed was to start feeling guilty over how he was impacting my game— and Tim was just the kind of guy to do that.

The brothers told me they had already booked their flight and would be leaving the day I played my next match—a quarterfinal against Jim Courier. That match could in many ways have been a celebration of sorts, even though Jim and I had become rivals. Now and then we even sniped at each other in the press. It was nothing serious, just two very competitive guys suffering from testosterone overload, each wanting his share of the spoils and rewards. But we still went back a long way together, and Jim's coach, Brad Stine, was friends with Tim and Tom. There was an American connection, a Bollettieri connection, all kinds of connections. But Tim's condition hung like a dark cloud over everything. And he was definitely leaving before the match.

At the last minute, someone decided that we all ought to get together for a "farewell dinner" for Tim, the night before I played Jim. It was a good suggestion and a nice gesture. The dinner took place at an Italian restaurant in downtown Melbourne. We made small talk about all kinds of things and tried to keep it lively and fun. The only subjects we wanted to avoid were Tim's condition and my upcoming match with Jim. But everyone was feeling very nervous for Tim, and the entire occasion was somewhat forced. It took some effort to keep up the jock banter. Tennis players thrive on the familiar, and this was foreign territory for us, emotionally; the added tension of knowing Jim and I were playing the next day didn't help.

Down deep, I had a terrible feeling that things were falling apart, but I was very lucky about one thing, from a purely selfish perspective. Paul Annacone, a pro who has always kind of looked out for me, was in Australia playing in his last Grand Slam event before he retired—in fact, he was playing only doubles. I asked Paul if he had any interest in staying on to help me out at the tournament until we knew what the story was with Tim, and he agreed to do it.

Very early in my career, our mutual agent, Gavin Forbes, made sure I got to know Paul. We got together now and then to talk about tennis over a meal, or at a tournament. In fact, during Wimbledon, Gus and I would go over to Paul's place at the St. James's Hotel to hang out and eat up all the ice cream Paul kept in his freezer. We stayed in touch as I matured and became a top player. The tour is a pretty cold place where everybody tends to take care of his own business. But Paul always took an interest in how I was doing, and he kept an eye on me; I felt it and appreciated it.

As luck would have it, a few weeks earlier, Paul and I had even been on the same plane to Australia. We talked a bit then, and he told me that after the Australian Open, he would try to get into coaching at the college level. But when Tim had to go home, he set those plans aside. It was a case of amazing timing, even though the circumstances were tragic. I have no idea what I would have done if either Paul had lost and gone home early, or decided not to make that last trip to Australia in the first place.

Paul is a soft-spoken guy who was even younger than Tim, and very easy to be around. He accompanied me to the site daily, although Tim remained my official coach. Paul would talk with Tim on the phone, and then act as a go-between, conveying Tim's ideas and implementing his wishes. Paul was willing to do this for as long as his help was required. We hoped that Tim would get his health issues sorted out and be back by my side in time for the next Grand Slam, in Paris—if not sooner. But the signs were ominous. In the locker room, I overheard some of the veteran coaches talking about brain tumors and cancer.

Tim left the next morning, and I slept in because I would be playing Jim at night, in the prime-time match. I didn't think much about the future. There would be other, better times for that. I had a job to do, and I was doing it in the way I felt would have made Tim most proud.

The retractable roof of Rod Laver Arena was open for our match; the conditions were close to ideal. Right from the start, Jim played well. He liked the court and playing conditions in Australia much more than I did, and on that night his forehands cracked like rifle shots in the still, warm air. There wasn't much to choose between us, but I dug myself into an enormous hole when I lost the second of two tiebreakers and trailed by two sets to none. That's as bad as it gets in best-of-five Grand Slam matches, especially against a player of Jim's caliber. The dialogue in my head went something like this: *Now I'm done. I can call it a day, have a shower, write it off to bad luck in the breakers. Or I can stay out there and, if I'm lucky, fight for another two and a half hours—just to get back into it.*

Something inside just drove me to keep fighting. I earned an early break in the third, and clung to the advantage to win the set. Then, in the fourth, it looked like I might be done when Jim broke me in the fifth game and held for a 4–2 lead. He was just two games from the match, but he was starting to cramp up (although I didn't notice at the time). With a game point to go up 5–3, Jim hit a double fault—one of just two from him in the entire match. Then he made two groundstroke errors and suddenly instead of 5–3 it was 4–all and I was alive again. I held serve, and broke Jim in the next game to take the fourth set.

I served the first game of the fifth set and led for the first time in the entire battle. The desperate straits I was in earlier had kept me distracted and preoccupied, but now that I had a bit of breathing room, things started to unravel. As I sat in my chair on the change of ends, I started thinking about Tim; I had a flashback to the hospital, and how vulnerable and sad Tim had looked. Moments later, I fell apart.

I had all this stuff pent up inside of me, all of these powerful emotions, and I had kept them bottled up. They needed to come out, they demanded to come out, yet it wasn't like me to let things out—and certainly not during a tennis match. So I didn't know where to go with those feelings, and what made it even worse was that as I struggled to contain my emotions, I realized how proud Tim would have been about the way I'd clawed my way back into the match.

When we started to work together, I was a so-so competitor, prone to getting discouraged. I wasn't a great come-from-behind player. But in this tournament alone, I had come back from two-sets-to-none deficits in back-to-back matches, and that had a lot to do with what Tim taught me, the work ethic he impressed on me, the pride he instilled, and the confidence he showed in my game. I could see his face, the eyes lighting up and his lips taking on this sneaky little smile as he told me—how many times he told me this—that my big, flat serve down the T from the ad side was just like the famous Green Bay Packers power sweep.

When Tim first floated that analogy, I just looked at him, puzzled. Maybe even rolled my eyes, wondering what kind of Tim-ism he was going to follow up with. I didn't know about any famous Packers power sweep. But Tim was from Wisconsin, and a rabid Packers fan. And he told me the punch line with relish: "You know it's coming, but there's nothing you can do to stop it."

Tim loved that line; he used it all the time, trying to pump me up before a big match. And there I was, trying not to think about any of that at two-sets-all and 1–0 up in the Australian Open quarterfinals.

Something in me cracked. All these thoughts and feelings came bursting out, the way liquid under pressure eventually blows out if its natural outlet is blocked. I was sobbing on that changeover and my shoulders were heaving. And then I had a sensation that ran contrary to everything I was feeling. Suddenly, it was like I was able to breathe again—to breathe, after not being able to for a long time. It actually felt good.

By the way, there's a myth about this entire incident, the idea that my breakdown began when a fan yelled out, "Come on, Pete, do it for your coach!" That isn't true. I didn't even hear the guy. Anyway, I struggled through the next two games, unable to control my emotions or tears. I tried to go on, as if nothing was wrong, but I couldn't do it. I had to step back to take a little extra time, try to gather myself. I didn't want to throw Jim off his game, but by this time he could see that something was wrong, although he didn't know what it was.

At 1–1, after the first or second point of that game, I had another minibreakdown, taking a little extra time before getting ready to play the next point. By then, everyone in the stadium knew I was going through something unusual and emotional. It was very quiet, I was struggling to pull it together, and then I heard Jim's voice from across the court: "Are you okay, Pete? If you want, we can come back and do this tomorrow."

I thought he said that with a little bit of that soft, sarcastic tone that Jim sometimes has—a tone that I knew well. I wasn't sure how to take his remark. The fans actually laughed about it. I didn't know what he was thinking, but I felt he wasn't happy about the way things were going. Maybe he thought I was cramping, and trying to buy time. Worse yet, maybe he thought I was stalling, hoping that the lack of activity would worsen his own cramps. But I didn't even know about his cramps until much later.

Jim's remark threw me off and it irked me. It also snapped me out of my awful state. I had to regroup, fast. Suddenly, instead of thinking about Tim, or struggling to fight back tears and welling emotions, I knew I needed to win the match, and I needed to win it right then and there. Jim had let me off the hook, and I sensed that his nerves were fraying; I had to stop wandering around like some sort of Hamlet, as much reason as I had to be distracted.

That was probably the longest ten minutes of my life, all of it taking place on this stage where almost twenty thousand people, including an international television audience, could see me writhing like a bug under a microscope. It was excruciating, but Jim's crack snapped me back into reality, and I responded well. I broke Jim in the eighth game of the set and made it stick; the match fell just two minutes short of the four-hour mark. As Jim himself said later, "At four–three in the fifth, either one of us could have collapsed, but he was the one left standing. Pete's pretty determined, and certainly at a Grand Slam he's going to do whatever's in his power to win."

I've never asked Jim just how he meant that remark about coming back to finish "tomorrow." We've talked about it through the media, and he knows that I took it as a caustic jibe, even though he has said that it was a spontaneous and sincere reaction to the unusual situation. One day, I guess, we could talk it all through, but that isn't even necessary. I never held a grudge about it. It was a tough situation loaded with a lot of stress for both of us. We were both big boys, we were intensely competitive, and sometimes big boys play rough.

After the match, I felt really embarrassed and very exposed. You know that feeling when you just want to cry and you need to talk to a family member? That's where I was. I needed to hear my mother's voice, and when I did, it kind of melted me. I called home and Mom answered. She tends to lapse into a compassionate drawl when one of us kids needs support, and I clearly remember how sad she sounded as she said, "Aw, Petey. I saw what happened. Are you okay?"

I just broke down and wept again.

. . .

Tim learned the result of the match while he was still en route to Chicago, changing planes in Los Angeles. He told reporters who met him at LAX, "I didn't see the match, and I didn't leave Australia by choice. If I'm not healthy, I can't help him. Pete deserves a lot of credit for coming back against a great player like Jim. I'm very proud of him."

The following day, the match and all the histrionics that went with it were all over the newspapers—the incident was the talk of Melbourne, and probably New York, Paris, and London. Walking onto the grounds, and in the locker room, I could feel people looking at me and talking about me, and all the attention made me intensely uneasy. I told Paul I had never felt so vulnerable in all my life.

If there was ever a tournament that I seemed destined to win, it was that 1995 Australian Open. But it doesn't always work that way. I beat Michael Chang in the semifinals, but ended up losing the final to Andre Agassi despite winning the first set. It was Andre's second consecutive Grand Slam title (and the only time in our careers that he beat me in a major final). I was emotionally drained by the day of the final, but that's no excuse. I've never blamed Andre for ruining the storybook ending, either. You live by the sword and you die by the sword.

After the tournament, some of the things I heard and read really bothered me. People were writing things like, "See, Pete Sampras really is human . . . he shows emotion!" or "It took the illness of his coach to bring out emotions in Pete Sampras and make him seem human . . ." I suppose that some of those comments were meant to be flattering. Some certainly were wrapped in stories that were otherwise positive descriptions of how I had managed to beat Jim. But I had the uncomfortable feeling that some commentators really did believe my effort not to show emotion meant I didn't *have* emotions, at least not to a sufficient degree. The inference seemed obvious: in some vague way I was less "human." Coupled with the Wimbledon "Sampras is boring" theme, this was a heavy one-two punch at my personality and nature.

I guess it was a sign of the times. Things in tennis and society had changed an awful lot since I was a little kid. It seemed that people increasingly craved sensation and they were also much more prone to letting it all hang out—letting their feelings be known, pursuing their goals with abandon, without apologies, oblivious to any message they were sending or how it reflected on them. This was supposed to be more "real" than cultivating discipline and behaving with dignity. In tennis, those floodgates had been flung open by Jimmy Connors and John McEnroe; in their wake, it was all about "personality." For me, it's always been about discipline.

Those who wanted me to show more "emotion," to be more "human," seemed to discount that there are many different personalities out there, and how they conduct themselves, in private or public, has nothing whatsoever to do with the depth or nature of their emotions—their "feelings." Actually, I never trusted people who were always talking about their feelings, or expressing their emotions. I don't think flying off the handle, pandering to sentiment, berating others, making crazy, diva-like demands, or telling people what they want to hear is a sign that you have deeper emotions, stronger feelings, or are more human. You're just less able to exert self-control, or are more demanding, or more willing to pander or make a horse's ass of yourself.

After that match with Jim, I often felt that if anyone lacked feeling, it was the people who stated so blithely that it took something close to a public nervous breakdown to prove that I really do have emotions. The match certainly showed that I was emotionally vulnerable, it just took an extraordinary situation to expose it.

· · ·

I learned in 1995 that life at the top was going to be extremely tough on a permanent, rolling basis. Who could have predicted Vitas's death—or the sudden illness of Tim? I knew very little about the big issues in life, and those two events rocked me. How was I going to react? By having a pity party? Withdrawing from the line of fire, brooding, letting my results suffer and then crying a river for reporters who could then write about how "human" I was? Tim and I were really getting into a flow when he fell ill; I felt more than anything else I needed to push onward and finish the job we'd started.

The Australian Open of 1995 was a brutal tournament, starting with Tim's collapse. I was lucky to be leaving Australia in the company of Paul Annacone, who agreed to stay with me until we knew more about Tim's situation. Shortly after Tim returned to Chicago, a further battery of tests confirmed what everyone most feared. He had brain cancer. The treatment was aggressive chemotherapy and possibly surgery, and the gravity of the situation was obvious. Yet Tim was resolved to beat the disease, and he was going to keep coaching me as long as he humanly could. I was all for that. I believed that keeping him involved would also help keep his spirits up.

I had a few weeks off before my next event, Memphis, and we worked out our plan going forward. Tim would watch as many matches as he could on television, and we would talk strategy over the phone before most of them. Paul would be on hand to help me out with the daily stuff—hitting, getting my rackets strung, booking practice courts, discussing what Tim told either of us. In the beginning this worked all right, but the situation inevitably went downhill as Tim's condition deteriorated.

Meanwhile, in a development I kept secret from everyone, I was battling physical problems of my own, although they were paltry compared to Tim's. For more than a year, I had been struggling with bouts of nausea and an inability, at times, to keep food or even water down. The situation started sometime in 1993, and was so aggravated by the spring of 1994 that I was unable to make the start time for the final of the important Key Biscayne tournament, in which I was to play Andre Agassi.

In a gesture I still appreciate, Andre agreed to postpone the scheduled 1 P.M. start of the final for an hour, while I took an intravenous glucose drip. I had been throwing up all morning, which I blamed on the pasta dinner I'd had the night before. The IV did the job, rehydrating me, and I went on to win the final in three sets. At the time, I wanted to believe that the episodes were somehow related to dehydration.

However, the bouts of nausea had started not long after I started taking Indocin to deal with pain in my serving arm. My arm problem probably started with a change Tim and I had made in our practice routine going back a year or longer. Up to then, I rarely served hard in practice, mainly because I just wanted to hit some balls, have some rallies, work up a sweat. Tim felt I needed to do more to keep my most formidable weapon in tip-top shape.

To Tim, serving easy in practice was like a baseball player wasting batting practice on bunting because he felt he was hitting too many home runs. It was nuts. Tim wanted me to keep developing my serve, and felt that if I trained it to work hard I would end up serving even harder, with better consistency, over longer periods of time (in this he was right). He convinced me, and Todd Snyder, the former ATP Tour trainer whom I had hired to work exclusively with me, also agreed that working my serving arm harder posed no long-term danger.

Tim's hunch was right. My serve improved, and became even more of a weapon. Unfortunately, the increased workload and all the hard serving suddenly did give me arm pain and ultimately a condition sometimes called "dead arm." My arm ached and throbbed, sometimes in the middle of the night, or during practice or in matches. It was just a dull, throbbing pain, very uncomfortable, like a toothache in my arm. And when it was bad, it affected my service speed and, of course, my enthusiasm and confidence.

I began to take Advil, in combination with the Indocin, a very powerful anti-inflammatory. I took them religiously after practice and matches. Pretty soon I was popping the Indocin and Advil cocktails before matches as a preventative measure. But as I got hooked on the Indocin, I suddenly found myself unable to keep food down. Before my 1994 Wimbledon semifinal with Todd Martin, I drank some water and promptly threw it back up. On the morning of the 1994 Grand Slam Cup final, I woke up feeling sick. I had the dry heaves but tried to force down breakfast anyway, and it came back up. I felt awful.

I was really settling into my number one position by then, however, and I didn't want to take time off; I wanted to give it the gas, so I just pushed on. Not long after that Key Biscayne match, I went to see my doctor in Tampa, and he ran tests on my upper gastrointestinal tract. It established beyond dispute that I had an ulcer, and the physician thought it was from a combination of stress and the Indocin. He said if I was lucky, and took the right medication, I could be rid of the ulcer in three months. So on top of Vitas's tragic death and Tim's sudden illness, now I had a three-pill-a-day regimen to follow.

B y February of 1995, it was pretty clear that this was not going to be a routine year. I had a lot on my plate, including Davis Cup. I'd told the USTA that I would be available for the entire campaign, which could be as many as four ties.

Some years the Davis Cup challenge appealed to me, and some

years it didn't. It never had anything to do with money. In fact, the money was lousy by any standard. We would typically get something like fifteen or twenty thousand dollars to play, and if our home ties earned money, we got a little additional revenue in a profit-sharing system. But trust me, it was minimal. Given that a Davis Cup tie is actually a full week's commitment (sometimes more, if you got there a day or two early), the pay was shockingly low for guys who could pull down four or five times as much for a one-night exhibition.

I understood the unique nature of Davis Cup. I had reasons other than money for running hot and cold on the competition. To win the Davis Cup requires a four-week commitment, which is the equivalent of two Grand Slams. You also aren't sure in advance who you're going to play round by round, or where the ties will be held. Fans often are confused by Davis Cup's unwieldy format and traditions. A number of times, I'd be part of a winning team only to have to explain to well-wishers or even reporters that we didn't actually win the Davis Cup that day—we'd merely won the tie to advance to the next one, months away. I understand that all that stuff is part of what makes Davis Cup compelling, but I just never fully bought into it.

My attitude might have been different if we had developed a Davis Cup team spirit comparable to that of the present U.S. squad, with Andy Roddick and James Blake leading. They have great team spirit and camaraderie, but then they aren't competing against each other for Grand Slam titles. My generation consisted of four Grand Slam champions (Andre, Jim, Michael Chang, and me) who were perennial top-five contenders, and a handful of lesser but still terrific players. We were rivals and competitors, and even though we all got along pretty well, we were always circling each other, sniffing, gauging our next moves. That doesn't lend itself to creating great team spirit, because most teams rely on a dominant leader (like Roddick), and none of us was inclined to play second fiddle to anyone else.

The comparison between Davis Cup, which struggles to get adequate exposure and public respect, and golf's hugely successful Ryder Cup is interesting: Ryder Cup is a one-week event played every two years. Davis Cup is an annual event, played in four rounds on a rolling basis in unpredictable places. I wish they would adopt a different Davis Cup model—play it in one place, over a specific period (two weeks would be ideal), and see what happens.

Davis Cup did grow on me (I ended up playing sixteen ties and helped win the Cup twice—that's a lot more than a casual commitment), but the way my singles career unfolded, Davis Cup became a constant source of tension. I knew that it wasn't feasible to focus on staying number one, winning majors, and also play a full four-week Davis Cup schedule. It was too much. So some years I committed to Davis Cup, and some years I declined. I skipped 1993 and was part of the 1994 squad that lost in the semifinals.

But there was another subtle factor at play in 1995. That year, my rivalry with Andre Agassi was entering a new peak phase. Just months earlier, at the 1994 U.S. Open, Andre completed his epic journey back from the netherworld of the rankings to become the first unseeded player to win the title. Then he beat me in the Australian Open final to start '95. People everywhere were dying to see Andre emerge as my rival. That was fine by me; I knew that any player is only as good—especially in the court of public opinion—as the quality of his competition. And Nike, the company that sponsored both of us, was at the head of the parade of people doing everything possible to fire the rivalry.

Andre, Jim, and I had all agreed to play Davis Cup in 1995, and as soon as the draw kicked out USA at Italy in the second round, it spelled trouble. The quarterfinal tie was scheduled for the out-of-the-way city of Palermo, Sicily, at the end of March—right after the two big U.S. hard-court tournaments (Indian Wells and Key Biscayne) left contenders like us tired and looking for some downtime before the European clay-court season.

The three of us all wanted to do what was best for Davis Cup, tennis, and ourselves. The bottom line was that nobody really wanted to go and play the Italians right after Key Biscayne, but there was pressure from various factions for us to win the Cup—how could you not win the Cup when you had Sampras, Agassi, Courier, and Chang as potential team members? It was sure to be a public-relations disaster if all of us skipped the event because we had other, more important fish to fry. We would look selfish and unpatriotic.

There was this, too: after Andre beat me in the 1995 Australian Open final, we both had the sense that the two of us would be battling it out for the number one ranking in the coming months and years. Very honestly, neither of us wanted to make a Davis Cup sacrifice that would ultimately improve the other guy's chances at the big tournaments, or over the long hunt for the number one ranking.

At Indian Wells in the late winter with Davis Cup looming, we all recognized we had a problem, so we took the unusual step of getting together—literally, in the same room—with Tom Gullikson (who had taken over as Davis Cup captain) and a few other advisers to talk things out. And we decided, face-to-face and right on the spot, that if nobody wanted to go to Italy but somebody had to go, the only fair thing was for *everyone* to go.

So we made that decision and held a big press conference, saying that Andre and I were both going to Palermo, with Jim waiting in the wings if needed. Over the next few weeks, Andre and I split the Indian Wells and Miami titles. With his win over me in Key Biscayne, Andre stripped me of the number one ranking. I'd end up chasing him all summer in hopes of getting it back.

But right after our Miami match, we hopped on a plane to New York—actually, we hopped on Andre's chartered jet, and that night paid his new girlfriend, Brooke Shields, a surprise visit on the set of her Broadway play *Grease*. We spent the night in New York, then flew by Concorde to London and took another private plane to Palermo for the tie.

The tie against Italy was a mismatch. The Italian singles players, Renzo Furlan and Andrea Gaudenzi, were solid top-fifty players, but nothing more. Granted, they were playing at home, on clay, before an Italian crowd that could be very vocal and unruly. But the way to neutralize that was to keep it from becoming a battle. That's just what we did, winning the first three matches to clinch by the second day of play.

We didn't have to worry about the semifinal tie until September, when we would be meeting a tough Swedish team led by Mats Wilander. At least we would get them at home—for Andre, literally at home, in Las Vegas.

With Davis Cup on the back burner for most of the spring and summer, and Andre much on my mind, I went to Europe with high hopes. Tim Gullikson knew how much it would mean, historically, for an attacker like me to win at Roland Garros, so we had worked extra hard on homework and preparation.

I played four events leading up to Roland Garros, and *lost* my very first match at three of them (I made the semis at Hamburg). At the main event at Roland Garros, I lost 6–4 in the fifth, in the first round, to Austrian journeyman Gilbert Schaller. It was a difficult time; I felt things pressing in on me from all sides. Andre was a new threat; he had snatched away the number one ranking that had been mine for two years. I was still recuperating from my ulcer, and, with the United States still alive in Davis Cup, I felt overcommitted. And then there was the Tim situation. He'd been unable to travel to Europe, and I missed him.

The good news was that my relationship with Paul Annacone was growing better all the time. Tim was still officially my coach, and it would stay that way until Tim made a miracle recovery—or the worst-case scenario came to pass. Paul and I knew that we had to prepare for the latter. I visited Tim a few times, and he put on a brave face, but he never looked better than the time before. We just wanted to make his life as productive and fulfilling for as long as possible while he fought his lonely battle.

In June, shortly after Roland Garros, Andre and I filmed that series of "guerrilla tennis" commercials that would punctuate the upcoming summer on the hard courts of the U.S. Open. Soon thereafter, I atoned for my poor showing on clay by winning the two big grass events, Queen's and Wimbledon. The Wimbledon title was my third straight, and while my four-set win over Boris Becker was unremarkable, I see it as a tipping point in my relationship with the grandest tournament of them all.

The first year I won Wimbledon, I was boring, and Jim—the guy I beat—was boring. It was a personality thing. The second year I won Wimbledon, the tennis was boring—the way Goran and I played in the final was boring. It was a technical, game-based thing. But by 1995, the club had gone to a slower ball, and while I survived another brutal, five-set serving contest with Goran in the semis, briefly reigniting the furor over power tennis, the final against Becker was played in such a glow of camaraderie and good sportsmanship that it pleased even the most sour of pundits.

The British loved Becker, and in this match he seemed to be passing the generational baton to me. The crowd must have felt that if Boris had such respect for me, I had to be okay. It also didn't hurt that despite the controversies in which I had been embroiled at Wimbledon, I spoke of the tournament only in superlatives—and meant every word I said. I was slowly winning the Brits over. I was gratified by the way the degree of respect increased, because my own affection for Wimbledon had increased by the year, regardless of my image or how Wimbledon fans felt about me. It was a great feeling to love the place—and finally to feel loved in return.

In my first few years at Wimbledon, I stayed at the St. James, which was one of the official player hotels right in the heart of London. But the smart guys, ever since the Bjorn Borg era, had found that the best thing was to rent a house in Wimbledon Village, an upscale suburb just up the hill from the All England Lawn Tennis and Croquet Club (that's the official name of the place where they hold Wimbledon; the tournament unofficially got its name from the town, much the way the U.S. Open, back in the day, was often referred to as Forest Hills). The house I first rented and then stayed in for many years was on Clifton Road, and it was—I still laugh when I think about this—owned by people called "Borg." Honest.

The Borgs were no dummies. They did nearly as well as their tennis-playing namesake because of the tournament. I paid around £10,000, which in some years was close to $20,000, just to stay there for the two weeks of Wimbledon. Over time, I paid more and started to take the place for a month, from just after the French Open through Wimbledon. I believe Roger Federer took over the Borg house after I opted out of our contract one year, and how could you blame him, with that history?

I've always been a little neurotic about air-conditioning; I like to sleep in a cool, dark room. So one of the first things I did when I set up shop on Clifton Road was go out and get a portable air-conditioning unit (the British don't like air-conditioning at all). I set that up in the bedroom, and it was waiting for me, year after year. I had a good shower at the house. Early in my career I had seen a French player relieving himself in the shower at a tournament, and from that day forward I never used the common locker-room showers. I always waited until I returned to my apartment or hotel, whatever the conditions, before I finally showered after a match.

I also had a chef, Kirsten, who was from South Africa, and whose more recent gig was cooking for Tiger Woods during the British Open golf tournament. Kirsten cooked my meals, and I was pretty easy to please: waffles and maybe a scrambled egg and one cup of coffee in the morning. She would sometimes make me a sandwich and I would brown-bag it to work, especially on days when it didn't make much sense for me to leave the grounds after a hit and before my match. The dinners she cooked were healthy, nutritious, and simple: chicken and fresh vegetables, pasta with homemade sauce, that kind of thing.

Once in a while, I'd go out to the village, or down another hill to the town of Wimbledon and the San Lorenzo restaurant, an Italian place that has been a fixture with the players for ages. Once in a while I might hit a movie, but that would be it. I'd go out maybe twenty-five percent of the time. Occasionally, I would go to the huge park called Wimbledon Commons, where I would train or sometimes just have a walk. It was nice and peaceful in the Commons, and the village itself, while lively, was surprisingly devoid of press and paparazzi.

Paul, meanwhile, stayed in a rental flat in London. It was because both of us needed our space. We were around each other all day, and it was nice to wake up in the morning and have privacy. I liked that, but I felt lonely at times, too. Sometimes I had nobody to talk to but Kirsten, with whom I'd chitchat a little, but that was it. My existence was a little monkish, my only break with routine consisting of inviting friends for dinner—guys like Paul or Todd Martin and his coach, Dean Goldfine.

I made a pretty famous crack once when I was asked how I liked London. I said that I couldn't wait to get back to the States, where I could get ESPN on television and a cheeseburger and fries at a diner. I was only half-kidding. British television improved over time; the dark, early years when there were only four channels, three of them showing six-hour documentaries on things like the Belgian lace doily industry, quickly gave way to the satellite age. The Borgs actually went and got a satellite dish and one of the first flat-screen televisions. When I saw it, I wondered, *How can they afford this?* And then I realized . . .

Kirsten made sure I got all the protein I needed in my meals. And for all my boasting about cheeseburgers, I always kept myself on a very short leash. I had one little ritual of indulgence. Every year on the morning after the final, I had Kirsten make me the classic English breakfast, which includes bacon, eggs, fried bread, sausage, beans, French fries, all this yummy greasy stuff that tasted great but always made me feel sick after eating it.

My other indulgence in years when I won was to return to my U.S. base in Tampa and immediately go to the local Checkers fast-food franchise for one of their great burgers and fries. I didn't drink wine at all, except at the Wimbledon Champions Ball. I drank mostly water, but treated myself to a Coke every now and then. And this wasn't just at Wimbledon; it was pretty much everywhere I played. I had very good discipline on the nutrition front, and I must say I often felt I had an edge when I saw these pros in the player's restaurant loading up on pasta with rich cream sauces, big steak-and-potato lunches, and cake and ice cream.

A maid would come in to do laundry and the beds three times a week in London. I liked wearing tennis gear that had been laundered at least once before. Usually when Nike introduced a new line (always right before a Grand Slam, so you had three or four new lines a year), they would send me fifteen to twenty shirts and pairs of shorts, and I would wear that stuff until the next new line came out. I wasn't like Ivan Lendl, who would wear a brand-new shirt for every match. It was funny; you would see Ivan sitting there in the U.S. Open locker room before he went out to play a big semifinal or something, and he would be messing around, trying to get that stupid little string and tag off the button on the new shirt.

I had a thing about tennis shoes, going all the way back to the time I paid dearly for changing to the new Nike Air models. Clothing and shoe companies often wanted you to switch to shoes that matched whatever line they were promoting, but I wouldn't have it. When I found the Nike Air Oscillate, which was pretty light but had good stiffness and support, I stuck with it. Nike sold plenty of them, too.

All the shoe manufacturers make special shoes for the grass-court pros, ones with a grid of little stubs on the bottom. They were like soft, tiny cleats. I didn't want the stubs to get too low (from wear), but I also didn't want to wear a new pair of shoes for every match, like some guys did. In general, I loved wearing worn-down shoes on most courts, but not on grass. So I would take a new pair of shoes, practice with them, and play one or maybe two matches wearing them. Then I would throw that pair away and break in a new one. So the most wear I got out of a pair of shoes at Wimbledon was one practice and two matches.

With Nike, it was important to stay on top of the company because as they changed lines and factories, you just never knew what you would get, sizing-wise. Jim Courier and I used to piss and moan about that. We'd say, "Do what you want to the color or pattern, but don't change the length of the hem on the shorts or the cut of the foot bed in the shoe." Sometimes I'd get a batch of shoes that came from a different factory than the last batch, and I could barely get my custom-made orthotic inserts into them. Of course, top pros tend to be more particular about things like the precise fit of their shoes or clothing, and we must have driven the Nike guys to distraction with our quibbles. Perhaps surprisingly, they didn't make custom shoes for us.

I was almost never hassled in Wimbledon Village. One time a

couple of kids came to the door and knocked, asking for an auto-graph, which I happily gave them. Each day, I'd just call the All England Club for my courtesy car, and in moments it was there. It took all of five minutes to get to the club to practice or play. The club itself was very cozy, even after the renovation binge in the late 1990s. The tradition there until the remodeling was that they had two locker rooms—a fairly big, well-appointed one for the seeded players (the "A" locker room), and a smaller one that wasn't even part of the main clubhouse/Centre Court complex for the journey-men, juniors, and others.

I made it into the A locker room pretty quickly, but the crazy thing was that it was not just tight, it was probably more crowded than the B locker room. You had all the seeded players in there, plus their coaches, and you had the former champions, some old guys, and club members. It was jammed. The guys would sit in there play-ing backgammon or cards, or telling stories. I'd mostly sit and listen. The most memorable thing about that locker room to me was it was a very short walk down a set of stairs and through a small holding room and there you were—right on the hallowed Centre Court.

That holding room is where they have that famous Kipling quote above the door: "If you can meet with Triumph and Disaster, and treat those two imposters just the same . . ." Everyone talks about that plaque and how much it means, how it sends chills down the spine of a player waiting to walk out there. It's pretty dramatic, because when you're in that room, you can look out the open door and see that green patch of Centre Court, all aglow in the sunlight, beyond the short, dark gangway. But the thing I remember most is the trophy—the singles trophy, which was always sitting right there to the left of the door.

Steve Adams is the attendant in that little room; his official job title is Master of Ceremonies and his task is to hold the players there until everything is ready. Usually, once you stage with your opponent,

Steve walks out onto Centre Court first to make sure everything is okay—that everybody in the Royal Box is seated, that the chair umpire is ready, that the crowd has settled, and that the net has been checked and secured. Then he returns and says, in this chipper, matter-of-fact voice: "Okay, we're all set, gentlemen. There is royalty; you must bow . . ."

Later in my career, Adams would sometimes turn to the poor guy standing next to me and say something like, "Oh, just follow Pete; he knows what to do."

And I'd be thinking, *How's that supposed to make this poor guy feel?*

M y third consecutive Wimbledon title was quickly overshadowed in 1995 by Andre's amazing resurgence, which picked up steam during the hard-court season. I was just another of his many victims as he went on a twenty-match summer tear that stunned all of tennis. Andre beat me in the Canadian Open as he went on a four-tournament run to enter the U.S. Open as the favorite. But that also put him under a lot of pressure. If he lost to me, all twenty-five of the matches he had won over the summer went right into the toilet, and the fact that he was number one went into the wastebasket. Andre, like me, played for the big moments and the big tournaments more than for the numbers and rankings.

So that created pressure, and I also felt that Andre *knew* I would be very tough at Flushing Meadows. I had the game, I had the motivation, I had the experience. I had everything needed to spoil his magical run. I was confident, despite Andre's superb level of play. The situation made great fodder for the press. But for me the bottom line was that I enjoyed playing Andre. Good as he was, and no matter what the score on a given day might be, he didn't really move me far out of my comfort zone if I was on top of my game.

We marched to the final to a drumbeat of inevitability and media hype. The weather on the day of the final was tricky, although you may not have known it if you were just watching, or even sitting in Louis Armstrong Stadium. It was a little breezy, and we started off feeling each other out, a little like two heavyweight fighters. I could sense that this was a huge occasion because the A-list celebrities had come out: John F. Kennedy, Jr., was there; so was Arnold Schwarzenegger and a host of others.

Andre and I jabbed at each other and built a feeling for the ball, game after game; both of us knew that as the set went on, one or the other would have an opportunity. At 5–4, set point to me, we had a nineteen-stroke rally, much of it forehand to forehand, that I remember as if it had just happened yesterday. It was one of the most important and significant points I ever played, and I won it with a sharply angled backhand winner.

Andre had maneuvered me into playing the kind of point that was his bread and butter, and I had not just escaped the trap to win the point; it won me the set. It was like a right hook that staggers a fighter. In tennis, a moment like that can cost you a lot more than the game. I think it probably cost Andre the next set, because I more or less cruised through it without being pushed, or feeling like I was being punished, physically. I won that second set 6–3.

With two sets in hand, my confidence soared. I had a commanding lead and just pulling even would cost Andre a lot. Still, I expected Andre to win his rounds as I would win mine. He played well to win the third set, but it took a lot out of him, and he still had a long way to go just to get on even footing. I had to be careful, though: if I went down a break in the fourth, it would be like an IV drip for Andre's flagging spirits; he would instantly revive and get a massive surge of adrenaline and confidence. I had to dial it up, but still play "within myself."

For me, dialing it up always started with improving the quality of my serve, either speed- or placementwise. One of the best things about winning your service points quickly is that you're in and out of your service game in the blink of an eye, and you can then focus and take even more chances on breaking serve. Conversely, your opponent feels pressure; he's so busy trying to hold serve that he barely has time to think of breaking you. This can be a big factor late in a set, and it always makes life tougher for a player whose own serve isn't a huge weapon.

Andre and I played close through most of the fourth set, but I was serving aces and held the eleventh game with ease. I sensed that the pressure might be getting to Andre, and got the key break for 6–5, after which I served out the match.

The win opened the floodgates for me in a number of ways. It was my seventh major, and it launched me on a run that would earn me six more majors in the next four years. The match also had a devastating effect on Andre. It put me up 9–8 in our rivalry, but more important it impacted Andre so badly that he soon fell off the radar—he admitted much later that it took him two years to recover from that devastating loss. It was too bad, because the match also certified my rivalry with Andre; nobody could push me and force me to play my best tennis the way Andre could. And nobody could call our rivalry hype cooked up by Nike anymore—it was the real deal, even though it was put on hold.

L ess than two weeks after the U.S. Open final, the Davis Cup squad reassembled in Las Vegas to host Sweden. The atmosphere in Vegas was relaxing. We gambled a little, and all gathered at Andre's house one night for a big dinner cooked up by a Vegas chef. After the meal, Andre took a few of us for a ride in the dunes and mountains around Vegas in his Hummer.

Our captain, Tom Gullikson, wanted everyone to be happy and

Top: That's me in the yellow shirt, with my older siblings, Gus and Stella, my little sister, Marion, and my parents, Sam and Georgia.

Above: As a kid I was pretty focused on tennis to the exclusion of just about everything else. Around school I was known only as "the tennis kid." But I truly loved what I was doing.
Robert Kenas

Left: I didn't see much of my dad as a child, because he worked two jobs. But as I got deeply involved in tennis, the game became a way to spend time with him.

Although he and I would grow apart, Pete Fischer was a big part of my early tennis life. In drafting various coaches and experts to teach me different aspects of the game, Pete was less a coach than a combination of mad scientist and general contractor.

In 1990 my game suddenly started coming together, and—not quite knowing what was happening— I found myself beating Andre Agassi at the U.S. Open for my first major title. After the thrill wore off, I found myself in territory that was unfamiliar and for which I was unprepared. *Associated Press*

Entering 1993 I promised myself that I'd never give up in a match ever again. Soon I'd taken my second major—and my first Wimbledon title! Looking back, that win was the day I finally learned how to get past my fear, and the beginning of my career as a dominant champion. *Getty Images*

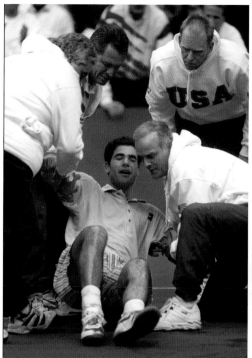

When Andre couldn't compete in the 1995 Davis Cup tie against Russia, I stepped up and played three matches on the slow red clay—including this grueling five-setter against dogged retriever Andrei Chesnokov. I collapsed on the court, immobilized by cramps, immediately after hitting the winning shot. *Associated Press/Sergei Kivrin*

Shortly after the 1995 Davis Cup, Boris Becker pulled me aside and said, "That Davis Cup performance in Moscow was unbelievable, Pete. That's why you're number one in the world, no question." Given the intensity of our rivalry, it was an incredibly generous thing to say, and one of the nicest compliments I've ever received. *Associated Press*

Andre and me filming one of Nike's brilliant "guerrilla tennis" commercials in Trafalgar Square. That iconic campaign helped to cement our rivalry—and it also captured the true nature of our relationship. *Associated Press/ Charles Miller*

Michael Chang was my friend and arch rival when we were juniors, and he became the first of the "Golden Generation" to take a Grand Slam title. *Michael Baz*

When my longtime coach Tim Gullikson died of brain cancer in 1996, I was devastated. Tim was a close friend, almost a big brother to me in my early years on the tour. And he was a real student of the game, a guy who played at a high level but also loved tennis with the purity of a fan. *Getty Images*

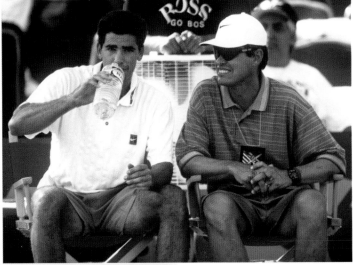

Alex Corretja and me after our brutal five-set battle at the 1996 U.S. Open, the match that became engraved in everyone's minds as my defining moment—my warrior moment. *Associated Press/ Kathy Willens*

Here I'm celebrating finishing a record sixth year in a row as number one in the world. Getting that record is still the accomplishment I'm most proud of. To me, greatness lies in going out there day after day and getting the job done. *Associated Press*

Jim Courier and I became close friends in our early days as pros, and he showed me how hard you needed to work to keep up on the tour. By the time our careers had blossomed and we found ourselves competing for majors, the friendship had cooled somewhat—the circumstances, and our personalities, were just too competitive for us to remain so close. *Getty Images*

In 2000 I battled through a painful shin injury to take a record-breaking thirteenth Grand Slam title at Wimbledon. When I climbed into the stands to hug my dad, this picture got printed far and wide, and my dad was amazed to find people in the street recognizing him. *Associated Press*

My wife, Bridgette Wilson, and I were married in 2000, and she agreed to put her career on hold to travel with me while I played out my last years as a pro. Neither of us was sure how much longer I'd have left.
Associated Press

In 2001 I found myself losing matches to an emerging new guard, the kids who would win majors and dominate the game in the years to come: Roddick, Safin, Hewitt, and, of course, Roger Federer, who knocked me out of Wimbledon that year.
Associated Press/Dave Caulkin

I'd been hoping that Wimbledon would help get my game on track after a rough start to 2002. But when I stepped onto the court for this early round match, I had absolutely no confidence and lost in five sets. Wimbledon, my last refuge, had turned into the focal point of my demise. *Associated Press*

Above: It was fitting that both my first and my last major final would be played against Andre. We were the oldest pair of finalists in the American Grand Slam in thirty-two years—I was thirty-one, Andre was thirty-two. We played a tough four-setter, and at the end I had the rarest of opportunities: to go out on my own terms. *Associated Press*

Left: A big part of my resurgence at the U.S. Open that year was due to my coach, Paul Annacone's influence. I don't think Paul's ever received enough credit for what he did for me as a coach. *Getty Images*

After the 2002 U.S. Open win, I found I just didn't have the appetite for the tournament grind and decided to hang up my spurs. Here I am at the retirement ceremony the USTA threw for me. I was touched and honored to see so many of my rivals present, and all of the pent-up emotions of the previous twelve months found release. *Associated Press/ Bill Kostroun*

Here I am with Bridgette and our sons, Christian Charles *(left)* and Ryan Nikolaos, at my 2007 induction into the Tennis Hall of Fame. Standing up there was an incredible honor and a moment I'll never forget. *Michael Baz*

In 2007 I played three exhibition matches against Roger Federer, who at the time had closed to within two Grand Slam titles of my fourteen. Much to the surprise of pretty much everyone, I won the third match of the series. And I had a great time hanging out with Roger, comparing notes and talking tennis. *Michael Baz*

With Rod Laver at a charity event in 2007. Growing up, I was conscious of trying to build my game in Laver's mold, and I still remember my dad's firing up the old film projector so we could watch footage of his matches on our dining room wall. I hope I've come close to living up to his legacy. *Michael Baz*

comfortable, so he volunteered to scrunch up in the back cargo area of the Hummer in a kind of crouch. Soon Andre was blasting up and down these mountains, the Hummer bouncing around like crazy—it was pretty much fun for everyone but Tom, who was getting thrown around like a rag doll in the back, bumping his head and shoulders and knees. All we heard from the back was, *"Ow . . . ooomph . . . eeech . . . arrraggghhhhh!"*

Tim, whose situation had continued to deteriorate, decided that he wanted to attend the tie—against his doctor's advice. The USTA and everyone else in tennis supported the idea, and Tim made the trip as a kind of unofficial cocaptain with his brother. It was great to see him near a tennis court again—great to see what being around the game and players could still do for his spirits. But he was looking very gaunt and hollow. Anybody could tell with one glance that he was not well.

Andre and I won our first singles matches, but the Swedes took the doubles. Andre showed up to watch that match with his right arm in a sling beneath his unzipped tracksuit. He had torn a chest muscle in his opening-day singles, and he was finished for the tie. We lost the doubles, but the following day Todd, replacing Andre, stepped in and crafted a tidy three-set win over Enqvist to clinch the tie. The USTA then asked the Swedish officials if they objected to Tim sitting on court alongside his brother (and our captain) during my meaningless match against Wilander. The Swedes, ever the good guys, agreed.

After the tie, the U.S. team room was awash with the usual assortment of friends, family, USTA types, ITF types, and garden-variety hangers-on. At one point, I glanced across the room and made eye contact with Tim. His face by that time was starting to hollow out, and his eyes—an intense blue to begin with—were practically burning. For a second, we looked at each other, and each of us knew what the other was thinking: This should be our moment. All these other people are extraneous. This is about the two of us, and nothing can take away what we've accomplished, or the trust we have. I've never forgotten that moment or that look. It's with me to this day as my enduring memory of Tim.

So it was on to Moscow for the November final, and I knew how much Tim wanted to see me lead the squad to a triumph. It was a tough ask, because the Russians, predictably, held the tie on very slow red clay, indoors. For them, it was the right move, even though Jim Courier and Andre Agassi could be as tough on clay as anyone. There was only one hitch—Andre was still nursing his chest injury. We hoped until the eleventh hour that Andre would be good to go, meaning that my job would be a manageable one: making sure we won the doubles, while Andre and Jim would do the heavy lifting in singles. I had confidence that we would win the doubles—I liked playing Davis Cup doubles with Todd Martin and, as ambivalent as I was about clay, I played doubles on it happily, with confidence.

We arrived in Moscow on a Saturday, six days before the Friday start. Andre had sent word that even though he couldn't play, he would attend the tie as a show of team spirit and solidarity. That sealed the deal. Tom declared that I was going to play singles unless, of course, I felt like I was the wrong man for the job, and made enough of a fuss about the decision. How's that for an awkward spot? What was I going to do, say, "Nah, Tom, I'm not up for it. Let Todd or Richey go out there"? I could see all the makings of Lyon revisited—a full-on disaster.

But the team spirit in Moscow was great, and fortunately for us, by then Russia was changing. We were well taken care of in a fine hotel with great food. Our comfort level with one another was high. And it really helped boost our morale when Andre showed up in Moscow, making the long trip at the end of a long year, even though he was destined to just sit on the bench without ever hitting a ball.

We even did a little sightseeing—we went to Red Square one day, and went through the line at Lenin's Tomb, where we posed for the usual PR pictures. I was happy to have my dad and sister Stella along on the trip. It wasn't that Dad was fired up about Davis Cup; he was just intrigued by Russia. I was like, *What am I, Dad, chopped liver?* But with him around, I didn't want to play lousy.

I opened the tie against Andrei Chesnokov, one of the era's most dogged retrievers. Chessy was a dirt devil who loved red clay; he specialized in running down every ball and outlasting opponents. He wasn't big, but he was lean and sinewy, with great stamina. Getting him on clay was a tough assignment at the best of times. It didn't help my cause that the red clay was not just slow, it was actually *muddy.* The Russians had watered the hell out of it, trying to make it as slow as possible. The only bright spot for me was that in that enormous Olympic stadium, the crowd wasn't much of a factor. They probably had close to twenty thousand fans in there, but it felt like far fewer because they were so far from the court.

Knowing how skilled Chessy was on clay, I started pressing right from the onset. I felt obliged to win points quickly, and made some poor decisions. That I wasn't in the best of shape also made me want to force the action. I wondered what I had gotten myself into—I wasn't even supposed to be playing singles! But in spite of all that, I was mentally into the match. I figured I'd just hang in there, let the ball ride, see what the day brings. It was just a tennis match, and the fact that I had no business winning it made my life easier.

The biggest thing I had going for me probably was that I was Pete Sampras, and Chessy knew it and I knew it. He knew what it would mean to beat me, the top player in the world (I had regained my number one ranking from Andre by then), with the hopes and national pride of all Russia riding on his shoulders in a Davis Cup final. Talk about pressure. Chesnokov won the first set, and I think that caused him to let down his guard and slightly lose his focus. Such things happen all the time; they're the mental equivalent of taking your eye off the ball.

I made just enough winners and won just enough points on the attack to keep Chessy a little off balance, and I won the next two close sets. Chessy regrouped—overall he was a good competitor with a strong mind and will—and took the fourth-set tiebreaker. But in the fifth set, I hit out a little more freely, and he got kind of stuck trying to figure out if he should force the action or let me take the initiative, hoping I might screw up, or tire.

Chessy took the latter course of action (which is always more tempting), the way baseliners often do. He basically left the matter in my hands. I didn't hesitate to take the initiative, and poured on the heat. I got to match point, but just as I whaled on a forehand, I began to feel myself cramping up. I ran to the net behind my shot. As Chesnokov drew a bead and let his passing shot fly, I lost control of my limbs, seized up, and collapsed.

Luckily, Chessy missed the pass and it was over. I had won it.

On the bench, the U.S. team, seeing that I was in agony, rushed to the court. If you've ever seen anyone cramping, you know it isn't a pretty sight. Cramps make you do crazy contortions, even though they don't do lasting damage. Our Davis Cup trainer, Bobby Russo, and our longtime team doctor, George Fareed, bolted onto the court; they started hauling me up.

Normally, Dr. Fareed is about as quiet a guy as you'll find anywhere. But he started yelling, "Get out of the way! Move!" He roared, "Coming through!"

It was like I'd been shot in the head or something, and they were trying to get me to the emergency room. Despite my discomfort, I found it terribly funny, and suddenly I was laughing my head off because Doc was making such a big deal out of it. They finally dragged me off to the locker room and gave me a pill that quickly helped stop the cramping, but every time I thought back to Doc Fareed's panicked reaction, I burst out laughing again.

Unfortunately, Jim lost the second rubber on Friday to Yevgeny Kafelnikov, leaving us tied at 1–1. When Tom decided that I would be playing singles, he penciled in Todd and Richey Reneberg as the doubles team. But with the score tied, Tom had second thoughts. Anytime the tie is deadlocked at 1–1 the team that wins the doubles goes into the final day of singles with a huge advantage—and much less pressure. That's one of the beauties of Davis Cup—the importance of doubles, the game that plays second fiddle to singles at regular tournaments.

Tom asked me how I felt about playing the doubles. I said, "Well, I've had better days . . . but yeah, why not?" So the next day, Todd and I went out and played a very solid match to take the doubles. The most valuable by-product of Gully's shrewd move was that it took the Russians by surprise. Suddenly they were down 1–2, on the brink of elimination and, despite their home-court advantage, looking at having to beat two of the very top players in the world. That clay was the surface probably provided little comfort after what I had done on day one. I was the dominant number one player in the world, and I had taken personal control of the tie.

I was first up on Sunday. I felt a little heavy-legged but I knew I was one match away from a great achievement. And I was going up against Kafelnikov, a guy I always enjoyed playing—a guy who was good, and who lorded it over a lot of guys ranked lower down, but who always admired my game. Now he had to beat me to keep his nation's Davis Cup hopes alive.

For no good reason I can name, I played a great match at the most opportune of moments. Call it fate. Call it lucking out. Call it whatever. The bottom line is that Yevgeny never had a chance. I got into the zone a little bit. Surviving that Chesnokov match had really loosened me up, made me feel anything was possible, and winning the doubles didn't hurt. I mixed up my game against Kafelnikov. I served and volleyed a bit, stayed back some, kept him off balance by alternately going for my big shots and then hanging back, seeing what—if anything—he could bring to hurt me.

I led 6–2, 6–4, and Kafelnikov's last glimmer of hope flashed by in the third-set tiebreaker. I went up 6–4, and then served an ace right up the middle to end it. Tom rushed onto the court, and he was very, very emotional. First thing he whispered to me was, "I wish Tim could have been here to see that."

It was a touching moment and seconds later the rest of the squad engulfed us, and we let it all hang out, celebrating on the court. Andre, who had borne the load with me all year, was there to share in the joy. I really appreciated that he had sucked it up and made the trip over. He could have blown it off, especially after seeing his amazing year go down the tubes after that devastating loss to me in the U.S. Open final followed by his chest injury.

It didn't seem like it at the time, but that Davis Cup performance would become a highlight of my career and a chapter in Davis Cup lore and legend. Yet it barely made the media radar in the United States. I'm not sure there was a single American reporter in Moscow— other than the ubiquitous Bud Collins. I still can't explain how the win came about, but I have a funny feeling that the desperate straits in which we found ourselves loosened up the team. We had nothing to lose and felt no real pressure.

Our celebration carried over to the locker room after the dead fifth rubber, and that night we had a function with the usual assortment of USTA and ITF bigwigs, and the Davis Cup sponsors. And that's a weird thing about Davis Cup. You feel this incredible camaraderie when you're in it, and this wonderful bond with the team, the coach, even the support personnel like Doc Fareed and Bobby Russo. You win, and the best moment is in the team room or locker room, before it's opened up to all the officials. You pop the champagne with your buddies, have a few sips, have a few laughs, and then get ready for the official banquet. After that, everyone goes his separate way. You don't even travel together, because you're usually headed for different places.

It's a lot like that classic Western movie *The Magnificent Seven*. You're an eclectic group of gunslingers who come together to save the town, fending off the bad guys. Then when the job is done, you all drift off down the trail. Like those gunfighters, you're a loner. A tennis player.

Chapter 7

1996

KEY MATCHES . . .

May 1996, Roland Garros

SECOND ROUND

P. SAMPRAS	6	6	6	2	6
S. BRUGUERA	3	4	7(2)	6	3

QUARTERFINAL

P. SAMPRAS	6	4	6	6	6
J. COURIER	7(4)	6	4	4	4

SEMIFINAL

P. SAMPRAS	6	0	2
Y. KAFELNIKOV	7(3)	6	6

July 1996, Wimbledon, quarterfinal

P. SAMPRAS	5	6	4
R. KRAJICEK	7	7(4)	6

September 1996, U.S. Open

QUARTERFINAL

P. SAMPRAS	7(5)	5	5	6	7(7)
A. CORRETJA	6	7	7	4	6

FINAL

P. SAMPRAS	6	6	7
M. CHANG	1	4	6

November 1996, ATP Tour World Championships, final

P. SAMPRAS	3	7(5)	7(4)	6	6
B. BECKER	6	6	6	7(11)	4

YEAR–END RANKING . . . 1996: No. 1

My Warrior Moment

I finished number one for the year for the third consecutive time in 1995, even though Andre held the top spot for most of that time. To clinch the ranking, I had to beat Boris Becker in the final of the Paris Indoors in November. If I had finished the year a close number two to Andre, the tenor of my entire career might have changed. For one thing, setting the record for years at number one wouldn't have become an all-consuming goal for me the way it ultimately did. But I'm jumping ahead.

Shortly after Davis Cup, I went on to Munich to play the Grand Slam Cup. When I arrived, Boris Becker pulled me aside and paid me one of the nicest compliments I've ever received. If you remember how serious Boris could sound—how downright presidential—you'll appreciate this. He looked at me and said, "That Davis Cup performance in Moscow was unbelievable, Pete. That's why you're number one in the world, no question." Given that our rivalry was intense (I had beaten him in the Wimbledon final just months earlier), it was a generous thing to say.

As the months and years passed, I would savor and treasure that Moscow Davis Cup accomplishment with increasing joy—I was especially pleased that it had occurred on clay. This was one fruit of the commitment I embraced after the 1992 U.S. Open final.

A few important threads of my career ran together in 1995. There was the emerging possibility that I might break Jimmy Connors's long-standing record of finishing number one for five years in a row—a mark that some thought untouchable. It was also the official start of the glory days of my rivalry with Andre; it just went to a different level when we split those two hard-court finals at Indian Wells and Miami. We were over the hump; we were a hot topic in sports conversations, among general sports fans as well as tennis nuts. And we presented enough of a contrast to make people feel passionate about why they preferred one of us to the other.

The sad part for me was that all of that played out against the background of Tim's illness. Although everyone, including the media, was respectful of our privacy, people invariably asked about Tim and expressed their sympathies. I had to bear a great deal of sorrow and uncertainty in 1995, and I believe I handled it pretty well. The public appeared to see me in a warmer light from that point on. I think they felt more empathy toward me.

But there was a price to pay for the way I overloaded my competitive plate in 1995, and the first payment came due just weeks after the Davis Cup final in Moscow, at the 1996 Australian Open. I entered that event after having had less than a month of "off season" following the Grand Slam Cup (I pulled out of that with an ankle injury), and there was no way I was ready, much less eager, to play.

I made the trip, though, and I played and ended up losing in the third round to an Aussie, Mark Philippoussis. The conditions were perfect for an upset: Mark had an adoring home crowd behind him and it was a night match, with some eighteen thousand fans jammed into Rod Laver Arena, hungry for an upset. Mark just overpowered me—he was in the mythic zone, and when that happens to a player who has as big and versatile a game as Philippoussis, you're in trouble.

Down deep, I didn't feel too badly about the loss. I'd done my best. It might have been different if I'd been able to have six or eight weeks off to recharge my batteries and prepare for the new year. It also might have been different if it were any other major but the Australian. I never really liked playing in Melbourne, and my results over the years reflected it (I won just two titles there). This surprised many people, because on the surface the Australian Open might have looked like the perfect Grand Slam for me.

The Aussies have a great tennis tradition, yet even their icons tended to be regular, plainspoken, understated guys, somewhat like me. That was an immediate affinity I felt with Australia. The Australians also are a friendly, easygoing people, and the atmosphere at their major is laid-back; that also suited me. You could get gut-shot in the street there and if you crawled up to a guy for help he'd probably say, "No worries, mate!"—and then do all he could to help. The facilities at Melbourne Park, including Rod Laver Arena, are modern and first-class. You don't have that feeling of chaos and crowding that characterizes the other majors; even the media presence is considerably smaller. So you have a little less of that intensity and crazy pressure.

My beef with the Australian Open started with the balls. The balls always seemed to play a little differently down under. It was like they couldn't decide whether they wanted a fast, hard ball or a soft, slow one—one that fuzzed up like a kitten, or had a tighter, shorter nap and flew faster. One year the balls left little black marks on the composite surface, like you see on a squash court.

In Melbourne, you could always count on a few days when the temperature pushes the one-hundred-degree mark, and even though it isn't very humid, the heat can be draining. It was a special problem for me, because I secretly suffered from thalassemia, a mild disease common to men of Mediterranean descent. It's basically a blood-iron deficiency that causes anemia, and those who have it are prone to wilting in intense heat. I knew thalassemia ran in my family, but chose not to deal with it until fairly late in my career. Curiously, the guys who did best down under were the Swedes—people from a cold northern climate who appreciate and love the sun and its heat in the winter. The Russians are usually competitive there, too.

Another unpredictable thing about the courts at Melbourne Park was the Rebound Ace surface (which was replaced by Plexicushion for 2008). Rebound Ace was a rubber compound that they painted over the typical hard-court base of asphalt. The surface provided a little cushioning and slowed the bounce, but it did strange things in the heat. It was so hot in Melbourne one year that a TV crew cracked an egg on a court and, using time-lapse photography, recorded it frying. The heat made the Rebound Ace very sticky. Gabriela Sabatini once blew out an entire tennis shoe while making a change of direction (the shoe stuck and tore as she pushed off). Others took nasty tumbles and turned ankles.

Yet the conditions in Oz can change in the blink of an eye. The difference between playing day and night matches there is huge (the Australian and U.S. opens are the only two majors that have night tennis, and the retractable roof over the Laver Arena means you can have night *indoor* tennis). The surface reacted easily to ambient changes of any kind; it was simply a different court when the temperature was a comfortable seventy-five or eighty degrees—which was often the case during the night matches that followed scorching afternoons. To me, the Australian major was a crapshoot in the areas where I most preferred consistency—the surface, the balls, and the ambient conditions.

In Australia in 1996, on the anniversary of Tim's collapse, all the old wounds associated with that event were reopened. So I didn't really mind leaving Melbourne and putting all that behind me. Back at home, Tim was going downhill fast. I frequently found myself taking stock and realizing what I was losing.

When you're a top player instead of just a guy hell-bent on improving and figuring out your game, you are not hiring a coach purely for his command of the x's and o's. Those are usually sorted out in the first six or eight months. After that, it's all about how you interact with and influence each other; it's about the confidence and trust you build, and about loyalty.

By the time Tim collapsed, our relationship was about things other than how to return on grass, or how to throw your chest out in a Grand Slam final. But I didn't really think about that part until after he became ill. Tim had gradually become my stability—the guy I talked to (to whatever degree I talked), and in whom I confided in my own limited way.

I was troubled in the winter of 1996, and a little dispirited, but I did win two indoor winter tournaments after my failed Australian campaign, San Jose and Memphis. In the former, I rolled through Andre 6–2 and 6–3. But after Memphis in '96, it's all a blur. Tim was dying; by then it was a matter of "when" not "if." I sleepwalked through the big outdoor hard-court events in the States, and earned my appearance fees in Hong Kong and Tokyo by winning both—much to my own surprise.

As the European clay-court season loomed, time was running out for Tim. Our system of Tim being the coach and Paul being the messenger had completely disintegrated, because it had gotten to the point where Tim had lost his capacity to think clearly. It became tough to talk with him—about anything. The process was heart-wrenching. Although my emotional state affected my play, it had nothing to do with Tim no longer being able to function as a coach. I was very comfortable with Paul Annacone by then, and felt my game and approach were in great shape.

I visited Tim a number of times at his home in Chicago. The last time I saw him, just weeks before he died, was the hardest. He could barely hold himself erect in his wheelchair. His hair had fallen out, and he was all swollen up—basically, he was waiting to die. On our drive back to the airport, I sat in the backseat, while he was helped from his wheelchair into the front, beside the driver. Whenever the car made a turn, his body listed in the opposite direction; he had no strength left. When he talked to me, he had to move his whole body to face me. He struggled for words, remembering less and less. Everything that made Tim who he was just slowly and inexorably drained away. I remember getting on the plane and looking back, out the window, and seeing him there all by himself. I was alone, too. Slowly, tears started to roll down my cheeks.

Tim died on May 3, 1996. It was the first time in my life that I'd lost someone who was like a family member; I had never even attended a funeral. Tom Gullikson asked me to speak at the memorial service, but I didn't want to do it. I told Tom, "I don't know what I'm going to be like at the funeral. I don't want to break down again in public, and I don't want to see this ceremony become about me, so I'm going to say no for now." But when I was at the funeral, surrounded by so many of our shared friends and loved ones, I knew I had to speak. It was the right thing to do.

I told a story about Tim's extremism when it came to his hobbies and interests. He was always reading different books that had self-help or spiritual overtones; he read about fasting, the Tao, Zen, and stuff like that. So once when we were at my home in Tampa, Tim spontaneously declared that he was going to lose ten pounds in seven days. He had read about how to do it somewhere. So he went to the local GNC store and got this awful, dark green stuff that you were supposed to mix with water and drink. It looked like pond scum, some kind of algae or something—and this was a guy who was addicted to Diet Coke. From 7 A.M. to 10 P.M. every day we were together for six years, Tim seemed to have a can of Coke in his hand.

So Tim slammed back the pond scum. A few moments later, he got up and went into the other room. I figured he needed to make a phone call or something. But over the noise of the television in the living room I heard this awful noise and realized it was Tim, throwing up. I ran to the other room and there he was, slouched against the wall, white as a sheet, and still puking up this vile green stuff.

Rome was coming up fast, but I needed time to mourn Tim, so I pulled out. I did enter the World Team Cup event just to get a little match play before the French Open, and I lost two matches: one to Bohdan Ulihrach, the other to Yevgeny Kafelnikov. So I went into the French Open without a single win in a clay-court match that year, while my rivals in Paris had battled their way through the entire European clay-court circuit, from Barcelona to Monte Carlo to Rome to Hamburg.

When the draw came out for Roland Garros, I just looked at it and went, "Wow." It was as tough as it could get. On form, I would play two recent French Open champs, starting in the second round with two-time winner Sergi Bruguera. It was time to step up; I knew that's what Tim would have wanted me to do. Paul wanted me to attack relentlessly, and the conditions for that strategy were good. It was hot and dry and the court would be playing fast. I might be able to attack and pressure Bruguera, although he was a great defender and could run down anything.

The Parisians are astute fans and tennis aesthetes; they like players who are stylish, daring, or flamboyant. They understood what a coup it would have been for me, a serve-and-volley player who played a relatively clean, elegant game, to win the ultimate clay-court title—and the only Grand Slam that had eluded me up to that point. But most important, they were well aware that I had just lost Tim, and their sympathy for me was obvious. Their press, led by that great sports daily *L'Équipe*, was all over the story. Tim had just died, yet because of all the publicity and the endless questions, he was more alive in my mind than at any time since before he became ill.

Inspired by the outpouring of concern, respect, and support, I beat Bruguera 6–3 in the fifth. I know Tim would have been proud of the way I attacked and kept the pressure on. I kept my head up for the entire match, and I really felt Tim—and the French crowd—pushing me through the rough parts of that battle. In the next round, I beat my friend and Davis Cup doubles partner Todd Martin, and I lucked out a bit to get Aussie Scott Draper in the fourth round—Aussie attackers just didn't pose the kinds of problems on clay as the European grinders did.

But in the quarters, I was up against Jim Courier, who played extremely well on clay, especially Parisian clay. He was a two-time champ at Roland Garros, and a dominant guy there for half a decade. I lost the first two sets, which was suicidal given the quality of my opponent. But I felt oddly confident and calm, as if Tim were looking over my shoulder, telling me that it was okay, everything was going to work out. And in reality, I was striking the ball well and putting myself in position to win points. I was getting my backhand to his backhand, which was always the key to playing Jim, who loved to dictate with his forehand. I felt I was outplaying him, but for one thing: I was missing a few volleys here and there, and generally failing to close.

Things changed in the third and fourth sets. I started to finish effectively, and everything else fell into place. Soon I was dominating, although I was also beginning to feel the physical toll. But emotion and inspiration pulled me through. After I won the match, I said something in the press interview about feeling that Tim was watching and helping me. I stated that as fact, and it just added to the developing story. Beating Jim gave me a semifinal berth opposite Yevgeny Kafelnikov, and I liked my chances in that one. I liked them a lot.

But a weird thing happened in the forty-eight hours before I played the semi. I had cravings—unbelievable cravings—for grease. I would have killed for an old-fashioned cheeseburger, or a big pizza, or even just a couple of sunny-side-up eggs. For two nights, I had trouble sleeping, the desire was so powerful. It was truly bizarre, and as I think back, the only logical answer is that I was lacking something critical in my diet—probably fat. I may have needed to replenish something I'd lost over a week and a half of tough matches, sweating under a strong sun. Maybe I lacked salt. I know an ultramarathoner who stops after twenty miles and inhales a burger or a pizza. He told me his body needs it, so that's what he does. Looking back, I know I should have found a Pizza Hut in Paris and feasted on a greasy pie.

But, disciplined guy that I am, I held out. I kept to my typical, healthy playing diet right down to limiting myself to one cup of coffee. Then I would go to the tournament site, practice, and, if I was playing late in the day, have a sandwich (usually turkey) and maybe eat a banana. That usually did it for the day, with a light pasta dish, perhaps with chicken on the side, for dinner.

When Friday rolled around, I was scheduled to play the early semifinal match. Playing the first semi in Paris is a drag. It's a late crowd in Paris, especially in the choice seats gobbled up by corporations. Frenchmen are not likely to pass up a long, lavish lunch in the corporate hospitality area just to catch the first hour or two of what is usually at least a six-hour center-court program. So in Paris, you can find yourself playing a Grand Slam semifinal that has all the atmosphere of a second-round day match in Indianapolis or Lyon. It's a bummer to play for a place in a Grand Slam final under those conditions.

The upshot of the scheduling was that I didn't have that great atmosphere to pull me through. The serious and passionate fans who come during the early rounds are scarcer when the corporate crowd decides to start paying attention (usually from the quarterfinals on). The lack of atmosphere threw me, and so did the conditions. It was hot; the sun was blazing in a cloudless sky, and there wasn't the slightest breeze. Of course, a fast, sun-baked court would help my game, but the heat could also drain me in a long clay-court grind.

As it turned out, I didn't have to worry about stamina. I served well at the start, picked my spots to attack, and made good use of my forehand to force the action. Kafelnikov hung in there without worrying me. We went to the first-set tiebreaker and it was close, but I lost it—theoretically, no big deal. And then everything just imploded. I didn't get a game in the next set, and won just two in the third. It was by far my most puzzling and distressing Grand Slam loss, and it occurred against a guy with a tendency to get tight in big matches—especially against me.

I still can't really explain why the wheels fell off. I just hit an unexpected physical and mental wall. I was powerless to play better. I believe it had something to do with diet, which would help explain those bizarre cravings I'd had—and suppressed. Whatever the reason, I just had nothing left, and I knew it as those games rolled by. That's truly a terrible feeling, especially when you've got twenty thousand people watching live, and millions more watching on television. Even more especially when the ongoing story of my unstated but very real desire to win it for Tim was such an obvious part of the plot. I had nothing in my legs, nothing in my head, nothing left anywhere. And when the mercy killing finally was over, it only felt worse. I felt empty like I never had before, utterly depleted.

I was stunned. Down deep, I'd felt that it was my time at the French Open, and that was all bound up with having lost Tim. I thought it was meant to be, especially after my wins over two worthy former champions. During that entire tournament, I felt like Tim was still alive. Tim and I were going to win the French—it was going to be another team effort, like getting over the hump and winning Wimbledon. I'd even had these conversations with him in my head during my matches at Roland Garros, and they helped pull me through.

During the Kafelnikov match, however, there was nothing but a resounding, deep silence. I didn't think about this during the match, but I guess the silence probably settled in because my attempt to hold on to Tim, my fantasy that I could keep him alive, expired.

Despite having been to Tim's funeral, I hadn't really faced up to or accepted the fact that he was gone. Two matches too soon, I had a devastating reality check.

When I hit the wall against Kafelnikov, and felt my dream—our dream—blow up in my face, it really did sink in. Tim was gone. Our dream was gone. It was gone for good.

If anything good came out of Tim being gone, it was that Paul was finally free to shed that "interim coach" label and carry on as my full-time coach, a job he had accepted when we discussed the subject in the last days of Tim's life.

Paul had been a solid, crafty pro with an interesting game. He didn't move all that well and his ground strokes were suspect; I always kidded him about having to recruit practice partners because he just couldn't keep enough ground strokes in play to give me a workout. But Paul had a great feeling for the game, a fine serve, and a terrific volley. He lived by his wits, specializing in kamikaze tennis as a chip-and-charge player who was always betting that he could get to the net and make more volleys than an opponent could make great returns and passing shots. It was not an easy technique to execute; on a bad day, you could look downright foolish, kind of like a cavalry on horseback charging a tank battalion. He was one of the last great practitioners of that style.

When chip-and-charge tennis worked, it was a bold and exciting thing to behold. It created enormous pressure and made guys very uncomfortable. In any event, you had to respect a guy who took big risks instead of sitting back and getting pounded 6–3, 6–3 by anyone who moved better or had more consistent groundies. Paul won three singles titles, a doubles major (the Australian Open, with Christo van Rensburg), and he climbed as high as number twelve in singles.

I had taken my last big strides as a player under the watchful eye of Tim, and under his tenure I grew from a boy into a man. What I needed in Paul was a companion and an adviser, an equal who understood me and my game, and who understood other players and their strengths and weaknesses. If Tim put the finishing touches on my technique (among other things), Paul focused on strategy, helping me figure out the best ways to deploy my weapons and neutralize those of my opponents.

Paul was less social than Tim. He was soft-spoken and reserved, although if he knew someone well enough he loved to talk about things—and always on a pretty high, philosophical level. Paul always thought before he spoke, and he was incredibly patient. He took the high road in any conflict or controversy. We were more similar in temperament than Tim and I had been, which by that time was an asset.

Paul never got the credit he deserved as my coach because of the level at which I was playing when he assumed the reins. Some people thought all Paul had to do was carry my rackets to the stringer, warm me up for matches, act as a go-between with the press, and make sure our dinner or plane reservations were in order. But I definitely needed—and got—a lot more than that from him, starting with the way he handled his role. Paul was very good at handling the media. He was both open to them and understanding of their jobs, but he wasn't in love with the sound of his own voice, and he always downplayed his influence on me. He wasn't a guy to pump up his own tires. Reporters liked and respected Paul, and that helped my cause with them, too.

Paul knew that different people need to be handled in different ways. He could coach me, or he could coach Andre. He was a good reader of character and temperament, knowing what I needed to hear and how to say it. And that is a huge—repeat, *huge*—part of being a high-level coach. You have to understand a guy and work within his comfort zone, avoiding the temptation to change him or make him conform to how you want him to be—even when you know that kind of change would be beneficial. His bedside manner was great.

Paul didn't have to say a lot, although he had a lot to say; he chose his words carefully and never overcomplicated things. He was a good reader of character, and he quickly figured out that I didn't really like to talk about my tennis a lot—I was kind of possessive about the game. He also knew that I didn't like to make a bigger deal out of things than necessary, partly because he was like-minded in that way.

It was tough for Paul to keep himself in the background while Tim was ill, for the simple reason that the press was always after him to talk, and Paul didn't want to overshadow Tim. What might have been even harder for him was to hang back in deference to Tim when it came to coaching me. Paul had his own thoughts about my game, but he was careful to avoid conflict with Tim. He had been supremely loyal, to Tim and to me. He kept the faith.

Paul was a great tactician, although I often resisted his strong emphasis on attacking tennis. That was because I took a lot of pride in my all-court abilities. Paul always wanted me to be aware of how I was losing points—not just after but during matches (which can be very difficult to do in the heat of battle). I think he believed that the awareness would lead me to play more forcefully and aggressively.

Tim was great when it came to my game; Paul was great when it came to the games of guys I would have to beat. His strategic solutions to the problems various players presented were gems of perception, a remarkable combination of simple yet subtle. He would suggest or say the kind of things that might make you want to smack your forehead and think, *Now why didn't I think of that?*

For example, against Andre Agassi, Paul felt I should play to Andre's forehand side—go to the forehand to open up the backhand court. In fact, that was always my key to beating Andre. But in order to work his forehand, I had to threaten his backhand—I had to soften up that side. So Paul always wanted me to start a match by establishing the wide serve on that ad side to the backhand. That would make Andre think a little about protecting that wing, opening up the serve down the center stripe. The overarching idea was to prevent Andre from employing his favorite strategy—smacking back a forcing return that enabled him to set up shop near the middle of the court, with the intention of dictating with his forehand.

Paul tried to get me to chip and charge more, not at 4–all, but at 1–all, even against Andre and his awesome passing shots. Paul felt it wasn't worth the risk chipping and charging on big points against a quality passer, but he wanted me to plant that seed in Andre's head, make him think that I might attack at any time. This became a recurring theme no matter whom I played. He basically said, "Show him that you're Pete Sampras, and that you can attack at will."

I did take some pleasure in beating guys at their own games— dominating a baseline grinder from the backcourt, that kind of thing. Sometimes that drove Paul nuts, because there were times when it made my own life a lot harder than it needed to be. I would get into these long rallies, maybe lose the match, and Paul would later just say, "You know, you looked awful good—losing."

It wasn't exactly the same as my dad saying I played "lousy," but I felt the rebuke in that comment. I looked good . . . losing. The key wasn't "looked good," it was . . . "losing." He used that word intentionally. Early in our relationship I told Paul, "Don't sugarcoat things. You've got to be honest with me." He did that, but in his own way, which always was intended less to make me feel bad than to make me think.

Paul was adamant about keeping me from becoming a predictable player, even while he encouraged me to establish my straightforward "big game" against every opponent. So at times it was a fine line to walk between playing serve-and-volley on autopilot and mixing up my game. Paul always wanted me to establish a tough, low-percentage shot, the backhand up the line (it's much safer and easier to go crosscourt, partly because the net is lower at the center). He felt I was technically sound enough to do that. Because of the quality of my second serve, he also wanted me to serve and volley with it more than I did.

On grass courts, Paul believed that my key to winning was the way I returned second serves. He was especially forceful about that when it came to guys like Goran, or Richard Krajicek. He often said, "If you return his second serve well, you'll beat him, no matter how many aces he hits. You'll wear him down. If Goran serves three aces in a row in a game, so be it. Move on, forget it. Don't get discouraged, and just keep looking for that second serve, because it's going to come, and it will give you an opening."

Paul impressed that on me so strongly that after a while, when I saw a second serve at Wimbledon I was like, *Wow, this is it*—it was as if I was looking at a winning lottery ticket. So I would attack the second serve, often with great results. I overcame the temptation to play it safe, which means I also overcame the fear of blowing a big opportunity.

On my own service games, Paul wanted me to put the hammer down as hard and often as I could. I guess this was part of Tim's legacy, that "Green Bay Packers power sweep" thing. Serving at 40–love, you can take a point off if you want, but Paul was big on me winning a game like that at love. The better you served, he reasoned, the more pressure you put on an opponent. He really wanted me to eliminate the sloppy double fault or shanked volley, even when I could afford to make the error. And he was right. I know that when a Goran or Krajicek or Michael Stich got to 40–love and held easily, I would always think, *Sheesh, this guy is tough; I didn't have a sniff at that service game and it went by in a flash. I'd better make sure I hold here.*

We very rarely analyzed potential opponents in a complex, by-the-numbers way. I can only remember one time that we actually watched a tape of a match—it was before I played Vladimir Voltchkov, a surprise semifinalist at Wimbledon in 2000. And it was only because neither of us even knew if the guy was a lefty or righty, never mind what his game was like. We didn't have formal strategy sessions. If there was something on my mind, I would just bring it up over dinner, or after a practice session. Just throw it out there to see what Paul had to say. I would sometimes ask what Paul thought an opponent was going to try to do against me, and found he was very good at those predictions.

Tim Gullikson always wanted me to hold my head high and show no weakness to opponents, but Paul took it one step further and liked for me to be slightly arrogant—you know, take that attitude, *I'm Pete Sampras and you're not.* He felt I was too self-effacing, too nice. He would say, "These guys are afraid of you, and you need to know that and exploit it." He was right. I never went out there afraid of anybody, but I didn't always take full advantage of my reputation and presence, either.

I could go either way on that issue. It wasn't like me to be more assertive, and I was uncomfortable consciously trying to cultivate the image that I was. I didn't want to misrepresent myself, and I never wanted to be perceived as cocky. I also felt there was a definite value in being so low-key that it made my opponents nervous, made them just look and wonder what I might be thinking. The way a Boris Becker strode around the court with this natural air of entitlement probably motivated guys to try to beat him. I didn't want to intimidate guys; it was just as valuable, in my mind, to make them nervous.

Besides, if I didn't act like I owned the world, it was more likely that I wouldn't feel that I did. It was important for me to do that, because by the time Paul was my full-time coach, one of the big dangers for me was letting my own press clippings go to my head. I took special care to play every tournament, week after week, as if it really mattered. I always went out there taking nothing for granted, feeling like I had to prove myself. I actually enjoyed that, maybe because it ended up giving me some extra positive reinforcement when I did win. I never felt blasé after beating someone.

There were periods, of course, when I became a little tired or bored with the typical pro's routine, and I wanted Paul to be hard on me if he thought I was slacking off. A few times I hit a plateau, careerwise, and started taking shortcuts. It just happens; you need to go on autopilot once in a while. Paul recognized when that was the case, and called me on it. He knew my mind, even though a champion's mind isn't always that easy to know.

Like I've said, Paul never got the credit he deserved. But in the end, I know what he did for me. I won ten of my fourteen Grand Slams with him, and he guided me with a firm hand through some of the most heartbreaking, challenging moments of my career.

As much of a blow as it was to lose in Paris, there was always Wimbledon. When Paul and I arrived in England a few days after losing in the French, I appreciated the cool climate and those beautiful grass courts. It was like deleting every recent file on my mental hard drive and starting over. I really needed to regroup after the shocking collapse in Paris. The year was halfway over and, like most years, I would judge it a success or failure depending on whether or not I won a major.

I skipped all the warm-up tournaments for Wimbledon in 1996, hoping to regain my stores of stamina and energy. Things started to click for me when the tournament began, and although I lost a set to my Davis Cup buddy Richey Reneberg in the first round, pretty soon I was firing on all cylinders. I hammered Mark Philippoussis in straight sets in the round of 16. I rolled through Cédric Pioline, losing just ten games. In the quarterfinals, I would be playing Richard Krajicek, the rangy, tall, hard-serving Dutchman who was always a threat on fast surfaces. He could pop up at any time and win a tournament, looking like the second coming of Pancho Gonzalez. At other times, he was just another big guy with a good serve who didn't seem to have the confidence or drive to win, week in, week out.

I felt that Richard was a little nervous as we warmed up under leaden skies. But he held his own through the first seven or eight games, each of us taking care of his serve. Everything was fine, in my book. I was making him work on his service games, and I was getting pretty good looks at his second serves. I had break points here and there, which was encouraging even when I didn't convert them. I had played many matches like this before on grass. The trick was to stay alert, focused, and confident, because my chance would come. I was getting to him, I felt pretty sure about that. It was just a matter of time.

But before we could finish the set, the rains came. We had a break of a few hours, and that gave both of us a little time to think and regroup. When we returned to the court, he was a different player. He was suddenly going for his shots, especially his second serve. Whether he knew it or not, he was taking me into the territory I least liked to visit. My m.o. called for me to approach even the most lethal serve-and-volleyers with the expectation that I'll get a good look at some second serves. If that happened, I could beat them. The strategy worked against Goran Ivanisevic, it worked against Boris Becker, and it worked against Stefan Edberg. But when it became harder for me to get a sniff at a second serve, it created a chain reaction. If I couldn't get to his serve, that put more pressure on mine. I think Richard sensed that, and his own excellent serving freed up the rest of his game, especially his return game. And that's how it almost always works.

Krajicek won the first set 7–5, breaking me once. It emboldened him, and suddenly he was getting hold of my serves with his back-hand return. Plus, his passing shots were impeccable. I lost the second set 6–4, and was relieved when it started to sprinkle again, because the light was fading. I knew we would never finish the match that day, and I really needed to regroup.

Yet instead of thinking, *Tomorrow's a new day, I'll get back on track—no way he can stay hot like that . . .* I had a strange sense of foreboding. I didn't feel good about the way the match was going, and knew I was in a big, big hole. Paul worked double time that night to get me back up, to restore my confidence, but he couldn't pull me out of it. Although I was still in the match, I was feeling negative.

When we returned to play the next day, we just continued where we left off. Richard came out bombing away, and I immediately got discouraged, thinking, *Hey, this is what I do to people on grass.* Long story short, he closed me out. All the credit to Richard for getting the job done. He played a great match, technically and mentally. And it was some balm for me to see him go on to win the tournament—if you're going to lose, you may as well lose to the guy who's going to run the table. I've never watched that match on tape, but I'd be curious—just to see if Richard's game really did change as much as I believe it did after the rain delay.

At the end of that day, three of the majors were gone, and I had yet to win one. Although I wasn't exactly thinking I had to win a Slam for Tim, others frequently brought up the subject. To me, though, that wasn't the point. It was simple: win or lose, the French Open had been "our" major—the Tim major. I fell short of honoring Tim with a win, so the movie didn't end the way everyone expected. But that didn't change the magical moments or emotions I experienced at Roland Garros, and it didn't change the way I felt about Tim or the right way to honor his memory. When I won my next major, I could make a pretty speech about "winning one for

Tim." It was what everyone wanted to hear. But I wasn't going to do that; it would have been phony. And I kept that promise to myself.

The summer hard-court season leading up to the U.S. Open was always low-key. As hectic as the Open is, the tournaments leading up to it are laid-back affairs of the heartland. Indianapolis and Cincinnati are two of the biggest events, yet you can drive from one venue to the other in an afternoon, and each one has a little bit of that air of a county fair. Some of us players had a running joke when we got to Indy or Cincy. We'd just look at each other, shrug, and say, "Same shit, different year."

Although I lost in the quarterfinals at Cincinnati to Thomas Enqvist, I won Indianapolis, improving my career record against Goran to 8–6. Going into New York, I felt good about extending my streak of winning at least one major per year to four. And the draw opened up nicely for me. The only name player I would meet before the quarterfinals was Mark Philippoussis, whom I handled in straight sets. That put me into the quarterfinals against Alex Corretja, who was known primarily as a clay-court grinder, but who also put up some good results on hard courts. I expected a tough match.

There was very little backstory going into the match. Most people, at least in the States, figured I was a shoo-in to beat Corretja. But at the quarterfinal stage, I always worried about anyone I played, and I took nothing for granted. The one thing that may have helped shape the day was the fact that I went out there low on fuel. I remember that I ate lunch in the players' lounge, but then the match before mine went unexpectedly long. It was just about 4 P.M. by the time I got on court. I should have snacked more—consumed a cookie, a banana, a hunk of bread—before taking the court.

It was a pretty warm day, but nothing like the real corkers you sometimes get at the Open. I was sweating a lot, though, and Alex was bringing plenty of game. He drew me into a baseline battle and made me work very hard. Alex was using the most basic strategy a grinder can bring to the fast-court game. He was just kicking in his first serve to my backhand to keep me from taking control of the point with an aggressive return.

When he did that, I was less likely to smoke the return, and he could immediately run around his backhand and engage me in a forehand (his) to backhand (mine) rally, keeping me pinned to the baseline. If I went bold and tried to go down the line with a big backhand to his open, forehand court (remember, he was standing way over on the backhand side), he could run over there and smack a winner crosscourt with his best shot. If I attacked, he would have a good look at a passing shot.

A grinder like Corretja really knows how to suck you into his game plan. That was something Paul took pains to stress: "This is what these guys like to do, this is what they love—it's their only chance to beat guys like you or Becker or Edberg, and that's why you have to disrupt that strategy. You have to chip and charge, or go for that big backhand down the line. You have to keep them out of their comfort zone, because if you don't, they will keep you out of yours."

But I was being stubborn against Corretja, ignoring Paul's sound advice. I was playing into Alex's hands and I knew it, but I was holding my own, and I was determined to beat the guy at his own game. For a long time, I was content to rally and wait for my opening to hit the big forehand. I built a lead of two sets to one, but early in the fourth set I was starting to feel uncomfortable. I didn't like the way the points were going—Alex wasn't backing off at all. I was having to work really hard to get to the net to finish points. As I tired, a little bit of panic started to creep in.

Alex had imposed a template on the game, and it was making me uneasy; I was stupid to have played along for such a long time. I was a bit mesmerized. I knew I should change something, but by then I was fatigued, feeling pressured and stressed, and unsure how to get out of the rhythm I had established. And when your mind fails, all you have to fall back on is your will and character.

Midway through the fourth set, I started losing my legs. They were heavy, with little of the usual spring left in them. When that happens, your game inevitably declines. You no longer get up as high when you serve, and you don't get that explosive first step to the ball. You don't move corner to corner effectively, or change direction that well. And when an opponent sees that, he uses it as emotional fuel, even if he's also tired. This was shaping up as one of those matches that I would have to find some way to save—whatever it took.

After three straight 7–5 sets, Corretja won the fourth 6–4. As we slogged through the early games of the fifth set, I started drinking Coke. I needed something—a pick-me-up, a little sugar, a little caffeine—and I needed it pretty badly. Underneath it all, I was aware that this was my last chance to win a major in 1996, and it was slipping away. That self-inflicted pressure made things worse. I was bruised, battered, and exhausted, but I was still able to put one foot in front of the other. I was able to keep fighting.

I hit a wall late in the fifth and felt like I was going to die. But I knew in the back of my mind that I had one chance to win—one chance at salvation. This was the U.S. Open, and that meant that you played a fifth-set tiebreaker. I kept telling myself to hang in there and just get to the tiebreaker; the match could not go on forever. I hung on and got to the breaker, but by then my head was spinning and things were getting a little blurry around the edges. I then told myself that whatever else happened, I could get through this. It could be as short as seven points. It was just a tiebreaker; I had played a million of them before, and none of them lasted forever.

At 1–1 in the tiebreaker, all the pain and distress and nervous energy got to me and I got sick. My back was cramping and my legs felt like they were made of wood, and not entirely under my own control. I remember playing a tough point and all of a sudden I had this realization: *Holy shit, I'm going to throw up. I'm going to puke— in front of the whole friggin' world!*

It was coming up and there was no way I would stop it. I staggered back from the baseline, and up came the Coke and acid and whatever else—thankfully, it wasn't much—that was still in my stomach. By the time it actually happened, though, I didn't care. I didn't really hear or see anything. I didn't care how I looked or what anyone thought. I was in my own little world of pain, and as bad as it was, I wasn't going to quit the match.

When you throw up like that, and it's happened to me in training sessions, it's a sure sign that you took yourself to the absolute limit—the point of no return. But I needed to push on, I had to get through a few more points. I was staggering around, my senses dulled and my body aching. I remember playing a hard point and getting through it, and then it would take me two points to recover. I was aware enough to think of only one or two things, strategywise. I had to put all I had into the serve and, if I saw a forehand, I had to let the sucker ride.

We lurched along to 6–6 in the tiebreaker, with me serving. It was time to decide things. I went for broke on my first serve end and missed. My second serve went wide to his forehand and, to my everlasting good fortune, Alex guessed backhand. There was nobody home. The ace brought me to match point. By that stage, the atmosphere was totally supercharged. People were leaning over the railings in the stadium, hanging into the court, screaming encouragement at me. I didn't know it, but all over the United States and the world, things in many places came to an utter standstill as people got sucked into the drama of it all.

And then Alex blinked. He did the one inexcusable thing, under the circumstances: he double-faulted at match point. I won without having to take that additional step—one that I might not have been capable of making.

I left the court completely spent, dehydrated, disorientated, and vaguely aware that I had made a spectacle of myself. I went right into the doctor's office under the stands in Louis Armstrong Stadium and collapsed. They immediately hooked me up to an IV bag. Paul went to gather my things from the locker room, and when we finally opened the door to leave the doctor's office, I saw a sea of faces, members of the press who had staked out the room.

But I didn't need to talk to the press that day; they already had their story and it was one that more or less wrote itself. The Corretja match quickly became engraved in everyone's mind as my defining moment—my warrior moment. And I was lucky, because other players have won matches like that, but few have done it at such a conspicuous, crucial moment. If I had played that very same match against Alex in the second round at Monte Carlo instead of at the U.S. Open, I doubt it would have had anything like the same impact. It might have been a footnote in the roundup section of most U.S. newspapers.

But it had occurred in the quarterfinals of the U.S. Open, a Grand Slam event and my native major, in the prime-time slot right after Labor Day when everybody was back from vacation, under the gaze of the international press corps and before an international television audience. So it became something special, something the entire world saw and everyone commented on.

The New York crowd had been a tough nut for me. I'm not sure they were ever all that fond of me or my game. They were accustomed to blustery, bombastic showmen who were great competitors, but not necessarily elegant or classic players. It's hard to beat a pair of acts called Jimmy Connors and John McEnroe. Sure, I had this easy, natural game. I had won half a dozen majors. But I wasn't very Broadway. I wasn't very flamboyant. They weren't sure what I really had in the way of grit, and didn't understand the degree to which I was a fighter. Unlike Connors, I had made no widely disseminated remarks about leaving my guts out there for them. Being typically skeptical New Yorkers, they had never been sure what they were buying.

After the Corretja match, they were finally sold.

I went on to win the U.S. Open (my eighth major) of 1996 but I was troubled by how I got sick on the court, and how weak and ill I felt. I thought back to the ulcer that went undiagnosed earlier in my career, and wondered if something else might be wrong. Was this a physical problem, or a mental one related to the stress I put myself under when I decided to try to shoot the moon in tennis?

It had freaked me out that I went all the way to the Open before I bagged my slam. I had set a high bar for myself in previous years, and you never really want to lower it—you want it to stay in the same place, or go higher. Maybe I was getting a little obsessive and unrealistic; maybe I was setting myself up for an inevitable fall. But I couldn't help myself. I would finish number one for the fourth consecutive year, just one behind Jimmy Connors's record of five. I realized I wanted that record but, unlike, say, winning Wimbledon or the Davis Cup, getting it meant two more years of struggle. Two more years of, first of all, playing enough tournaments to keep myself in the hunt.

I talked all this over with Paul; I told him what I wanted to accomplish. We decided that I needed to take a few steps back, think over my mental and physical approach to the game. I needed to pace myself, without losing drive or intensity. I had to embrace the mission, but not put too much pressure on myself, because that would tear me up inside. Was it possible to reconcile all those conflicting desires? We didn't really have an answer, but we agreed that the first thing I needed to do was get myself checked out, physically. In the back of my mind was a word that I feared a little, and had chosen not to deal with: thalassemia.

As I've noted, this mild form of anemia afflicts people of Mediterranean descent. It causes fatigue, especially in the heat, and I'd certainly battled listlessness and loss of desire on some very hot days—including during my seminal first win at Wimbledon. But you know, nobody wants to go to a doctor and be told that he's got something wrong, something that would justify underperforming. I knew that thalassemia occurred in my family. My mother, Georgia, and sister Stella have it, although the Sampras men do not. I chose to ignore the possibility that I suffered from it until right after the Corretja match.

Within days of testing, blood work revealed that my red blood cell count was abnormally low—a sure sign that I was suffering from the condition. It wasn't life-threatening, but it could certainly affect my on-court performance. However, it was easily addressed. I had to start taking iron supplements and ramp up my intake of meat, eggs, and other protein.

This would have been just something else to deal with until Tom Tebbutt, an enterprising journalist and tennis nut from Toronto, broke a story in *Tennis Week*, a small bimonthly magazine published out of New York City. He speculated that I suffered from . . . thalassemia. I have to hand it to Tom; he did his homework. I was a little annoyed, but I had to be impressed. Somehow he had heard about the disorder and started poking around. He had a doctor and some other folks confirm that thalassemia could easily have been a factor in my breakdown in the Corretja match. Then he just connected the dots and nailed me.

I don't recall that Tom ever tried to confirm the story with me before it was published, but that was okay. I would have denied it— as I did after the story came out. I felt bad; I tried never to flat-out lie, but I also wasn't about to admit to having it. I just didn't want my rivals to have that information and take comfort in or motivation out of it in any matches I might play in the future. In fact, the first person I eventually admitted it to was Peter Bodo—my collaborator for this book—in an interview for *Tennis* magazine that we did in September of 2000.

B ut despite this eventful end of the Grand Slam season, 1996 had one last spectacular moment in store: my match with Boris Becker in the final of the year-end ATP World Championships. By then, Boris and I had a lot of history and a lot of respect for each other. Now I had to play him indoors, in Hannover, Germany, in a huge match before a German crowd that adored him. The circumstances would inspire Boris, I knew that. While I felt that our games were similar and that I did most things just a hair better, I also knew that if he got on a roll on his home soil he could take me out.

The atmosphere in the arena in Hannover the night Boris and I played was electric. Outside, it was bitterly cold, but inside, the arena was brightly lit, warm, packed with fans, and sizzling with anticipation. One feature I enjoyed about that event and venue was the way the players were introduced. Instead of emerging right onto the court from a tunnel, as at most events, we walked together down to the sunken court from street level, which was the *top* of the arena. And we came down the same aisle as a ticket holder going to one of the better courtside seats.

The entire arena was dark but for a spotlight on us. Boris and I took that long walk down to the court with fans screaming on either side. The roar of the crowd was deafening; I got goose bumps from the sheer intensity of the moment, and thought this must be exactly what it's like for a couple of heavyweight fighters wading through the crowd to take the ring for a title fight. The flashbulbs were exploding all around, flesh pressed in on all sides.

Boris returned well from the start, which was always a huge factor for him. And his serve was popping. I knew right off the bat that it was going to be a very tough, long night. But I was serving big, too, and if the fast indoor carpet was ideal for Boris (hey, we were in Germany), it suited me just as well. Boris broke me to win the first set; I narrowly averted disaster by winning the next two sets, although I won them only in tiebreakers. It had to be demoralizing for him that I hadn't broken his serve and he had broken mine, yet he was down two sets to one.

By the same token, my two sets to one lead didn't mean all that much to me. *Would I ever break the guy?* I wondered. *What if my luck in the tiebreakers turned?* But as the fourth set developed, I sniffed a few chances. I got the feeling that the match was right there, at my fingertips. A shot here and there and I could break. But Boris held me at bay and tenaciously held his serve all the way to the fourth-set tiebreaker. And when he won it to force a fifth set, the place erupted. It was like a volcano, spewing out this intense, guttural chant: *Bor-is, Bor-is, Bor-is . . .*

We went into the fifth, and the situation was starting to get to me, mentally. I had yet to break serve, and now we were even. We continued as before—each man holding serve until we got to 4-4. At that point, the door opened a hair for me. I got him breakpoint down on his serve, and he responded by going big—he hit a heavy serve to my backhand but I caught it perfectly and drove it back, up the line, for a winner—and my first break. As relieved as I felt, it was equally heartbreaking for Boris. When I reached match point in the next game, we had a point that reminded me of that great, long point Andre and I played in the U.S. Open final of 1995. It ended with Boris missing a backhand and just like that, it was over.

We had a long embrace at the net, and some kind words for each other. At that point our lungs were still burning and we were panting. Physically, it was one of the most punishing, demanding matches I've ever played. That's how it was with Boris—he always manhandled you, and most players simply couldn't take the physical beating. The German fans were great—I think they loved it: they saw two of the great players who dominated in the 1990s playing power tennis at a very high level at the same time, in a wonderful atmosphere. And they got a great if slightly anticlimatic ending.

I watched that match on DVD a few years later, and felt it was as good and exciting as I had remembered. It was an epic battle, bitterly and boldly fought in an attractive glow of sportsmanship and, I think, respect for the game. It was a peak moment in my career. People in Germany and the United States still contact me about that match, or mention it in conversation. It may have been the closest thing I ever played to an ultimate match—not necessarily in terms of execution, but as an example of a transcendent tennis moment.

When the match was over, I allowed myself a special treat. I grabbed Paul Annacone and we hopped on a private plane, going from Hannover to London, and then on the Concorde to JFK. Back then, I had a time-share in a jet, and my own plane was waiting in New York; it took me right to Tampa. My reward was to get home quickly and comfortably.

1997–1998

KEY MATCHES . . .

January 1997, Australian Open, final

P. SAMPRAS	6	6	6		
C. MOYA	2	3	3		

July 1997, Wimbledon, final

P. SAMPRAS	6	6	6		
C. PIOLINE	4	2	4		

August 1997, U.S. Open, fourth round

P. SAMPRAS	7(4)	5	6	6	6
P. KORDA	6	7	7(2)	3	7(3)

July 1998, WImbledon, final

P. SAMPRAS	6	7(11)	6	3	6
G. IVANISEVIC	7(2)	6	4	6	2

September 1998, U.S. Open, semifinal

P. SAMPRAS	7(10)	4	6	4	3
P. RAFTER	6	6	2	6	6

YEAR–END RANKING . . . 1997, 1998: No. 1

Wimbledon Is Forever

I won the Australian Open to launch my 1997 campaign, a pleasant surprise given the way I felt about the tournament. I took extra pride in the win for a couple of reasons. In the round of 16, I played Dominik Hrbaty in a five-set war that I eventually won 6–4. The on-court temperature during that match hit 135 degrees Fahrenheit. Today, with the "extreme heat" policy in effect, they would have stopped the match, or closed the roof on Rod Laver Arena. Given what had happened at the U.S. Open just months earlier in my match with Alex Corretja, I was glad to survive that test of stamina in the infernal Aussie heat.

It was also encouraging for me that while the Australian major is a hard-court tournament, in '97 it was dominated by slow-court players. After Hrbaty, I beat, in order, Al Costa, Tomas Muster, and Carlos Moya, to take the title. Each of those guys had won—or would win—Roland Garros. That gave me hope—maybe my fate at Roland Garros, the one slam that continued to elude me, wasn't sealed quite yet.

Back in the States after my successful campaign down under, I added two tournament wins to make it a pretty good little roll, although I lost in the first round at Indian Wells. That was another tournament, like the Australian Open, where the conditions were less attractive to me than you might think. While I won the event a number of times, and Indian Wells was pretty much my "home" tournament, geographically, I didn't like the combination of wind, dry air, and ball pressure that you had in the Southern California desert. I always felt like everything flew on me, like I wasn't quite in control. I preferred Miami, where the humidity made the air thicker, but I felt like I had greater control.

I went to Europe in pretty good shape, but I didn't win a single match in three tries going into the French Open. What's worse, in Rome I got a phone call from my sister Stella that really threw me for a loop. Pete Fischer, the coach who had shaped and orchestrated my development, had been arrested and charged with child molestation. One of his former patients had stepped forward to bring charges (Pete, you'll remember, was an endocrinologist with Kaiser Permanente, specializing in growth-related issues in young boys). The news freaked me out. I'd lost Vitas Gerulaitis and Tim Gullikson in a short span of time, and now my original coach was in disgrace. It was a repugnant charge, and I wasn't sure what to think. Could it really be true? With the bombshell weighing on my mind, I failed to win a match on clay until I survived for two rounds at Roland Garros before falling to Magnus Norman.

The charges against Pete Fischer really baffled me. Although Pete was a single guy, he usually had, and frequently talked about, girl-friends. He was actually engaged at the time he was arrested. Nothing in Pete's life or habits suggested that he was anything but a typical guy. He fit in fine in the locker room. He was brainy, he worked hard, and led a very disciplined, straight-and-narrow sort of life. I'd never seen him act out of character or in a way that indicated that he was not what he appeared to be. Sure, he was arrogant, but that was neither here nor there.

I'd spent a lot of time at Pete's house, usually with my brother, Gus, when I was a kid. I never had an inkling that he was capable of this kind of crime. But as I thought about things and reviewed my childhood experience, I saw some red flags. Pete always surrounded himself with boys; he was around them day and night, whether at his job, at the Kramer Club, or at his home. He sometimes organized ski trips to Mammoth Mountain. I went on one of those trips, and it was all boys. But it was a good mix, with some older boys along, too—kids who would be more on guard about sexual predators.

My parents trusted Pete, and until the time we parted ways over money, nothing unseemly ever happened to harm our relationship with him. I was sure of one thing—I'd always been special in Pete's eyes. I think he saw me as different from other kids and maybe that was something that kept any other impulses he may have had in check. There was also my dad. He was savvy, and hands-on as a parent, if not a tennis coach. It would have been very risky for Fischer to try anything inappropriate.

By the time Fischer was arrested, he was long gone from my life. I didn't feel obliged to call him, and I didn't see him until I returned from Europe. My father, though, spoke with Pete periodically, and stood by him. I think it was out of sheer loyalty for the role Fischer had played in our family and in my career. My father really appreciated that. In turn, Pete turned to my family for support when the scandal broke. He resolutely clung to his claim of innocence, and my dad treated him as if he was innocent until proven guilty.

When I returned to the States, my family told me that Fischer wanted to get together with me, to explain his situation. I reluctantly consented and suggested to Pete that we meet for lunch at a café in Torrance, Mimi's. The meeting was uncomfortable. I didn't want to believe the accusations against him, but I also didn't have the guts to look him in the eye and demand that he tell me the truth. Everything he said suggested that the charges were false, but he acted a little strange during lunch.

Once he became comfortable, he told me that while driving to Mammoth in the recent past, he had found "Mother Mary"—I presumed he meant the New Testament Mary, the mother of Jesus. This was odd because Pete was a Jew and a committed atheist—you wouldn't find a more rational, black-and-white man on the planet.

Just as strikingly, he was actually divulging feelings, something he had never, ever done before. I didn't know what to do with all of this.

I think if Pete were still in my life, I would have needed more definite assurance of his innocence. But while I felt I owed him a certain amount of support, it was only because of the past. I supported him as a friend, and I even lent him some money (which he did eventually pay back). I know he went to our house for dinner a few times before his trial, but by then I was back on the road, playing, so my family had to bear the brunt of that situation. Thankfully, the press didn't make a big deal out of the scandal. I was in no way connected to it, and it had been years since I had a relationship of any kind with Fischer.

This much was certain: Pete's life was in ruins, and he didn't have many friends left. Neither my parents nor my siblings talked much about the case; we all just kind of supported Pete through the dark times as the trial loomed and his fate hung in the balance. Once the shock of being charged wore off, some of Fischer's signature arrogance crept back in. When the trial rolled around, my father attended for a few days. I admired that in Dad; he could very easily have cut Fischer off and left him to swing in the breeze.

The trial ended when Pete accepted a plea bargain that reduced his jail term to six years, of which he served four before being released. He told my dad that he took the plea bargain because he didn't trust his fate to "twelve people from Norwalk" (the California site of the pending trial). I guess Fischer was saying that he didn't think he could get a fair trial in such a conservative place. It was an odd tack to take for a man who claimed he was innocent and who had so much to lose in the event of a conviction. In addition to doing hard time, he would lose his license to practice medicine and leave himself open to civil litigation. A guilty plea destroyed the life he had built just as effectively as a guilty verdict. The only difference would be in the amount of time he served.

Right before Fischer went to jail, he spent a little time at our house. His fiancée was still in the picture, but she would soon leave him. He talked about jail in an almost upbeat way, saying crazy things, like he was going to learn French, use the time to expand his horizons. Meanwhile, we were thinking, *Pete, whatever the truth is, you're going to prison. Your life is ruined. It's going to be horrible. How could you get yourself into this?*

After Fischer went to jail, he started writing me letters. I could barely read his handwriting in those long, rambling communications. They were often written after he watched a match I played. I read a few of them, or parts of them. He was very complimentary. He reiterated that I was going to make people forget Laver, just writing the same stuff he used to say.

The European clay-court season had been a disaster, the Pete Fischer scandal had thrown me for a loop, and Jonas Bjorkman of Sweden had bounced me out of the big Queen's Club tournament. But Wimbledon . . . Wimbledon was a different story. It had become a place of refuge for me, and I really needed that in '97.

I rolled through my first three opponents at Wimbledon, giving up an average of a shade over ten games per five-set match, meaning I was winning three games to one against my average opponent. Although I had struggled on grass in the past and would struggle on it again in the future, in 1997 the game just felt . . . easy. It felt so easy that when I beat my rival, Wimbledon hero Boris Becker, in the quarterfinals, he made a surprising declaration up at the net when we shook hands. He told me he had just played his last Wimbledon final—he was retiring.

I was stunned by that; I had no idea he was even considering it, although by then he was slightly past his prime. I learned later that it was just his emotions getting the better of him; apparently, I had played such a commanding match that he figured, "Why bother?" I was happy when, come 1998, he changed his mind and was back at Wimbledon.

Wimbledon is a place full of complex rituals and traditions, but the thing I most cherish about the tournament is the simplicity of tennis on grass. It's easy and natural. It's a no-frills undertaking played on a clean, elegant, quiet stage. That remained true even after the "grass tennis is boring" debate led Wimbledon to slow the game by changing the balls and grass mix. Although that process was on-going in the second half of my career, I hardly noticed. I played the same serve-based, attacking tennis from the beginning to the end of my Wimbledon career.

I like that grass-court tennis is (or was) serve-based, and I'm not just saying that out of self-interest. Historically, the game was always serve-based—the serve is the most important stroke in tennis. It's also the one over which you have total control, because the ball isn't moving when you start your shot. The entire game, including the scoring system, is built around the idea that having the serve gives you a big advantage.

It doesn't matter how good your backhand or forehand is, there's only one way to win a set or match. You have to break serve more often than you are broken. This is still true in the tiebreaker era given that the only way to win the tiebreaker is by scoring at least one "minibreak"—that is, winning at least one more point off your opponent's serve than he gets off yours. It's a bit of a shame that in this era of slower courts, great serving is not as well re-warded as it has been in the past, and that the coaches and players today overlook the extent to which a player with a great serve can build his entire game around the shot. To me, a match with a lot of service breaks is as unsatisfying as a match with none, because a great match is only supposed to have a handful of decisive moments (as entertaining as all the other points may be). It's just like a book or movie is supposed to have just a handful of key scenes or plot twists.

Although tennis on grass came easily to me, it was also mentally debilitating. I served and volleyed and returned, biding my time, trying to stay focused and positive. I tried to be ready for the moment when a little daylight came filtering through the crack in the door. Grass-court tennis between power players was often compared to a crapshoot. (In the 1991 Wimbledon semifinal between Michael Stich and Stefan Edberg, there was just one service break in the entire match, and the guy whose serve was *broken*, Stich, ended up winning the match! The scores were 4–6, 7–6, 7–6, 7–6.) But winning was anything but a roll of the dice. A better analogy is that grass-court tennis in my era was like an old-fashioned Western gunfight—you didn't want to be the one to blink, tip your next move, or fumble as you dragged leather.

On grass, momentum often shifted in the blink of an eye. No points anywhere else were big points in quite the way they were at Wimbledon, because you often got only two or three swings of the racket with which to win a set. At Wimbledon, a match might be determined by a sloppy second serve that leads to a service break early in the first or second set. You paid heavily for your mistakes on grass. Breaks were rare and precious, and I really felt the heat when I gave one away—and it was really dispiriting to blow a chance to score one.

People sometimes said that the "problem" with grass-court tennis during the years I dominated at Wimbledon was that a big server could just serve any opponent off the court. But the reality is that winning at Wimbledon was never *just* about serving big. The biggest servers in the game didn't win Wimbledon; the great servers who did take the title often won other majors as well. Goran Ivanisevic could serve me off the court anywhere, he was scary to play. Yet he only won one title at Wimbledon, and that was very late in his career. Roscoe Tanner, one of the most deadly servers of the Open era, got to just one Wimbledon final, and lost to Björn Borg.

Actually, Wimbledon has produced fewer one-slam wonders than the serve-neutralizing, theoretically "level playing field" of Roland Garros clay. The bottom line is that the big titles are almost always won by great players, because they have superior execution (everyone has great basic strokes) and the strongest hearts and minds, and they find ways to win.

Todd Woodbridge had a career singles run at Wimbledon in 1997, making it all the way to the semifinals. Although he is one of the all-time doubles greats, Todd had trouble translating his skill to singles. He had great technique and finesse, and he was very crafty. But he didn't make a lot of power and he didn't move great (in doubles, he only had to worry about half the court). Todd's weaknesses played right into my strengths, and I had little trouble with him. Once again, I found myself facing Cédric Pioline in the final.

I felt for Cédric, because even though he had played a previous Grand Slam final against me at the U.S. Open, this was different— no tournament feels as historic as Wimbledon. There was no pressure on him; I was the prohibitive favorite. His best chance lay in going out there and just letting it rip—what did he have to lose? But that's easier said than done.

Once again, as in our U.S. Open final, Cédric seemed overwhelmed. I won the first two sets, giving up just six games. I was on top of my game and in touch with the Gift. It seemed like just minutes after the start of the match, yet there I was, serving at 5–4 in the third. I found myself thinking, *Wow, this is too easy.* I don't mean to be disrespectful toward Cédric. It was just that the match was on my racket, far sooner and with far less difficulty than I expected.

I had this flash as I got within two points of the match: *Man, this is so big, what I'm doing—this is it. Wimbledon. It's huge. . . .* And I was immediately overcome by this feeling of insecurity. I panicked, like someone having an anxiety attack. I thought, *Is it really supposed to be so easy? Am I missing something here? Is this all going to turn out to be some kind of joke or hoax, on me?* In a very real, visceral way, it was like a great dream, the kind in which you feel omnipotent, but a part of you knows that at any moment you might wake up and destroy the illusion.

But I didn't wake. I coasted across the finish line in straight sets, giving up a total of ten games. It was a fitting end to one of the least eventful or significant of my Wimbledon tournaments. I didn't have any epic battles or showdowns with career rivals. Yet my performance at Wimbledon in 1997 may have been my best, in terms of having full control of my game and using it to maximum advantage for the longest sustained period. One stat said it all: I served 118 games, and held 116 times.

I had every reason to feel confident about the U.S. Open a couple of months later. I was playing some of the most dominating tennis of my career, and I had a great draw for the year's last major. For starters, I sliced my way through three relative unknowns—Todd Larkham, Patrick Baur, and Alex Rădulescu, losing just thirty games (numbers almost identical to my previous Wimbledon stats) as I cruised into the fourth round and came up against the mercurial Czech player Petr Korda.

It rained on and off on the day we would play. It was a herky-jerky match in every sense, including the way we played. I was playing okay—I won the first set in a tiebreaker. But then I lost the next two sets, reviving just in time to win the fourth 6–3. When I rolled to a 3–1 lead in the fifth, I think everyone (myself included, to be honest) thought we had passed the turning point. But I have to give Korda credit. He hung in there. He was right at my side, hitting his unpredictable and sometimes dazzling winners each time I threatened to open a bigger lead. He broke me back, forced the tiebreaker, and won it 7–3 to take the match.

That was one of Korda's signature, streaky performances, on a day when my own nerves were a bit frazzled and thin—mostly because of the somber, gray atmosphere and the annoying rain delays. I had two majors already that year, and taking the U.S. title would have made '97 my best year, productionwise. And to rub salt in the wound, Korda didn't even play his next match because, he said, he was sick. Like almost all top players, if I was going to lose I wanted it to be to the guy who would win the tournament.

Korda would go on to win the Australian Open in 1998; it would be his lone Grand Slam title. But shortly thereafter, he tested positive for performance-enhancing drugs in what was the first high-profile drug suspension in my era. He was subsequently fined and suspended from the game.

Steroid abuse wasn't a big story in tennis until many years later, so I'm no expert on the subject. But I believe that 99 percent of the tennis players are, and always have been, clean. It isn't in the nature of most players to mess with drugs—tennis players who make the tour level are shaped in an information-rich environment, usually by people who are sophisticated and knowledgeable; they aren't naive or ignorant of the long-term dangers posed by performance-enhancing drugs the way some young players might be in some of the more popular sports.

Also, tennis is less about strength than quickness, so the premium on building muscle isn't that high. I don't think the NBA has a big performance-enhancing-drug problem either, because basketball and tennis are both more about quickness and good hands rather than about big muscles and strength. But I've come to learn that performance-enhancing drugs do have some subtle benefits for a tennis player. They enable him to train hard and recover faster— that is, to build a fitness base and stroking discipline with stamina they don't naturally possess. Still, guys who practice the most, or who have the most stamina, aren't the big winners.

I'm not naturally a suspicious person, but one thing that troubles me whenever there's a doping controversy is the way guys *always* have the excuses: I drank my wife's medication by mistake; the doctor wrote the wrong prescription; the testing procedure was flawed. In other words, the dog always eats the homework. I really have nothing but contempt for guys who get caught and try to wriggle out of it that way. I took a lot of pills in my time, including all kinds of vitamins, and always went to a doctor to have them checked out to make sure they were legal. And that was well before doping raised its head as a serious issue. It can be done. I'm tired of the excuses you keep hearing, and see no gray area—it's up to you to test clean; if you test positive for steroids, you should be penalized, unless there is some clear and overwhelming mitigating circumstance. End of story.

The other thing for me was that I could never cheat. I just couldn't justify taking an unfair or illegal advantage, and doing so would have messed with my mind so much that it would have wiped out any good that drugs might have done. Even if I was sure other guys were doing it, I just wouldn't take steroids for ethical reasons. Not even if everyone around me egged me on, telling me that everyone else was on them, not even if it meant the difference between keeping up with the pack or falling behind. I realize it's easy for me to take that high ground, but I believe that's how I would have felt if presented with the option.

Here's something else. It's rarely the top guys who pay for the sins of the dopers. One thing drugs can't do is make you a Wimbledon champion, or give you a game to beat Roger Federer. The guys who really get hurt are the players in the doper's peer group, where boosting your ranking by just a few notches, or going an extra round or two at some events, can make a big difference, ranking- and money-wise. Whatever Korda ingested during that period, it didn't catapult him to the top. He was always in the mix near the top of the game, and I had struggled with him in the past (four years earlier, he'd beaten me in the Grand Slam Cup 13–11 in the fifth).

I realize now that doping might have played a role in our U.S. Open encounter (Korda was, after all, caught less than a year later). It was a long, debilitating match, played under strange conditions, in which a little extra strength might have provided him with a critical advantage. We'll never know, because only Petr knows the truth about what he was—or wasn't—doing. I bear him no ill will, and just write that loss off as one of those things.

After that U.S. Open disappointment, I played one of my best Davis Cup matches ever, against a strong, young Australian team on the hard courts in Rock Creek Park, Washington, D.C. I beat Mark Philippoussis and Pat Rafter in my two singles to lead the United States into the final against Sweden. We would lose that final, partly because I had to retire with a leg injury in the middle of my opening match against Magnus Larsson. I did, however, win the two big year-end events, the Grand Slam Cup and the ATP World Championships. In the process, I couldn't help notice that I was seeing more new faces all the time—guys like Patrick Rafter, Greg Rusedski, and Carlos Moya. . . . I was beginning to feel like a veteran.

I finished as number one for the fifth year in a row in 1997, tying Jimmy Connors's record. My mission for the coming year, regardless of my parallel quest to break Roy Emerson's record for Grand Slam singles titles (with ten, I trailed him by two at the end of '97), was to become the only man ever to finish number one for six years running. Unfortunately, I got off to a pretty slow start.

I had an easy draw at the Australian Open, and didn't lose a set until the quarters, where I lost a match I'd just as soon forget to Karol Kucera. A few weeks later, I won just six games off of a resurgent Andre Agassi in the big indoor tournament in San Jose. In the two major events of the late winter, Indian Wells and Miami, I took losses from Tomas Muster and Wayne Ferreira, respectively. Both of them were in early rounds. I had just one tournament win before the tour moved to Europe for the spring, and that was at my old standby—Philadelphia.

I was picked apart by Fabrice Santoro in the second round at the big Monte Carlo tournament, so I returned to the States and scooped up a win on the green clay of Atlanta. Green clay, or HAR-TRU, is a U.S. phenomenon. The loose surface dressing is more granular and slippery than the brick dust of red clay, so the court plays slightly faster. Along the way, I beat a nice clay-court player from Paraguay, Ramon Delgado, in two tiebreaker sets. Buoyed by my win, I returned to Europe and got to the third round of the Italian Open before my countryman Michael Chang sat me down. I felt all right about my game going to Roland Garros.

I was reasonably confident, and I had a kind draw in Paris, starting with my pal Todd Martin in the first round. However a match with Todd went, I was always comfortable playing him, and this time I was on my game and I rolled into the second round in good shape. I found myself up against Delgado, the clay-court expert I'd beaten handily on clay just a few weeks earlier in Atlanta.

During the match, all of my unresolved issues with clay-court tennis began to play on my mind. Paul sat by, horrified, as I lost a first-set tiebreaker and then went down winning just seven games over the next two sets. It wasn't just that I lost, it was how I lost—I looked like a fish out of water, flopping around in the dust on the floor of the Philippe Chatrier Court Centrale. I was playing a guy who was barely inside the top hundred, and who would eventually fall off the ATP computer-ranking chart without ever winning a singles title (his career record in singles was 94–103). Yet I was the one who played with slumped shoulders and a lack of fire in my belly. It was one of the most negative performances of my career.

I had survived and overcome difficult moments before, but this time I really recognized that my time in Paris was running out. I had plenty of good results to call upon from the past to try to change my own mind, but that didn't work. I could neither convince nor fool myself. That Delgado match was the straw that broke the camel's back as far as Roland Garros went for me. Even for me, thinking about Roland Garros raises more questions than it answers.

One thing I know for sure is that the year when I actually made a big effort to do all I could to win in Paris was a mess. In 1995, I had set up my tournament and training schedule with an eye toward doing well at Roland Garros. I did it partly to placate critics as well as friends, all of whom thought I had to target the event if I wanted to unlock its mysteries. The strategy didn't just backfire, it blew up in my face when I lost my first match to Gilbert Schaller. Tim and I had expected to make a run in Paris that year, and the loss really hurt my long-term confidence as a clay-court player.

The situation was perplexing. I periodically put up some fine results on clay (I had won the Italian Open and Kitzbühel, and led the United States to that key 1995 Davis Cup final win in Moscow), but it was almost like they came out of the blue. Tim died shortly before the 1996 French Open, and that inspired me to make what would be my best run there. But let's face it, that was an extraordinary circumstance. The cold reality is that after 1996, I was never really a factor in Paris—even if I happened to go a round or two.

My problems on clay were related to my versatility, and the confidence that was so helpful to me on hard courts. I could win from the back—I had beaten French Open champs like Jim Courier and Sergi Bruguera from the baseline. So I was reluctant to heed the advice of Paul and others who thought my only chance to win was through attacking. Sometimes I did feel obliged to attack, and felt comfortable embracing that game plan. At other times, I tried to feel my way into matches from the baseline, not entirely confident but hoping I'd hit upon something that would help me crack the clay-court code.

I never really evolved in Paris, never made progress toward a comfort zone. I was accustomed to feeling totally in control of my game—that's how it was at Wimbledon and the U.S. Open. On grass and hard courts, I just had this mentality: bring the gas—serve big, push the action, notch it up, and see if the other guy can take it. On clay, though, you have to back off the gas a little, even when you're playing attacking tennis. You need to be more patient, awaiting your opportunity. I didn't really feel comfortable playing within myself that way. When I played well on clay, it was because I was reasonably calm, and just felt my way around in matches—it wasn't that different from how I played on hard courts.

But there was always pressure on me, some of it self-imposed, to win in Paris with an attacking game. A part of me wanted to come in all the time, the way Stefan Edberg did. His daredevil attacking style carried him all the way to the final one year, which was further than I ever got. But when I rushed the net behind every decent serve, I'd often feel uncomfortable, like everything was happening too fast. I don't think I was a great mover on clay, and that was a subtle factor in my struggles. I found the surface was a little slippery and uncertain underfoot, so I played a little too upright, at least compared to a guy like Yannick Noah (the Frenchman who won Roland Garros by attacking the net in 1983). Noah played from this crouch, like a big cat always ready to pounce. I was often ill at ease, even up at the net.

Paul was always after me to attack the net in Paris, but I resisted his advice. In fact, the year I beat Jim from the backcourt, it was as much to prove my point to Paul as anything else. But the reality was that I couldn't win from the back consistently enough to beat the very top players in the three or four successive rounds it takes to win a major. One year, I decided to embrace the chip-and-charge strategy that Paul thought might work, but I was picked apart by Andrei Medvedev. So much for that.

Clay gave my opponents additional advantages. They could expose my backhand—my weaker shot—by getting to it with high-bouncing balls. Having to hit those high backhands gives one-handed backhanders fits—just look at the problems Roger Federer has had on clay with Rafael Nadal. In Roger's case, the problem is exacerbated by the fact that Nadal is a southpaw. Late in my career, technology was also starting to catch up with me. I played my entire career with that extremely small-headed racket. Not only did I ignore the potential benefits of evolving racket design, the advances in rackets helped level the playing field for opponents who were more inclined to adapt.

Because I never settled into a clay-court game plan, every match was like a Rubik's Cube. I always had to start from square one. I confess that after my loss to Delgado, I never saw Roland Garros through the same eyes. It seemed like it just wasn't meant to be. It wasn't like I just mailed it in—that wasn't my way, and there was too much to gain from winning in Paris—but after that Delgado match I had the gnawing feeling that I'd run out of options.

In the end, maybe the truth just caught up to me. Maybe I just plain wasn't good enough on clay to win Roland Garros, and I never caught the lucky break or hot streak that might have landed me on the champion's podium even for that one critically important time.

At Wimbledon, I had a good run, beating Mark Philippoussis and my friend and frequent practice partner Tim Henman in back-to-back matches starting in the quarters.

In the final, I was up against Goran Ivanisevic—again. But this time, there was something funny in the air. Underneath my calm, confident exterior, a part of me sensed that maybe it was Goran's time. He'd come so close, so often. Wimbledon was the tournament that mattered more to him than anything else; he was bound to break through at some point. Although the speed of the surface was changing by then, he and I were going to bang aces even if we played with water balloons. We still had that mentality, and maybe that was a big part of why we were able to play that way despite the changing times. Goran had put on a fierce display of power serving in his semifinal, outlasting Richard Krajicek 15–13 in the fifth—after he had failed to capitalize on two match points in the fourth set.

Goran won the first set of our final in a tiebreaker, and he had two set points in the second set. My premonition seemed about to come true, but then he missed a critical shot by inches, and I ended up squeaking out the set in a tense tiebreaker. Getting out of that jam to even the match at a set apiece was huge, and it left me feeling better. Maybe my instincts were wrong. Goran had chances to really put down the hammer, in classically brutal grass-court fashion, but he had faltered.

With Goran, I always expected a lapse here, a sloppy error there. The name of the game was staying focused and eager enough to pounce on those opportunities. We continued to trade bombs and split the next two sets on the strength of one break each time. In the fifth set, I could see that fatigue was getting to Goran. He hit just two of his total thirty-two aces in the fifth set, and I closed it out comfortably, 6–2 in the fifth.

Goran was disconsolate after the loss—he blamed it on a loss of energy stemming from his inability to close out Krajicek in four sets in his previous match. I made a point of expressing my sympathy for Goran in the press conference afterward, saying: "There was almost nothing that separated Goran and I from each other at this stage of the tournament. I just managed to squeak this one out." But like me, Goran was a realist. He knew he'd had me and let me off the hook. As he said afterward, "This time, I had the chance, because he didn't play well. In ninety-four, we played two sets, and then the third set, he killed me. [The scores in that final were 7–6, 7–6, 6–0.] But today was very close—a lot of everything. It was interesting, but now it's the worst moment of my life. You know, I've had some bad moments, when you are sick or when somebody dies, but for me this is the worst thing ever, because nobody's died yet."

Although there were undercurrents of discontent following this typical grass-court service battle, more people seemed to appreciate the icy, minimalist majesty that Goran and I produced in our Wimbledon matches. They were unlike most of the other matches that either of us had played there. One of the career statistics that gives me the most pride is that I was 3–1 at Wimbledon against my most consistent and dangerous rival, Goran.

I was within one match of Emerson's record twelve Grand Slam singles titles as I left Wimbledon, and there was no better place to equal his mark than at the U.S. Open. But I lost at Flushing Meadows to the swashbuckling Australian with the samurai topknot and zinc-oxide war paint, Pat Rafter. I would have made the rest of my life that year a lot easier if I had managed to win in New York, because it would have spared me having to undertake a late-season push to clinch the number one spot for a record sixth consecutive year.

As I looked at my prospects for the fall of 1998, I realized that I had no appetite for the indoor European events that take place after the Grand Slams are all done. Six or seven years earlier, I wanted to win everything. For years, the mileage on my odometer had been building up, and while my engine hadn't lost any pep, my shocks were getting worn and things were beginning to break. For an athlete, that means injuries, or moments when the mind just snaps and fails to focus in the correct, relaxed way that helps you win tennis matches. All those years at number one took a lot out of me, and had me thinking a lot more about peaking at the right, choice times of the year—meaning, for the Grand Slams.

Nevertheless, I was determined to make a push for that ironman record of most years at number one. It may not be as spectacular a record as the Grand Slam singles title mark, but in many ways it's more significant because greatness begins and ends with going out there, day after day, and getting the job done, learning to live and survive with that target on your back. The essence of greatness is consistency.

I'm often asked to name the GOAT (Greatest of All Time), and to me there are five guys in that conversation if you count guys who played at least a significant portion of their careers in the Open era that began in 1968. In all honesty, I just don't feel qualified to judge the great players of the amateur era, when top players turned pro and were barred from playing the Grand Slams. My five guys are Rod Laver, Björn Borg, Ivan Lendl, Roger Federer, and—no arrogance intended—me. My reasoning is pretty simple: to me, the GOAT was not just a guy who won X number of titles, or who finished on top X number of years; he's also the one who came closest to dominating his main rivals throughout his career.

Some people may ask, "Lendl?" Well, yes, because Ivan really transcended the game in his time. His record against Connors was an amazing 22–13 and against McEnroe he was 21–15. How do you argue with that? And Connors had a nemesis in Borg, while McEnroe was manhandled frequently by Lendl. The only thing Lendl lacked was good PR, and the charisma people want in a great champion. He was in the final of the U.S. Open eight consecutive years—and the Open is thought by many to be the most demanding of the majors. So those are my top guys, with all due respect to Connors, McEnroe, and Andre Agassi, whom I put in the second five of my all-time top ten.

It's interesting to compare the feat of breaking Emerson's singles title record (twelve Slams) with the accomplishment of finishing at number one for six years in a row. A player can equal Emerson's record by winning two majors a year for six years. That isn't too great an ask, given that a great grass- or clay-court player could win just one tournament on a less desirable surface to get those two majors. Six years is a pretty reasonable window, given that McEnroe is the only one among the great players who won all of his majors in a span of *fewer* than seven years (Connors won majors almost ten years apart). Seven years is twenty-eight Grand Slam events; to win twelve is a massive achievement, but not unthinkable.

So you're really talking about a month of great tennis out of every year and you have your twelve majors. The rest of the time, you can hide, relax, or plot your strategy while marshaling your resources. But you can't do that if you want to finish number one. You don't get that top spot unless you play and win a lot of tournaments and matches over the course of the year. Most players would trade majors for consistency any day, much like most baseball players would rather be on a World Series winner once than a team that finishes tops in its league for years but never takes the fall classic. But the best of players win big, and they win often. They grind.

Ultimately, it was grinding that almost undid me in that period in 1988 when I was driving to capture that sixth straight year-end number one ranking. I played seven post–U.S. Open events in Europe in the fall in an attempt to hold off Marcelo Rios, who was making a big push for the top ranking. At the start of the year, I had no intention of playing some of those events (Vienna and Stockholm pop right to mind), but I ended up asking for wild cards into them. As the year progressed, Rios kept closing on me, and I became border-line obsessed with the record.

The European circuit in the fall is no picnic, even at the best of times. It's cold, it gets dark early, and you're playing night matches in massive arenas under artificial lights. At the end of the long, hard Grand Slam season, that ambience can leave you feeling like you're living in some strange, parallel universe. That last big push to secure the record started on a down note when I lost to Wayne Ferreira at Basel. I bounced back and won Vienna. I pulled out of Lyon with a minor injury, but then lost a heartbreaker of a semifinal (in a third-set tiebreaker) at Stuttgart to Richard Krajicek. To make matters worse, I could have clinched the year-end number one ranking by winning that event.

So it was onto Paris, which is where I started to lose it a little bit. The general fatigue that contributed to my inconsistent results was starting to get to me at a deeper, psychological level. The stress was causing my hair to fall out in clumps. Yet nobody in the States seemed to care—there wasn't a single reporter representing a U.S. news-paper or magazine covering this drive. By contrast, the European press was all over it. It was the dominant story of the fall season, and it just brought that much more pressure to bear on me.

Finally, realizing that I just couldn't internalize it all any longer, I called Paul's room in the hotel from my own and asked him to come by. This was a watershed moment for me, because I had never before showed the kind of vulnerability I was about to exhibit. Paul came into my room, wondering what was up. I confessed, "Paul, I'm struggling here. I feel like I need a therapist or something. This race is so close, I've worked so hard to get this record, but I'm thinking these crazy things, like, What if I don't get it? How am I going to deal with that?"

Paul looked at me, dumbfounded. It wasn't an easy situation for him—it ran utterly counter to the relationship we had established over many long years. He didn't know what to say at first, but in reality, he didn't need to say anything at all. I was the one who needed to say things—I just had to articulate and off-load all that anxiety. I explained that this was an emotional thing I was going through. I felt this huge sense of pressure, a different kind than I had felt trying to win a major title, or as I closed on Emerson's record. I dreaded what might happen if I didn't get the record. What was there to dread? Good question.

There was a sobering practical dimension to this, though. My effort to set a new mark was six years in the making, and if I failed, it wasn't like I could try again the following year. This was the most all-or-nothing situation I'd ever been in; if I didn't accomplish my goal, it would be a career shortcoming that was bound to haunt me for life, and more rather than less because I had come so close to achieving it. This hunt had grown into an obsession; it became a weight I carried around in my chest all fall, getting heavier and heavier. Eventually, I needed to exhale.

Paul took that information and went and thought about it, and then set about getting me ready to run the last leg of the race. It's not like there was a lot he could do, but understanding how much I had tied myself in knots over this would lead him to maybe deal with the situation on his end a little differently. Basically, Paul provided a place where I could go to be vulnerable, and his quiet encouragement and understanding of what I was going through were very welcome. I felt better after talking with him. To the extent that I needed an emotional anchor—an unfamiliar need, for me—he became it.

None of this had anything to do with the tennis part, the forehands and backhands, even though I was playing tired, erratic tennis—up one day, down the next. However, the ATP was trying to capitalize on the story, ostensibly for my benefit as much as theirs. They were asking me to do all these interviews, including prime-time European news and chat shows. That was just what I needed—to waste my energy and downtime in the evenings going on chat shows with the French Larry King.

I was really tense. I asked the ATP to leave me alone, without divulging how much I was struggling. They kept pushing, and it all came to a head when they wanted me to do this one show that, the ATP told me, was France's most popular evening news program. I put my foot down and refused: I'll do anything you want during the daytime, but after dark I just need to shut down. I had a big knockdown, drag-out fight with the ATP PR guy David Higdon, and ultimately even Mark Miles, the CEO of the ATP Tour, got into the discussion. Ultimately, I relented and did the show.

Unburdening myself to Paul helped, and it gave me a little extra surge of energy and confidence, even though it didn't suddenly restore my game to its customary effectiveness. I put my all into it, and got to the final of the Paris Indoor. But again a chance to seal the deal eluded me as I lost to the hard-serving Canadian-turned-Brit, Greg Rusedski. Nothing was settled; Rios was still riding my tail pretty hard. In fact, we were heading for a showdown in the ATP Finals, with the top ranking—and my coveted record—on the line. I wondered, *Did I have enough gas left in my tank?*

Stockholm was next. I hoped to put a little more distance between Rios and me, but the tension was excruciating and I finally snapped. It was during my match with Jason Stoltenberg. I got so frustrated with my play that I destroyed a racket. It was very funny, in a way— people were so shocked I did it that nobody even said anything. Even the umpire was baffled; he didn't even warn me, much less issue the appropriate code violation and fine (for "racket abuse"). I think people just blinked and said, *Naw, that wasn't Pete Sampras I just saw doing that. Pete Sampras doesn't do that kind of thing.* I ended up losing the match.

Ultimately, it was Rios himself who ended my agony. He hurt his back and pulled out of the ATP Championships after playing just one match, rendering the race moot. He couldn't catch me if he didn't play. It was an anticlimactic ending to one of the more interesting situations that that tour and ranking structure kicked out, and that diminished the impact of my achievement. But I couldn't have cared less. I was glad that it didn't come down to a final showdown; in my frazzled state I don't know what might have happened. I felt like hopping on a plane and going home after Rios announced that he was closing down shop for the year, but it wasn't the right thing to do. Glad and relieved, free of stress and pressure, I went on to reach the final of the ATP Championships, losing to Alex Corretja.

When I evaluate how I was able to win so many matches over so many years, a few things pop up as keys to the accomplishment. First, I trusted myself and the Gift. Throughout my career, whenever I made a critical mistake, I just wiped it off the hard drive. I don't really know how I developed that ability to move on instead of dwell upon, but I had it. My guess is that it was some mental function, rather than an emotional one—a kind of extra-high focus on success. And a lot of it was sheer will.

If you train yourself not to let things get to you, they don't—although you probably need to be predisposed that way for the training to work fully. I never got into it with umpires, even though seeing the guy in a chair take a pretty crucial point away from you can sting like a slap in the face. Guys lose it over that, and I know just how they feel. But I think I received just one official code violation in my entire career—many players have gotten more than that in a single, relatively meaningless match. Maybe I'm just built a little differently, but a big part of my mentality and, ultimately, success, was making a conscious decision not to lose it in front of others.

Part of that had to do with keeping a competitive advantage, a lot of it also had to do with my personal pride and how I wanted the world to see me.

Distractions are another daily threat to winning matches. But nothing intruded on my mind when I was on the court, and it was as simple as that. Girlfriends, coaching problems, family issues—I was almost always able to block all of it out, and it wasn't even like I had to work at it. That's a huge help if you want to perform at peak level consistently. I was all business on the court, although I did draw on memories, conversations, and even vows made to myself when I needed them. It was always positive, not a distraction that blunted my focus.

Anger? I would have been faking it if I took to strutting around screaming, with the veins popping in my neck and my eyes bulging. As a kid, I threw the occasional tantrum, but as I became more of an attacking player and grew into a man, that behavior kind of dissipated somewhere along the way. It just comes to a point where you are who you are, and you recognize it. Pundits and fans sometimes wondered why I didn't show more anger or emotion now and then, and the answer is simple: I didn't feel it—or if you prefer, I didn't *allow* myself to feel it; I internalized it instead.

But I experienced frustration and felt the sting of criticism as much as anyone. I can keep score with the best of them when it comes to remembering who's a friend and who's a foe. I've got as much of a sense of justice and fairness as anyone, but I always subscribed to that old expression: Revenge is a dish best served cold.

With rare exceptions, anger is an impediment to playing well and winning matches. I remember seeing Goran Ivanisevic lose it a few times in our many matches at Wimbledon. I would watch as he broke a few of his sticks, and at that point I always felt that I had him. The meltdown told me that I had broken my opponent's composure and will. I now had him exactly where I wanted him.

I also didn't want anyone to be able to read *me* like that. By being opaque, I may have made some of my opponents a little more cautious and fearful. But that dynamic wasn't an orchestrated strategy. I never tried to intimidate anyone, and I never played mind games. My biggest weapon was being myself; I showed that I could meet and handle the most nerveracking of situations in a calm, focused way—my natural way. Being cool with no frills or affectations won me a lot of matches.

Early in my career, I marveled at the way John McEnroe would complain and stall, and suffer no repercussions in his game (in fact, he often played better when he was on his worst behavior). His outbursts didn't bother me as much as they irked others, because I wasn't easily distracted and always felt confident about how our games matched up.

Andre Agassi sometimes lost it in our matches—I remember one year in San Jose, he cracked two rackets, fought with the chair umpire, and called him a "motherf#$@&%r." Watching that happen, I sat back in my chair and thought, *Okay, Andre's finished.*

I tried very hard to keep everything simple, and that meant staying at arm's length from many things, including nontennis relationships and activities that could distract me. I didn't do many charity events or appearances, I didn't respond to business overtures, I didn't chase women. I felt I had to make certain sacrifices that others would or could not: I moved to Tampa and made it my home and base for most of my career because it was the best location for training, and it took me away from the distraction of friends and family in Southern California.

But I missed my family—often powerfully—and didn't especially enjoy training for the Australian Open in Florida during Christmas. Maybe I should have had someone to talk to about this stuff, a therapist or something, because putting on the blinders and internalizing everything, denying myself even the simple, harmless things like Cokes and cheeseburgers, being unable to talk to anyone about feeling vulnerable in my game, or being afraid to find outlets for my feelings of insecurity lest it water down my drive took a physical and mental toll.

After I broke Connors's record, I was free to focus on what most people thought was a greater task and more noteworthy accomplishment: besting Emerson's record twelve Grand Slam titles. That required as much planning, work, determination, skill, and luck as any other goal, but it wasn't as all-consuming an assignment. I could get that record without playing at the level I had set for myself over the last six years. From 1999 onward, I didn't worry that much about the rankings, or my performance in sub–Grand Slam tournaments. Most of the regular tour events simply ran together in my mind, win or lose. At the same time, a whole new cast of rivals was emerging and I began to lose more matches.

1999–2001

Chapter 9

KEY MATCHES . . .

July 1999, Wimbledon, final

P. SAMPRAS	6	6	7
A. AGASSI	3	4	5

July 2000, Wimbledon, final

P. SAMPRAS	6	7(5)	6	6
P. RAFTER	7(10)	6	4	2

September 2000, U.S. Open, final

P. SAMPRAS	4	3	3
M. SAFIN	6	6	6

July 2001, Wimbledon, fourth round

P. SAMPRAS	6	7	4	7(2)	5
R. FEDERER	7(7)	5	6	6	7

September 2001, U.S. Open, quarterfinal

P. SAMPRAS	6	7(2)	7(2)	7(5)
A. AGASSI	7(7)	6	6	6

YEAR–END RANKING . . . 1999, 2000: No. 3

Catching Roy

I was so worn out by my push to break the consecutive-years-at-number-one record that I skipped the Australian Open, and was content to tread water through the spring events. I reached just one semifinal on my way to London's grass courts, but then I won at Queen's Club and entered Wimbledon with a chance to equal Roy Emerson's record of twelve Grand Slam titles at the tournament I loved best.

At this time, Andre's final resurgence was in full swing. He made a huge statement at Roland Garros in 1999, winning the title to become just the fifth man in tennis to post a "career Grand Slam" (winning each of the Grand Slam events at least once). I had a good draw at Wimbledon with a relatively easy first week. The demands of grass-court tennis created a smaller pool of contenders than you get at, say, the French Open, although the downside is that anybody with a big serve at Wimbledon threatened to upset a contender. It was hardly surprising to me when I saw that, just as in 1998, I would be playing Mark Philippoussis to get at (probably) Tim Henman in the semis.

I knew that Philippoussis was getting ever more dangerous. The previous fall, his big forehand and powerful serve had carried him to the U.S. Open final. In our Wimbledon match, he was on fire in the first set, winning it 6–4. But he went down, hard, at 1–2 in the second set, and suffered a terrible knee injury that would severely impact his career.

Henman was next, and at some level I felt for him. He was a

class act; a friend, golfing buddy, and frequent practice partner. The British hadn't produced a male Wimbledon champ since Fred Perry, and Tim was as close as they had come. He was always in the hunt, making the quarters or better, but the big upset, combined with a little luck in the way of opponents, always eluded him.

Some pundits trashed Tim for not making that big breakthrough, but I felt that given the hopes of the Brits and the pressure that put on Tim, he not only handled the situation with great dignity, he actually played above his head at Wimbledon. I sat him down at the tournament myself three times (twice in late rounds), and the next best thing to winning a tournament is losing to the champion. People sometimes asked me if it was tough to douse my friend's dreams as often as I did, and I have to confess: not one bit. It was like beating a buddy at darts, or a game of H-O-R-S-E. You just played, the better man won, and that was it.

The last man standing between me and equal status with Roy Emerson was my main rival, Andre. It had rained on the Saturday women's final, so the match between Lindsay Davenport and Steffi Graf was scheduled to finish on Sunday, as a prelude to our final.

A Wimbledon final abounds in traditions and rituals that can really add to the pressure you feel before you go out to play. There's that whole thing about having to wait in the small holding room, looking at that sign bearing the Kipling quote above the door. Then, when you're finally sent on court, it's with empty hands—an attendant carries your racket bag for you, all the way to your chair. It's a nice gesture, but it makes you feel even more exposed and vulnerable. As you walk out there to play a Wimbledon final, arms dangling at your sides, you realize there's no turning back. There's nowhere to hide. This is the test of your tennis life. That's part of what makes winning Wimbledon so special.

Centre Court is the epicenter of Wimbledon's mystique. It's a cliché, but the place really is like the cathedral of tennis, and entering it you quickly get a sense of your own smallness in the grand scheme of things. But unlike the world's great cathedrals, Centre Court is surprisingly small (before the ongoing renovation, it seated about twelve thousand), and the roof over the stands adds even further to the sense of intimacy (for 2009, Centre Court will have a retractable roof that covers everything).

In comparison, the Rod Laver Arena at the Australian Open is antiseptic, featureless, and, seemingly, vast. When you're standing at the baseline looking across the net, it seems *miles* to the wall at the far end of the court. And that makes the actual court seem smaller than it really is. I always preferred architecture that made the actual court of play seem *larger.*

The Philippe Chatrier Court at Roland Garros is also huge, with a lot of space around the lines of the court. That always added to my feeling that I couldn't really control what went on in there—it was too much territory. That uncomfortable feeling is somewhat legitimate, too, because on clay you actually do play on a much larger court—at least in terms of how much space you use. You often play from much farther behind the baseline on clay, you chase balls farther than on any other surface, and you're often pulled wider from side to side.

That leaves Arthur Ashe Stadium at the USTA Billie Jean King National Tennis Center in New York, and while it's the most imposing of the Grand Slam venues, the court and space around it, surprisingly, are just about right. I guess those towering walls make the court feel smaller. Many players beef about how hard it is to concentrate in Ashe because of the restless, chatty New York crowd, but that was never a problem for me. However, I liked the old Louis Armstrong Stadium court (which was the main court before Ashe was built and is now the secondary feature court) even better, probably because it felt a little smaller—although nothing like Centre Court.

There was a definite psychology at play in this. The smaller a court appeared to be, and the closer the far side seemed to be, the faster the court seemed to play. And that always gave me extra confidence, because I liked fast tennis. I wonder if the illusion affected my opponents as well.

At Wimbledon, the court is completely and inescapably the center of attention—there's no plane noise and no JumboTron or complicated digital scoreboard to distract you with stock prices, NFL scores, or ads. The space around the court at Wimbledon is limited, and the backdrop is dark, with very little advertising or busy features. The dark background also makes the pale green grass look extra-inviting; aesthetically, grass courts have it all over a dusty stretch of clay, or bland hard courts.

I enjoyed the relative "softness" of the court; it was terrific to feel that sod gently give way beneath my feet with every step. I felt catlike out there, like I was on a soft play mat where I could do as I pleased without worry, fear, or excessive wear and tear. Centre Court always made me feel connected to my craft, and the sophisticated British crowd enhanced that feeling. It was a pleasure to play before them, and they inspired me to play my best. Wimbledon is a shrine, and it was always a joy to perform there.

As it turned out, Lindsay upset Steffi, and the crowd didn't seem to know how to react. The atmosphere as Andre and I took the court was muted, and a little strange. It was the kind of thing that rarely happens at Wimbledon, where they know how to give every match its due. But because of the rain, things were a little off. There was still an abundance of empty seats because many people decided to take a break between matches. Those in the stands were probably still trying to process what they'd just seen, and weren't ready to focus on something else.

Andre and I felt our way into the match gingerly, just like the fans. We held serve to 3–all, but then Andre got hold of my serve a few times and had me pinned, love–40, in the seventh game. I somehow survived that scare. Andre served the next game with new balls, and a funny thing happened. He missed a few easy balls and I hit a few good returns. It might have been that he was distracted by having let me off the hook in that previous game, but whatever the reason, just like that, I had a break and I held serve to go up a set. It was a classic grass-court reversal of fortune.

My confidence was ignited, and Andre's style of play fed the fire. He was my most dangerous career rival, but he was also one of the few baseliners I played in a Wimbledon final. He gave me a little more time to play my game than I got from the likes of fast-court heavies like Richard Krajicek or Goran Ivanisevic. As much as I enjoyed dominating with my serve, I also liked playing points on grass, especially engaging in rallies that stretched my legs and tested shots like my running forehand.

Andre liberated my game, and that felt great. On grass, if I was playing well and my opponent was not, and on top of that he was also staying in the backcourt—well, that made things seem pretty easy for me. As well as Andre was playing that year, and as great a returner as he was, I felt no real pressure to hold my service games. I knew that even in the event that he broke me, I'd have chances to break him back. When I played Andre, I always knew I could get into his service games.

The beginning of the second set was the backbreaker for Andre. I got an early break and drifted into the zone, that place where you play as if clairvoyant, in a calm trance and with all the time in the world to make your shots. I served huge (first and second serves) and pulled the trigger on fierce backhand returns. That enabled me to take control of the backcourt, which turned the conventional wisdom about my confrontations with Andre upside down.

There was an interesting technical reason for why I was able to get into rallies with Andre on grass and still feel on equal footing. On a hard court, Andre's ball always came in quicker; I often felt a little rushed. But on grass, despite the reputation of the surface, Andre's shots sat up a bit. I felt I had a fraction of a second longer, which was just enough time for me to get a good look and crack at the ball.

This effect was most pronounced on Andre's second serve. When he kicked it on a hard court and got it up high, I would either have to chip it or play it defensively, because I couldn't get over on it. But on grass, which deadens the bounce, that serve doesn't get up as high. So I was able to drive through those returns from a more comfortable position. If I got hold of his serve with a good return to start a rally, it was like, *Here we go—let's see who moves better.* I always felt I was a little better of a mover and athlete, even in the backcourt—especially on grass.

Sometimes when the court was brown and hard, the ball would skid or leap the way it might on a fast hard court. But even then, if the ball hit certain areas of the court, I found I had a better look. This is a pretty good example of the way court speed is a more complex, tricky issue than it may appear. Our generalizations about "slow" and "fast" are influenced by other factors, including spin and stroking mechanics.

My shots flowed freely in that second set, and I was able to use my entire arsenal. We played highly entertaining tennis, but Andre was unable to get back that early break and I won the set 6–4. The third set was another exhibition of great shotmaking by both of us, with Andre hanging in there all the way. Unfortunately for him, I was as close to unstoppable as I would ever be. I won the third set with commanding tennis 7–5.

The fact that I'd tied Emerson's record didn't mean all that much to me in that moment. There had been so much talk and speculation about the issue by then that I felt tapped out. To me, it was just another feature of the match, like how many aces I'd hit, or how the result affected my career head-to-head record with Andre. But I did take pride in producing tennis that was as close to perfect as I felt I could get.

By this stage in my career, I'd even come to enjoy the once-dreaded Champions Ball that takes place on the night of the men's final (both singles champions are expected to attend, although the days when they shared the first dance are long gone). At first, the ball seemed a real drag—the last thing I wanted to do after the stress and effort of winning Wimbledon was to get dressed up in a tuxedo and hobnob with elderly British gents and ladies who belonged to the All England Club. Also, giving a speech of any kind had been a daunting challenge for me ever since I was a kid, and the champions were expected to speak. I never had any idea what to say, and I worried that I had to come up with something special instead of just speaking from the heart.

But over time I came to understand that going to the Champions Ball was part of the whole package; it was a sign of respect for the tournament, as well as those who put it on. Over time, I became friendly with John Curry (the former head of the AEC) and his wife, as well as some of the other club members. Sometimes I'd have a glass of champagne or a glass of wine, and one time I smoked a cigar with John. Eventually, I came to enjoy the ball, and attending was a way that I could express my gratitude toward the club. Besides, I was a disciplined, clean-living athlete. It wasn't like I was dying to rush out of Centre Court after the final to hit the London clubs.

One thing about the Champions Ball that always struck me as funny was that after the speeches, various dignitaries (like the heads of various affiliates of the International Tennis Federation) invariably got to ask for pictures or autographs. This was kind of weird; here were all of these bigwigs, some of them twice my age, and most of them very successful in their own right, acting more like star-struck kids than adults. One year, I had the pleasure of meeting the iconic actor Charlton Heston, who was a member of the AEC. I was genuinely touched when he praised my attitude and style of play with strong, heartfelt words. Some others were just blowing smoke and mostly wanted a picture with me so they could hang it on the office wall. I didn't mind. It's part of a champion's job.

After I beat Andre in 1999, I spoke to the crowd at the Champions Ball from my heart, and for once it was an easy speech to deliver. I basically said that the match I'd played was less of a tribute to me than to Wimbledon, and the kind of tennis the place could inspire me to play.

The match with Andre also completed my 180-degree swing in the public eye. I had morphed from boring, bullying pariah into the best thing to hit grass-court tennis in twenty years. Yet I knew it was all because Andre had pulled it together and played up to his potential in making the final. After a few years of overpowering performances, I was able to show that I wasn't just overpowering; I could beat a baseliner of the highest order, using tools other than my big serve.

I don't want this to sound bitter, because I don't feel bitter at all. What I am, really, is bemused. The bottom line on my "image" at Wimbledon is that I really didn't change that much over the years, and neither did my game. The thing that changed was my opponents (and the games they played), and the *perception* of me and my game. The lesson in all of this is hard and it isn't pretty, and I'm not sure how you teach it to your kids, or how I'll teach it to mine. But if you win enough, people are going to come around.

That's the one thing everyone ultimately understands and respects: winning.

• • •

Fueled by my dream Wimbledon, I was looking to break the Grand Slam singles title record at home, at the U.S. Open. I was probably at the absolute height of my tennis powers, and secretly felt that my game had quietly jumped a notch in the mid-1990s. My second serve, in particular, had improved, and I felt I could hold my own from the baseline with anyone long enough to strike with my forehand and attack.

I tore it up on the early hard-court circuit after Wimbledon, winning two events. Then, in Indianapolis, I suffered a minor leg injury in a quarterfinal match with Vince Spadea. I didn't want to jeopardize my chances at the U.S. Open, so I retired when we were even at a set apiece.

That was all right. My hard-court game was dialed in, so I had no plans to play any more tune-up events before the Open. On the Friday before it started, I went out to practice at Louis Armstrong Stadium with Gustavo Kuerten. I hit a serve, stretched to hit a backhand off the return, and felt a twinge in my back. I shook it off and tried to play on.

But the twinge became a sharp pain, and after a few more points it was agonizing. I left the court and went straight to a doctor. Over the next two days, I tried the usual anti-inflammatory injections and remedies, but they didn't really help. The doctor said I should get an MRI, and it revealed a herniated disk.

I was floored. I felt confident that I would win the U.S. Open. I was on the cusp of breaking the Grand Slam singles title record. And I might have added a seventh year to my streak of finishes at number one—this time, without having to undertake another fall death march in Europe. All of it was now going up in smoke. I was looking at being off the tour for months, with the kind of injury that had permanently laid low many great players, from the Aussie icon Lew Hoad to that smooth Slovakian former U.S. Open finalist Miloslav "Big Cat" Mecir.

I felt like I'd been blindsided, because I'd rarely missed a major. I could hardly believe my bad luck. Thankfully, Paul Annacone had a long history of back trouble, and he walked me through what I might expect.

Dealing with injury is one of the toughest things for a professional athlete accustomed to the roar and din of the arena and the adrenaline rush of competition. It's a very depressing experience, and it takes all your willpower and faith not to sink into a bad place, mentally and even physically. I left New York and went back to Los Angeles, looking at a few months of therapy and, basically, laying around on the couch, alone.

My condition was so bad that at first I could barely walk; I was literally house-bound. And when all you're supposed to do all day is lay around watching TV or reading, it's pretty easy to let yourself go. The fridge, full of ice cream and pop, is nearby, and so is the telephone, the instrument that was invented so people could order pizza with ten toppings. I vowed not to slack off, though, and immediately started to take treatment that was heavy on icing and electrostimulation twice a day. That was followed by a regimen of exercises and therapy meant to strengthen my back muscles. It was tedious, painful, hard work. It was also a real wake-up call, telling me to take greater care of my body. I worked and worked, fighting off depression, mostly in the silence of my empty home.

But there was a bright spot to that otherwise terrible late summer—my injury was indirectly responsible for my wife and me meeting. While I was hurt, I was watching this movie, *Love Stinks*, with a friend, John Black. Bridgette Wilson, an actress in the film, caught my eye. Actually, she blew me away when I saw her. I thought she was stunning. John is a pretty well-connected guy, so I told him, kind of sarcastically, that if he really wanted to impress me with how much pull he had around Hollywood, he would have to get me a date with that Wilson girl.

A few days later, John called and told me it was a done deal—he had gotten Bridgette's number from her publicist, whom he knew. "Sure," I said, wary that this was going to be some kind of prank. I called Bridgette a few days later. She was very shy on the phone. I asked her out, and she suggested meeting at my place. I guess she wanted to check me out and not give away too much about herself.

Our first meeting was almost painful, it was so awkward. We were both tongue-tied, and we barely made eye contact. It was comical, or at least it would have been to anyone who wasn't either of us. Very soon after she arrived, she asked to use the bathroom, and as soon as she left the room, this is exactly what I thought: *Wow, she's really beautiful. If she can put two words together, I want to marry her.*

When she returned, I quickly realized that in order to make things less awkward we ought to go out. I suggested dinner at an Italian restaurant. The change of scenery—and getting onto neutral turf in a public place—helped. Gradually, we loosened up and had a wonderful dinner. Back at home after our first date, I was smitten—I knew she was the one. We started going out. I went from being down in the dumps about my injury to feeling great about pretty much everything, including my tennis future.

After a long, slow recovery, I found myself still eligible for the year-end ATP World Championships; I had clinched one of the eight highly coveted spots by August. I had just one match going into the year-end championships, a 7–6 in the third win over Francisco Clavet at the Paris Indoors—a result that wasn't exactly promising. In fact, I had to pull out of my next match (against Tommy Haas) in Paris because of back spasms—a minor problem that was linked to my long layoff.

I came within a few points of bombing out of the ATP Championships, because my first opponent in the round-robin was Andre, and he beat me like a drum (6–2, 6–2). Nicolas Lapentti took me to two tiebreakers in my next match, but I toughed out both of them to stay alive in the round-robin. I notched a win over Gustavo Kuerten in my final round-robin match, and that qualified me for the knock-out semifinals. After beating Nicolas Kiefer in my first match, I faced Andre—less than a week after he had tagged me two and two. I surprised him, winning in straight sets.

Despite my win in Hannover, Andre finished 1999 at number one, ending my record run. It was a well-earned coup. Andre had come back from the dead that year, careerwise, to win the French Open. He also bagged the U.S. Open while I lay on my sofa in L.A. nursing my sore back. We didn't really know it, but we were entering the last and greatest stage of our rivalry.

Andre certified that early in 2000, when he knocked me out in the semifinals of the Australian Open. Although I cared about each and every major, the loss didn't hurt that much. The truth is, I was starting to save myself and choose my spots like never before. A host of talented young players, including Pat Rafter, Lleyton Hewitt, Roger Federer, Carlos Moya, and Marat Safin were starting to develop dangerous games, and those new guys would be giving fits to old dogs like me, Andre, Boris, Goran, Jim, and Michael Chang. I still had majors in me, of that I had no doubt. Emerson's record was still unfinished business. But I was on the downhill side of my career, and I knew it.

I won Miami again in 2000, but it was my only title before the spring clay-court circuit. In Paris, Mark Philippoussis took me out in the first round, 8–6 in the fifth; I had not survived the second round at Roland Garros since 1997. Those good years, when I would battle guys like Sergi Bruguera and Jim Courier straight up, in tough, hard-fought matches, were a thing of the past.

My Wimbledon campaign in 2000 got off on the wrong foot. Somehow, while preparing for the tournament, I pulled something in my shin and developed a little inflammation and fluid under my skin. Also, Paul had picked up some new running shoes for me, and working out in them may have aggravated the condition. It was annoying, but seemingly nothing major—until I played and won my second round against Karol Kucera. In that match, I felt pain every time I put weight on my right foot. That night I had an MRI and the bad news was that I was having a fluid buildup in the irritated area.

I made a reference to the injury in the presser after the Kucera match, and the media were all over it. I felt enough pain and discomfort to consider pulling out of the tournament; it would have been crazy to jeopardize my longevity in a desperate attempt to break Emerson's record. On the other hand, memories of my enforced fall hiatus and the frustrations I experienced in Australia and France had me keyed up and unwilling to withdraw. I talked to former Wimbledon champ Pat Cash, and he recommended an acupuncturist he used. I also decided that if necessary, I would get shot up with cortisone, too. The drug knocks out inflammation and soreness, but it's also dangerous to use with any frequency or in large doses.

After my second-round match, I no longer practiced on the alternate off days for the rest of the tournament. I paid frequent visits to the acupuncturist, even though I didn't notice much of a change after the sessions, and I had myself shot up before matches. At times I still considered pulling out, but when I looked at the draw, I liked what I saw. It just kept opening up for me.

Ultimately, my path to the final went through Justin Gimelstob (third round), Jonas Bjorkman, Jan-Michael Gambill, and Vladimir Voltchkov (one of the all-time Wimbledon surprise semifinalists). It appeared easy, but the journey was full of pain and stress. I went out for every match without having hit a ball in practice (other than in the match warm-up). That made me uneasy. The constant pain was wearing on me; pain has a way of breaking down your focus and confidence. It can put you out of sorts and pretty soon your game is all over the place.

Pat Rafter emerged as my opponent for the final. A late starter as a Grand Slam contender, Rafter was at the peak of his career, and his relentless attacking style was especially dangerous at Wimbledon. Pat had won two U.S. Open titles by then, and he had done a brief stint at number one. He reached the ultimate plateau in the summer of 1999, almost a year to the day before we met in the 2000 Wimbledon final.

Rafter was a popular, classy guy, although he was one of the very few rivals with whom I had—for a time—a testy relationship. It all started back in 1998 when Rafter beat me 6–4 in the third in the final at Cincinnati. In the press conference, someone asked me what the difference was between Pete Sampras and Pat Rafter, and I said, "Ten Grand Slam titles." It was the wrong thing to say. I just got kind of uncharacteristically emotional there, following a tough loss. He took offense and I don't blame him.

Rafter also tagged me in the semifinals of the U.S. Open, just weeks after that Cincinnati incident; I guess my snide put-down had him all fired up. Then, when he became number one, he made some remarks to the effect that it was great for tennis that I was no longer number one. Of course, the press were all over that, and they wanted my reaction. I took the high road, and just said that if Pat had an issue with me, he could talk to me face-to-face. The next day Pat called and apologized. He admitted he was being a little vindictive, and I told him that my own remarks in Cincinnati the previous year had been arrogant and ill conceived.

We got along fine after that, although his game continued to give me fits. Pat was extremely crafty, and he could put a lot of pressure on me with his relentless, kamikaze-like net rushing. I had a lot of trouble with Pat's serve; it wasn't the pace or weight of his shots, and it wasn't the speed, because he hit the kicker (a relatively slow serve) almost all the time. It was the way he mixed up his serves, moved them around, and kept me guessing. He was an absolute master of picking his service locations. He'd kick one out wide, then the next one would be into the body. I'm glad he wasn't a lefty, able to kick it high to my backhand in the ad court. My life would really have been miserable then.

My folks had flown to London the day before the final to attend one of my Grand Slam matches for just the second time. The first time was for my 1992 U.S. Open with Stefan Edberg, so I can't exactly say this was a good omen. Throughout my career, they had chosen to remain in the background, partly because the hoopla surrounding a big tournament didn't suit them. I know they were very wary about being identified for the television audience. They felt that tennis was my deal, they were shy people, and they didn't want to appear to be basking in my glory.

But this particular tournament was different; they wanted to be present for me, and to share in my potentially historic feat. I asked my parents what I could do for them in London, and they said they just wanted to talk to me to wish me luck before the match and wanted to stay off the television. I told them I could handle the first task, but I had no control over the second. We did find them seats in the crowd, but the NBC cameramen searched and found them in the stands anyway. So I ended up 1–1 on the wishes.

Pat had played a great semifinal to beat Andre, and he came into the championship match riding an emotional high. We both played well at the start, thrusting and parrying for about forty-five minutes, to 4–all and then 5–all before the rains came. The rain delay had special significance for me, because it meant that the cortisone shot would be wearing off earlier in the match than usual. At this point, I was so close to winning the event that I was willing to toss caution to the wind and get another injection to get me through the final. But the doctor was pretty adamant about not doing that; he said we had touched it enough already. So after the delay I went back out, feeling considerably more uncomfortable than when we had stopped.

I had my hands full and then some: I lost my nerve a little and Pat won the first-set tiebreaker 12–10. The next set went to the tie-breaker as well. When Pat jumped to a 4–1 lead, I thought I was going to lose the match. It was a shame—my parents had come all the way to London, and it looked like I would fail to produce a win again. But Pat, faced with a match that could become the highlight on his résumé (you know how those Aussies are about Wimbledon), faltered. He had two set points at 6–4 up in the tiebreaker, but he failed to convert either. I guarantee that if he'd won either of those points, he would've won the title.

When I wriggled out of the jam and won the tiebreaker, the complexion of the entire match changed. Deep down, I felt I was going to win, even though it'd been a grueling, grinding battle to that point. That premonition lifted my spirits and game just a bit, while I felt that Pat's went down by a similar small margin. But that's the way momentum works, and that's grass-court tennis.

I was in control, but my foot was killing me. I wasn't exactly play-ing on one leg, but it was getting awfully close to that. The adversity just got me more fired up, once I sniffed the finish line. I reveled in the emotions I felt in those last few games. I was so into the moment that I actually enjoyed the pain. I had a fierce desire to drain every ounce of meaning and every sight, sound, and smell out of the moment. It was like, *This is it. Screw it, I'm going to get it done right here. I'm so into this. . . . Nobody said it was going to be easy anyway.*

I finally won it, 6–7, 7–6, 6–4, 6–2. It was dusk by then, and flashbulbs went off like a thousand lightning strikes. I looked over at Paul in the players' box. He gestured up toward the area where we knew my folks were sitting. I was disoriented, but I knew what to do next—I climbed into the stands to find and hug my folks. And those flashbulbs just kept exploding. The scene was surreal.

I learned later that Dad had been so nervous that he had left the match to go for a walk in Wimbledon Village. When he returned, he told me, he saw people milling around the grounds and he assumed that the match was over—that Pat had won. But that was just the crowd, preparing to come back into the stadium after the rain delay. The holdup also pushed the conclusion of the final into prime time in the U.K., ensuring that an amazing number of British people saw the end of the match.

Left to my own devices, I probably wouldn't have climbed into the stands. Thinking about it in advance, I would have said, "None of us likes to make a really big scene, and my parents would find it embarrassing. I don't think I'll do that." But when Paul signaled me, I knew immediately it was the right thing to do. Much like when I had been asked to speak at Tim Gullikson's funeral, my first reaction was to avoid drama and attention. But when the moment arrived in both those cases, I knew enough to do the right thing. As Paul said later, when I asked him why he had thought to signal me, "How often do you get to break the Grand Slam record, at a place that's been so good to you, in front of people who have been so good to you?"

The paparazzi got a picture of me hugging my dad. The image was printed far and wide, and it became well known. The following morning, Dad phoned from his hotel in central London and, sounding kind of amazed, told me that all kinds of people in the street recognized him—Sam Sampras!—and congratulated him.

Because of the magnitude of my accomplishment, I had all kinds of responsibilities right after the match. The ATP Tour officials were buzzing around, sifting through all these offers in what was a PR bonanza for both them and me: Charlie Rose, David Letterman, Larry King, *Today*. . . . Everyone wanted an exclusive interview. Because of the demands on my time, I was barely able to make the very end of the Champions Ball—in fact, I went there still dressed in my warm-ups. I made a brief speech and hurried back to my house in Wimbledon to have a shower and a glass of champagne with Bridgette, Paul, and my family.

Finally, I had a chance to unwind. It was just one of those moments in life when I sat back and, despite the pain in my foot, I had a big you-know-what-eating grin on my face, and I thought, *Life isn't perfect, but sometimes it's pretty damned close.*

We were due to fly out the next day. Meanwhile, the calls and faxes were pouring in, both at the house in London and my home in Los Angeles. I came late to the cell phone party, so those were the only two numbers where people could reach me. Todd Martin, Jim Courier, and Andre Agassi called to congratulate me. Michael Stich sent a fax, and so did Monica Seles.

Actually, Monica sent me lots of faxes throughout my career. We had an odd relationship that began in Los Angeles, shortly after Tim was diagnosed with cancer. Someone—it might have been a guy from IMG (the management firm that represented both of us)—called to say that Monica wanted to talk to me.

So within a few days, I was at a Los Angeles Lakers game and there she was, sitting nearby. We approached each other to exchange pleasantries, and in the course of the conversation I told her that I was flying back to Tampa the next day on a chartered private jet. She asked if she could hop on with me—at the time, she also was living near Tampa. I told her, "Sure, we're leaving out of Van Nuys tomorrow at noon."

I was a little surprised that she had invited herself along like that—after all, I hardly knew her. But I learned her reason soon enough. She wanted to reach out to me and talk because, just like I was losing Tim, she was losing her father, Karolj—also to cancer.

This was after Seles had been stabbed in the back by that crazy

German fan, and I could tell that she was going through some difficult emotional times about that as well. I was touched that she could reach out to me at a time when she was going through so much herself. And while I've never been very good at talking through things like that, we discussed our sick loved ones, and we talked a little about the stabbing incident. I realized that she was deeply shaken by it, and understood better why it took her such a long time to return to the game.

After that shared plane ride, Monica and I shared a bond of sympathy. She was a very supportive, encouraging friend, even though we never really spent much time together.

It was fitting that I would bag a record that was based to some degree on longevity against a player who wasn't on the pro radar when I won my first Grand Slam. The first requisite for achieving greatness is talent, but then it's about consistency. I faced a slew of gifted if not always complete players in my era, and I've included them all, with commentary, in the appendix at the end of this book.

In 2000, I had a chance to celebrate the tenth anniversary of my first major at the place where I won it, the U.S. Open. But Marat Safin, one of my new emerging rivals, ruined my moment. I felt good about my chances going into the match, even though I'd lost to the Russian upstart earlier that summer.

I didn't think I played badly in that U.S. Open final at all—Marat was just returning my second serves like they were nothing, he was popping his own first serve, and anything I got back, well, he would just hit the crap out of it. All I could do was mutter, "Too good," shrug, and hope he wouldn't be able to play that well throughout the match. But he did—just like that Sampras kid had in 1990. It was a great example of the adage, "What goes around comes around . . ."

I like to say that everyone has his window, and it all comes down to how willing you are to take advantage of the opening, and how long you can keep it open for yourself. Safin's window opened at Flushing Meadows in 2000 and he took full advantage, much like I had a decade earlier. He beat me with a demonstration that simply shocked and awed anyone who witnessed it.

At the time I lost to Safin, though, I had other things on my mind. Bridgette and I were to be married shortly after the tournament, and she'd agreed to put her career as an actress on hold and travel with me as I played out my string. I wasn't sure when I would quit, but I knew I wouldn't do it while I still believed I could contend at majors.

I started pretty slowly in 2001, losing to Todd Martin in the round of 16 at the Australian Open. I didn't reach a final until Indian Wells, where Andre rolled through me in straight sets. Andy Roddick beat me in Miami less than two weeks later. I made a note: another new face to remember.

The clay-court season was a write-off, and at Queen's I lost to Lleyton Hewitt in the semifinals. I got a great draw at Wimbledon. I had, in successive matches, Francisco Clavet, a clay-courter, Barry Cowan, a British long shot in through a wild card, and Sargis Sargsian. Beating those guys brought me up against a young Swiss guy I'd already heard good things about, Roger Federer. From what I'd been told, he was very talented, but he ran a little hot and cold. I expected to win, but very early in the match I realized that I was up against a kid with a complete game and talent to burn.

Early in the match, Federer was serving big and hitting the ball hard. He was also attacking—rushing the net in a way he would not do at Wimbledon in later years. It was a good, tough match. I had one sniff at a break point in the fifth set, but I let that slip way, and he played a great game to break me and ultimately win 7–5 in the fifth. Federer had halted my bid to equal Björn Borg's record of five consecutive Wimbledons, but that record didn't mean much to me.

I saw every Grand Slam event as an entity unto itself; five Wimbledons was certainly better than four, but whether or not they were in a row simply didn't matter much to me.

The loss hurt, but I had to admit I liked this kid's style. He was poised and dignified, yet he played with great flair. I was very impressed. The win was an important step in Roger's path to greatness, and looking back on it, this was the moment when the Wimbledon baton was passed from me to him. Roger also needed to know what he was really made of, sort of like I did after the Edberg fiasco of 1992. He had an inkling of it when he beat me.

I've gotten to know Roger pretty well in the last few years. He's a pretty modest, unassuming guy—nothing about him, other than his talent, suggests entitlement. I won a major on my eighth try, in just my second full year on the tour. Roger didn't win a major until his *seventeenth* try, midway through 2003, his fifth year as a tour regular. Since then, though, he's been more prolific than I was at my peak. He really took a quantum leap sometime shortly after our only career meeting. As I write this, Roger is poised to shatter my Grand Slam singles title record.

So a pattern was emerging. I was losing some matches to an emerging new guard, but they were the kids who would win majors and dominate the game over the years to come: Roddick, Safin, Hewitt, Federer. . . . And while I struggled week in, week out, I felt I showed up and gave a good accounting of myself at the majors.

When I was knocked out of Wimbledon by Roger Federer, it opened the door for Goran Ivanisevic, who beat Pat Rafter to finally get his long-coveted title. I was happy for Goran, because I liked him. He was a real grass-court warrior and a charismatic guy who was fun to be around. We got along fine, like opposites often do. I knew he could—should—have beaten me in that 1998 final, and he'd had a good chance to beat Andre in the 1995 final, too. It had to have been killing him to have blown those chances, but he put all the demons to rest in 2001.

Goran was a loose cannon. In the locker room, the players all dropped whatever they were doing and gathered around the television sets and turned up the volume when Goran was giving a press conference. He handled those sessions like a guy on a psychiatrist's couch, but always with great wit and charm. You just never knew what was going to come out of his mouth next—just like you never really knew what was going to melt off his racket in a blur, except for those aces you knew he was *always* going to hit.

A few weeks after Wimbledon, I sought Goran out in the locker room at Cincinnati and told him how happy I was that he finally got it—the big one, the one he'd dreamed about all his life. I think he was shocked to hear that, coming from me—we were rivals, we had never given each other much quarter, nor asked for any. But I just wanted him to know that I was genuinely glad for him; we had been through a lot together at that tournament.

Also, Goran's father, Srdjan, was an incredibly nice guy. He sat through all those tense, seesaw, nail-biter matches—most of which ended badly for his boy—without ever losing it, or showing the disappointment he must have felt. I never heard the guy utter a word of complaint, or make a harsh or bitter comment. He was a class act.

The situation I was in, careerwise, was perfectly expressed at the U.S. Open of 2001. It was one of the most interesting and challenging tournaments of my career, because in order to win I would have to beat three former U.S. Open champions—two dangerous guys who had shown themselves to be more or less oblivious to whatever edge my reputation theoretically gave me (Pat Rafter and

Marat Safin), and one deadly rival who just would not go away—Andre.

It was fitting that Andre was the last man standing when it came to my rivalries. Andre was toughest during that great summer of 1995, and then again near the very end of our careers, culminating with the night-session quarterfinal at the 2001 Open—a match that was the crowning moment of our rivalry and, to me, our toughest and greatest battle.

Volumes have been written about my rivalry with Andre, and from every perspective. In my heart of hearts, I know he was the guy who brought out the best in me. He had ups and downs, which accounts for why we didn't have more confrontations, especially in big finals. But Andre was still the gold standard among my rivals. Nobody else popped up as frequently, over as long a period of time, to test and push me to the max.

For most of our careers, we really couldn't have been more different—in personality, game, even the clothing we wore. Our lifestyles were radically different. Andre always seemed bent on asserting his individuality and independence, while I tried to submerge my individuality and accepted the loss of some personal freedoms. Andre was Joe Frazier to my Muhammad Ali, although the personalities were kind of flipped around because Andre was the showman and I was the craftsman. Wherever you lived, we were your neighbors: I was the nice, quiet kid next door on one side, and Andre was the rebellious teenager on the other.

Yet as Jekyll and Hyde as we were, and as much as people liked to emphasize the very real differences between us, there were powerful, deep similarities between us, too. The Gift we both had shaped our actions and lives, posing challenges as well as offering opportunities. First-generation Americans (Andre's father, Mike, was from Iran), we were both champions but outsiders who crashed a sport dominated for most of its history by white Anglo-Saxon Protestants.

That never bothered me, because the American Dream fulfilled its promise to my family, a few times over.

Because we had both been prodigies, we grew up in the public eye, under scrutiny. It was easy to stereotype us—Andre was the brash, flamboyant showman, I was the reticent, old-school, boring guy. Who was hurt more by the stereotyping? Who knows? What I am sure about, though, is that we were tough, albeit in different ways and with different goals. When we reached the top, we cast frequent, nervous glances across the divide between us. Andre and I always made it our business as individuals to know what the other guy was doing.

In late career transformations, I became more inclined to show my emotions and let fly the occasional attention-grabbing quote, while Andre shaved his head, which was not just a dramatic response to male-pattern baldness (another thing we shared) but something seemingly meant to send a message, calculated or subconscious. Andre had become a bit of an ascetic, embracing a monkish look to go along with a late-life, monkish discipline.

One thing was certain: Andre brought a lot of flair to a sport that needed it. And while it made him a huge star, it also brought him a lot of grief. It may sound crass to tennis purists, but it should be clear already that Nike played a significant role in both of our lives. We lived in a commercial era, and for most of our careers, we were both Nike guys. The company recognized that between us, we covered both ends of the tennis spectrum—the traditional values and aesthetics, and the envelope-pushing features of the Open era. If I was the heir to Rosewall and Laver, Andre was the offspring of Connors and McEnroe.

I had signed with Nike and first wore the firm's clothing at Wimbledon in 1994. In fact, I claim to be the guy who launched the long, baggy shorts craze, because that's what I liked and Nike thought it suited me. It didn't hurt that the shorts were a striking contrast to the gear Nike created for Andre. Who can forget those black shorts with the fluorescent pink compression shorts underneath?

Over the years, I hit rough patches with Nike and often felt that the company didn't do very much to market me, especially in contrast to Andre. But Nike did its best to capitalize on our rivalry. One of my few off-court run-ins with Andre was engineered by Nike. In 1993, Nike had this exhibition before the French Open, and Phil Knight (the founder and then CEO of Nike) got together with a few clients, including Jim Courier, John McEnroe, and Andre. Phil told them that he wanted to stir up a little controversy. Andre, who was in that period when he frequently said provocative things, obliged Phil. He said of my rise to number one, "Nobody should be ranked number one who looks like he just swung from a tree."

The comment became public overnight, and when it was brought to me I refused to rise to the bait. I shrugged. Andre could say what he wanted, it made no difference to me. So the ploy kind of backfired, and it left Andre feeling uneasy. He wrote me a nice fax a few days later, apologizing for the remark and telling me how much he respected my game.

Because Andre was so flamboyant, he seemed to get an inordinate amount of Nike's attention. Once, in a fit of pique, I told one of Nike's top executives, "Listen, I'm not one to cry much, or complain. I'm a quiet guy. But I've had my moments—in Australia with Jim Courier, in Flushing Meadows with Alex Corretja, getting sick and all that . . . those weren't moments I created or set up to make myself look a certain way. I'm not doing any of this on purpose, or to project an image other than what I am. So what more do you want from me, as an athlete? You tell me Nike is all about performance, so what more can I do?"

However, one of the good things about all the exposure and attention Andre got was that it took pressure off me. I was content to operate outside the limelight as much as I could. The difference between us that way also helped keep the rivalry from becoming too intense, which was a real danger because, unlike, say, Roger Federer and Rafael Nadal, we were from the same country. All in all, I think we did a great job over our careers of keeping things under control. We had no public feuds. It was a dignified rivalry, with very little trash talking. The truth is that even though one or the other of us might get in a little snit from time to time, we basically liked each other.

The best expression of our commonality was in the most successful commercial exploitation of our rivalry—that wildly successful "guerrilla tennis" television ad campaign of 1995. That was a series of commercials in which Andre and I jumped out of vehicles in unlikely urban locations to set up a net and play tennis before astonished passers-by. It was drive-by tennis before "drive-by" was part of our vocabulary.

The campaign was brilliant, and it was an enormous success. And it worked because, instead of "Pete or Andre?" or "Pete vs. Andre" driving Nike's promotions, it became Pete *and* Andre. There was a welcome, counterintuitive feel-good message conveyed in them. The commercials helped further interest in the game and our rivalry. It also caught the true nature of our relationship. We had plenty of differences, but we were friends.

Much later that year, after the U.S. Open and the Las Vegas Davis Cup tie against Sweden, Andre invited me to fly with him on his private jet on a trip to Los Angeles. Andre was on the cusp of that long slide into the depths of the rankings, brought on by my win over him in the U.S. Open final of '95. (He bottomed out at number 141 in the fall of 1997, setting the stage for an equally remarkable resurgence.)

I sensed on that flight that Andre was struggling. He quizzed me very closely on how I lived my life, and seemed dumbfounded to learn that I had moved to Tampa solely for my tennis game. I told him that I missed my family, and Southern California, but considered it a necessary trade-off. He admitted that he wouldn't give up living in Vegas, or his lifestyle, in order to be the best player in the world. The contrast was clear and striking, although Andre made that point at a time when he was feeling a little disillusioned by the game.

Through all of that, though, I always believed something that others, particularly people who didn't know Andre very well, doubted. I always thought that Andre was a sincere guy. When we spent time together out of the limelight, he was always honest and frank—and I respected him for that.

Davis Cup was always a good time when Andre was around. He was, at times, downright exuberant. He frequently let his guard down in Cup practices, screaming and yelling about any little thing, just for the fun of it. He seemed to get a kick out of stirring things up, creating drama, taking little things and making a big deal out of them. He was emotional, and he liked to whip up others' emotions.

At other times, we sat around in the locker room and talked about this or that, mostly about sports, and it was very comfortable. Andre was inquisitive. He liked to compare notes on players and he was eager to see how others perceived the same things he was thinking about. Andre had a great grasp of strategy; it was a great asset, given the type of game he played.

I respected Andre for another big reason as well: I knew what he was capable of doing on a tennis court.

Much like at the U.S. Open final of 1995, Andre and I were both on top of our games the night we met in that 2001 U.S. Open quarterfinal. But there were great contrasts in how we approached and played the game.

Andre had to think a little more about the nuances of the game than I did. Against top guys, he needed to set things up for himself in order to play his most effective game. At his best, Andre was the consummate puppet master, jerking his opponents all over the court. Thankfully for me, he was also a little bit at the mercy of what his opponents could do.

My game, by contrast, was much more about what I was going to do, and whether or not the other guy could stop it. The big question for me on every surface but clay was, *Okay, what do I do to break the guy?* That was because I always felt confident that I could hold my serve. Andre didn't have that luxury—at least not to the same extent that I did.

Andre pushed me so hard that he forced me to add a few things to my game—things that I rarely needed against most other guys. I had to play a lot more serve-and-volley on my second serve against Andre, and I had to go more often for that risky backhand down the line instead of playing it safe and going crosscourt. Andre also could expose things in my game that other players could not. If I wasn't playing well against Andre, I would lose—there was no bluffing through.

The way I saw our matches, he was a great hitter and I was a great pitcher. If I didn't throw strikes, he would hit the ball out. It was tough to break Andre because, while he didn't have a huge serve, he served smart and at times very well. He would often hit a second serve instead of a first, kicking the ball wide to my backhand. Surprised, I would chip it back and if it floated he would pounce on it. And that's what Andre liked to do most of all, set up shop in the middle of the court, where he would not have to do a lot of running, and yank you from corner to corner, dictating—preferably with his forehand.

Andre always hit a few aces here and there, and he was good at serving to spots where he could get control of the point from his first touch after serve. If I couldn't get the return to his backhand, he would run around and smack that forehand and that was it—

then I would have to lace up the track shoes. But if I could get on the offensive with Andre, things usually worked out better. That was easier said than done, because he played from inside the court and hit a pretty flat ball, so he didn't give me a lot of time to set up and hit my shots.

Even when I was playing well, I had to really mix my serves, pick my spots, and—contrary to the conventional wisdom—confront Andre's terrific forehand. Most guys stayed away from Andre's best shot, but I wanted to get to it in order to get him moving. If I was able to hit my backhand deep and hard to his forehand, I could start doing damage because the flow of play almost demanded that he go crosscourt—bringing one of my best weapons, the running forehand, into play. That gave Andre something to fret about, because I could make him move with my forehand, and he wasn't an exceptional mover.

I also sought to get into forehand rallies with Andre. Those were athletic hitting contests in which I felt I had an edge, however marginal. On my service games, I liked to mix it up, especially on the ad side. I loved going down the middle with the big serve—my strength to his (the forehand). But Andre was such a good returner that I could only pull that off if I established the wide serve early on, just to keep him off balance.

Andre was such a great hitter that I was constantly forced to mix it up—go for the second serve out wide to his forehand, or just put a little something extra on the ball. Late in our rivalry, I started to serve and volley more often on the second serve. He was a tough guy to chip and charge, but I did a little of that, too. I threw in lots of double faults when I played Andre, because he forced me to try to execute at the very edge of my comfort zone.

When I volleyed against Andre, I felt that if I could get the racket on the ball, I would be okay. I liked my chances if I could poke the ball deep to a corner, or even hit a drop volley. I never felt Andre's defense was that great. If I got him running to a corner, or changing directions, I felt I had him. The big danger was hitting a second serve only to see Andre get that return down low, to force a defensive volley. You just didn't want to mess with Andre's passing shots.

The overarching theme, in my eyes, was that if I could make it a test of athleticism and movement, things would break my way. I had the fast-twitch-muscle advantage. By contrast, Andre had amazing eye-hand coordination; he was unrivaled as a ball striker. The idea was always the same: avoid becoming the puppet on the end of Andre's string. Avoid getting into those rallies in which I found myself trying to get the ball to Andre's backhand, while he's cracking forehands and jerking me around the court.

We had a tremendous crowd for our big quarterfinal in Flushing Meadows. Word must have gone out all over Wall Street, the Upper East Side, and Central Park West that this was a potential classic, for all the scenemakers, movers and shakers, and celebrities were out. The best thing was that you could feel this respect and appreciation for tennis in the air. It wasn't the usual noisy New York crowd, being semiattentive. Everyone seemed riveted and there were moments when you could have heard a pin drop.

Andre and I gave them their money's worth—this was a battle pitting the best serve-and-volleyer against the best returner and passer. It was different from our final of 1995, because I attacked more—in fact, I attacked relentlessly. I think I served and volleyed on every single service point I played for more than three straight hours. That takes its toll; that constant stopping and starting, leaping and lunging, sudden directional changes, and bending low can be debilitating.

That match also represented the longest period of time over which Andre and I both played really well at the same time. We each had our little lulls and hiccups, but nobody lost serve for more than three hours. I had chances to break Andre in the first set, but I blew it. I lost the first tiebreaker, but I came back to win the next three. It was a blunt and sometimes brutal battle that was decided most of all by execution and mental focus, rather than strategy or the way our strokes matched up.

In a way, that high point of our rivalry was also a microcosm of our decade-long battle. I held a six-win edge in our rivalry (20–14), although if Andre had not taken significant breaks from the game we might have played fifty times. I performed a little better in the majors, holding a 6–3 edge. He won all of our clashes at the Australian and French opens; I won all the ones we played at Wimbledon and the U.S. Open. We met in five major finals, and I won on every occasion but one, the Australian Open of 1995. We had a few epics.

In the long run, I was just a little better at those giant moments, just like I was on that sultry New York night when Andre and I played our masterpiece.

2OO1—2OO2

Chapter 10

KEY MATCHES . . .

September 2001, U.S. Open, final

P. SAMPRAS	6	1	1		
L. HEWITT	7(4)	6	6		

June 2002, WImbledon, second round

P. SAMPRAS	3	2	6	6	4
G. BASTL	6	6	4	3	6

September 2002, U.S. Open, final

P. SAMPRAS	6	6	5	6
A. AGASSI	3	4	7	4

YEAR—END RANKING . . . 2001: No. 10

2002: No. 13

One for Good Measure

Unless you're very young in your first big final (in which case not having time to think can be a good thing), you need time to savor and process a victory and get yourself into a proper competitive frame of mind for your next match. It's especially true in the late stages of major events, and doubly so in the late stage of your career, when recovery time is longer. In the final of the 2001 Open, I would be playing Lleyton Hewitt, a scrappy, fleet, superbly fit Aussie.

It had been a draining second week for me. After beating Rafter and winning that epic four-setter over Andre, I handled Marat Safin with relative ease. I think he felt the pressure of the situation. Instead of swinging freely and painting lines, he seemed a little inhibited. I won in straight sets. He was probably going through the same thing I experienced in the year after I won my first major.

I had to play Hewitt in the final barely twenty-four hours after finishing my semi, and by that point my brain was already slightly fried and my legs were feeling a little heavy. For a veteran, that twenty-four-hour turnaround at the Open is one of the toughest assignments in tennis, mentally as well as physically.

Hewitt was just twenty, and he still had peach fuzz on his face. With his long blond hair and clear blue eyes, he looked like a teenage surfing or skateboarding champ, and he played with a healthy disdain for etiquette, forever punctuating his better shots—sometimes even errors by opponents—with gut-wrenching screams of "Come awwwwwwn . . ." A year earlier, I had barely managed to contain Hewitt in the U.S. Open semis, winning two of my three sets in tiebreakers. He was now a year older, a year wiser, a year hungrier—and a year stronger.

Arthur Ashe Stadium was playing fast that year, and pundits didn't recognize the degree to which the conditions, while good for me, were tailor-made for Lleyton's game. Although Lleyton was a very consistent baseliner, he was least dangerous on slow surfaces like clay. He was slightly built and not very powerful, so he could be roughed up and beaten down in a simple war of the ground strokes and stamina. Opponents could also attack his serve on slow courts to take control of points. A faster court gave Lleyton more openings to attack from the backcourt, in classic counterpunching style.

Lleyton returned well enough to be sure of getting a few looks at breaking my serve. At the same time, being able to hold his own serve by popping in a few aces and making it harder for me to hit forcing returns would take a little pressure off of him to hold. And he liked to have a target, forcing him to hit passing shots. My style played right into his strengths.

Lleyton took full advantage of the conditions and played a good first set, taking the tiebreaker 7–4. I was beat, out of gas, emotionally as well as physically. It quickly turned into a rout in which I won just two more games the rest of the way. It was my worst loss by far in a major final, and it began the debate over the state of my game. Some pundits thought I was slowing down. The Pete Sampras they watched in the U.S. Open final against Hewitt looked like a tired, vulnerable tennis player, at a loss for a strategy to employ against his bright-eyed, bushy-tailed, not-yet-twenty-one challenger. It was an accurate assessment, but it was more of a comment on the tournament I'd had than my general physical state.

I didn't look tired because I was old, or losing focus, or banged up. I looked tired because it had been an ultrademanding week filled with very tough opponents and a back-to-back semi and final. I didn't exactly feel slow out there during the Hewitt match, but I felt like I was having to work awfully hard for the points that I won. I struggled and heaved and tried to dig into my reserves, but there was too little left to call upon.

In Lleyton, I saw a feisty young gun who was zeroed in on the target on my back and determined to take his shot at greatness. I saw a pugnacious and gifted Aussie battler aware that he was facing his window, determined to make the most of it. Hewitt seized the moment; I was the last person who could begrudge him that or rationalize away the fact that he just plain ran me into the ground.

My days were numbered. On the other hand, there are a lot of numbers.

T he loss to Hewitt in the 2001 Open meant that for the first year since 1992, I would fail to win a major. Guys were closing on me; my appetite for daily combat was diminishing. I didn't exactly think about retiring—two fourth rounds and a runner-up in the four Grand Slams wasn't a shameful record. But people talk, and it was difficult to block them out. I felt I still had at least another push left, but I didn't want to delude myself. After the loss to Hewitt, I decided that a coaching change might give me the inspiration and motivation to have one more good run.

The problem was that I would have to let go Paul Annacone, the coach who had shepherded me through my greatest years. The one thing that I will always cherish Paul for is his loyalty. I think I earned some of that loyalty with my own behavior; I don't think I ever treated Paul like the help, or took advantage of him to do things for me that I should have done for myself. I put my money where my mouth is as well; Paul was probably the best-paid coach on the tour, and worth every penny of it. But I'm a tennis player. When it came to my career, I was a selfish, obsessive individual driven by naked self-interest. And in late 2001, after seven years with Paul, I had a gut feeling that I needed a break.

Paul was in a tough if comfortable position. He would have been crazy to leave on his own, because there was nothing left on our "must do" list. As much as I wanted to win the French Open, we both knew that my window was closing. It would take a miracle. I was destined to call it a career within a year or two anyway. Why would he want to walk away now, when he could just coast to the finish line with me? And where could he go that would be a step up? Beyond that, we had a great relationship.

But relationships go stale, and deep down you know it when they do. It would have been all right, too, if I had been content to coast to that finish line. But deep inside, I wasn't ready to yield. I knew I had something significant left to give. I began to feel that maybe the coziness of our relationship was holding me back at a time when what I probably most needed was a kick in the ass. And I knew Paul wasn't going to kick. He probably would have been surprised to know what I was thinking, and that may have been part of the problem.

I'd always hired and fired my own coaches and agents, and now I was facing the toughest call I'd ever had to make. Paul and I were friends, our families were close. We had accomplished great things together. But I was searching for those last bits of greatness left in me, and ready to make some difficult choices in pursuit of them.

So, late in 2001, I called Paul up and told him in pretty straightforward fashion what I was thinking; I needed to make a change in my coaching situation. I had thought about it for a long time and it kept coming back to that. It was not that Paul had any shortcomings; I just told him that I needed some fresh blood. My confession blindsided him completely. He was in shock, and I felt horrible.

Given his reputation, Paul was able to find work right away as a top coach with the USTA. So I felt some relief about that. Meanwhile, I started calling around. I tried Bob Brett, who had coached Boris Becker and Goran Ivanisevic, but he was busy with his European sports camp operations, and enough of a veteran not to want to go back out on the road, even with me. I tried Tony Roche. Similar story. I finally hired Tom Gullikson, and he traveled to Australia with me in early 2002. I lost a tough match in the round of 16 at the Australian Open to Marat Safin; he won in four sets, the last two of them tiebreakers that he won 7–5 and 10–8.

I felt after that trip that things weren't working out with Tom, through no fault of his own. I had just left a coach because he was too much of a friend, and I couldn't shake the feeling that Tom fell into that same category. We had been through an awful lot together. I decided to part with him and hook up with Jose Higueras, who was willing to do the job—as long as he didn't have to travel much. Jose prepared me in the California desert for the big spring U.S. hard-court events and the clay-court season in Europe. He strongly felt I could benefit from going to a racket with a larger head than the 85-square-inch Wilson that I had used all of my pro career. But I didn't want to complicate things at that late stage in my career, and wasn't willing to risk the switch.

The spring was unexpectedly rough. I lost in straights to Lleyton Hewitt in Indian Wells, and to Fernando González in my second match in Miami, without taking a set off either guy. A week after Miami, I played Davis Cup on an outdoor grass court in Palm Springs and lost a five-setter to clay-court expert Alex Corretja—a guy whose career record at Wimbledon, in the few years he actually bothered to play, is 2–3. The year suddenly began to shape up as a nightmare. I was in trouble. And then something clicked. I played Houston, on clay, and beat Andre Agassi and Todd Martin before losing to Andy Roddick in the final.

My Houston karma didn't carry over to Europe: I won exactly one match in four events, and I didn't even enter the French Open. On top of struggling with my form, I had to deal with a changing situation at Nike. Jeff Schwartz, my agent at the time, assumed that Nike would be interested in working out some kind of long-term deal with me. As the all-time Grand Slam singles champion and a guy who represented old-school values and appealed to an older, more conservative crowd, I felt I could have a long shelf life.

But there were other realities at play: tennis (a favorite of Nike founder and CEO Phil Knight) was falling out of favor. I may have been the all-time champ, but it was the top players, and mostly hot young players, who moved product. Over the years, Nike had paid me a lot of money, I had hit my earning peak, and, all-time singles champ or not, if I failed to contend at Grand Slams, my value would plummet. Nike came back to me with an offer that was essentially a hefty pay cut.

I was so angered that I called Phil Knight. I told him that I felt I'd been a model Nike athlete. I had also shown great loyalty; I never fished around for a better deal. I had shown good faith, going all the way back to that first year and the problems we had with the new Nike Air shoe. There were no arrests on my résumé, or any rumors about unseemly behavior, on or off the court, at any point in my career.

When Andre and I were doing our thing, and helping market Nike products in the process, the scuttlebutt was that the tennis division was making something like $500 or $600 million a year. Those numbers, if at all accurate, showed that we'd been a good investment. Most important, I had produced the Grand Slam singles title record for a sponsor that had always emphasized that it was, first and foremost, about performance. If I wasn't a prized client for a company that professed to be about excellence, who was?

Phil said he understood my disappointment, and promised to

work on the situation. But the handwriting was on the wall. It was clear that the tennis division wasn't doing all that well anymore. I assumed that Phil, despite our good relationship and his genuine love for tennis, was under pressure from the bean counters up on the Nike campus. They had shelled out a lot of money over the years to Andre and me. When it came to budget slashing, I was a prime target. The cruel, underlying reality is that, in the endorsement business as well as the game, you are only as good as your latest results, and people are more interested in what you might do in the future than what you'd done in the past.

My contract was up at the end of 2000, and we still had no deal. I decided that until the issue was resolved, I wouldn't wear clothes with the trademark Nike "swoosh." At the 2001 Australian Open, I wore a plain white shirt with an American flag patch on it.

Gradually, though, I realized that my pride was getting the better of me, and I was getting a little too emotional about the issue. There was no denying that the Federers and Safins and Hewitts were coming on, just like I had come on in my early years, and they were the priority for Nike. I had the option of running off to look for a better deal, but at that stage in my career all it would have done is—maybe—bring in more cash, and I didn't do things just for the money. I had a few more conversations with Phil, and we eventually reached a deal. The experience was a reality check.

I traveled to London in 2002 in a familiar frame of mind, ready to use Wimbledon results to combat any sense of vulnerability or insecurity about my game. But deep down, I wasn't confident. I felt uneasy. I wasn't sure where my game was, and fretted that I was becoming the one thing I had taken such great pains to avoid being: unpredictable. You bet on good players; you go to the bank with great ones.

At Wimbledon, my managers got into a conflict with the Borgs over the escalating rental price of their home, so Bridgette and I rented a new house. It was light and airy, but the bed in the master bedroom was only a queen size. Bridgette and I are both pretty tall people (she's five-nine and I'm six-one), so we tried to get a king-size bed in there. We couldn't get it in through the hall, though, so I had to make yet another sacrifice for my career—sleeping apart from my wife. I was married to one of the most beautiful women on the face of the earth and every night, after we would watch a movie or linger at the dinner table, talking, I would reluctantly rise and basically say, "Well, I gotta tuck in now. Match tomorrow. See you at breakfast!"

My sleeping habits became something of an issue over the years, for which I blame Sally Jenkins, the author and sportswriter. I always liked Sally but, like some of the best writers, her great imagination can cause trouble. I once told her that I needed to sleep in darkness, in a very cool room, and she took that admission and ran with it. She was very dramatic about the way she wrote it up and made it sound like I needed to sleep in a mausoleum and didn't want to be touched. When I read her piece, I kind of laughed. You would have thought I was a vampire. Of course I like a cool, dark room—it sure as hell beats a hot, brightly lit one for getting a good night's rest. As for "touching," let's not even go there. But that became something I was known for: I was Pete, the guy who sleeps in the batcave, untouched. . . .

Bridgette was handling this entire frustrating European swing very well, given how much stress I felt and how little fun it must have been for her to be around me most of the time. She was pregnant with our son Christian by then, but we didn't tell anyone. However, she had morning sickness. In Europe, she couldn't really leave the hotel room for long periods. It was hard for her and hard for me, because she was sick a lot, and I had to try to juggle my needs as a player with my chores as a dad-in-waiting and dutiful husband. I worried about leaving her when I went to dinner or to the courts. Bridgette isn't a big shopper, so she wasn't dying to get into central London all the time. That made things easier. She became friendly with my faithful cook, Kirsten, and they did a few things around town together, but Bridgette largely spent most of her time around the house, or at Wimbledon.

Because play at Wimbledon doesn't start until after noon (except when the tournament has to make up rain matches), Bridgette and I stayed up until eleven or twelve every night. And on many of those nights in London we spent a lot of our leisure time just talking about what I was going through, because I was playing lousy and was preoccupied with it.

Bridgette knew by then how my mind worked, and she listened closely. She had opinions, but she had no interest in wading in and taking charge of my life or career. She gave me space to work things out in my own mind. So much of what she was doing was pure support for me that I often wondered if she wasn't also thinking, *Whoa, what did I get myself into here?*

At Wimbledon, I had a gimme first round against a young British player, Martin Lee. I had good reason to feel confident against my second-round opponent as well, Swiss journeyman George Bastl. I was stunned when the schedule came out on the evening before my match and I saw that I was being relegated to Court 2—Wimbledon's infamous Graveyard Court. I don't want to sound like a prima donna or anything, but that was a snub.

The assignment to Court 2 was made by Alan Mills, the legendary (and now retired) Wimbledon referee. He had always done right by me, and we had a friendly acquaintance, so I was shocked and angered when I heard that Alan had put me on Court 2 for the second-rounder against Bastl. From the time I first won Wimbledon, I had, like most multiple Wimbledon winners, played almost exclusively on either of the two main show courts, Centre Court or Court 1. There were solid practical reasons for that, including security.

Court 2 was unfamiliar territory to me. It was called the Graveyard Court because of the extraordinary number of headline-making upsets that had occurred on it. Those upsets occurred partly because of the atmosphere and conditions. Court 2 has limited seating capacity, but the crowd is very close to the sidelines, so you really end up feeling that you're in the boiler room. The court itself is usually more chewed up than on the main show courts, and there are numerous distractions, starting with the crowd noise from adjacent Court 3. Also, the terrace of the players' lounge overlooks Court 2. When there's an upset in progress, players and camp followers—a who's who of those present on the grounds—gather to watch from up there, like vultures perching on a cliff.

I felt that as a dominant champion for so many years, I deserved a little better. If I lost there, the headlines the following day would be sensational: GRAVEYARD COURT CLAIMS ANOTHER CHAMP! SAMPRAS BURIED ON GRAVEYARD COURT! Ironically, Tim Gullikson had added substantially to the lore and legend of the Graveyard Court when he upended John McEnroe there one year. Was there some kind of karmic payback afoot here? The answer was probably simpler. Perhaps the Lords of Wimbledon perceived a golden opportunity to add to the legend of the Graveyard Court, and thereby the event in general. I probably knew by then that the All England Club is *always* going to put its own interests—and glory—first. I just hadn't ever been on the losing end of that proposition before.

The road was getting awfully bumpy for me, at a time when it ought to have been smoothly paved. But all these struggles and setbacks contained important lessons in life, reinforcing many of the things I had always believed but never really had a chance to put to the test because of my status: People really don't care about you that much; basically, you're only as good as your last win; people often love what you do, while you can do it, but there's nothing really personal about it; many people are interested in you for what you can do for them, not necessarily because of who you are, or even how great you are; you may do special things, but you're nothing special; nobody in tennis is given a free ride based on past performance. Some of those truisms are fair and all of them are realistic. But tennis players are selfish and disinclined to see things objectively.

There was an outside chance that I could snap out of my funk at Wimbledon, but that prospect vanished when I stepped onto the court. I felt terrible. I had absolutely no confidence, despite my history at Wimbledon. What's more, I was paired against someone I had never played before. Throughout my career, guys had their best chance to beat me the first time we played. Once I had a good look at their style, and developed a feel for how they hit the ball, I was a lot tougher.

I was in trouble from the start; I lost the first two sets to Bastl 6–3, 6–2. The funny thing is that I was hitting the ball fine; there wasn't a thing wrong with my strokes or how they were landing. It's just that in front of a lot of people, I kind of lost my way. My confidence had been slowly eroding for months, and now big chunks of it were crumbling and falling off, almost by the minute.

Bridgette had written me a letter before the match, and tucked it into my racket bag. I read it in the locker room, but I was a little distracted before I went out to play and it didn't really sink in very well. So at one point in the Bastl match, I had a bizarre urge to re-read her letter; clearly, I was groping for something, anything to get me out of the negative space I was in. I pulled the letter out on a changeover and started to read it again. The first line was, *To my husband, the seven-time Wimbledon champ* . . . It was a letter of support and inspiration, in which Bridgette basically told me to remember who I was, and that this—playing tennis—was what I did best, and the thing I most cared about.

I tried to believe those words, I tried to take heart. I wish I had been able to read them, take a deep breath, and go out there and start serving bombs and drilling passing shots. But I was so mired in misery that I couldn't do it. Bridgette's kind, loving words had the opposite effect. When I absorbed the words, the letter kind of freaked me out; I had the sensation that my world was falling apart and thought, *How could this be happening to me?* I was incapable of mustering my pride or drawing inspiration from that sweet gesture by the woman I loved. That's how down I was.

But after the contents of the letter sank in, I felt a glimmer of hope. I pulled my game together long enough to win the next two sets. But I was never out from under the cloud. My funk slowly began to get the better of me again. Usually, when a guy blows a two-sets-to-love lead against a top player, he crumbles while the better player really pours it on. Bastl hung in there, though, and I was unable to pour on anything but sweat that could just as well have been blood—that's how much I was suffering.

In those crunch times, it's all about your mind and emotions, and my usual self-assurance and predatory gusto just weren't there. I lost the fifth set 6–4. I walked off Court 2 just another figure in the lore and legend of the Graveyard Court. I could've told myself that at least I was in good company, but you can bet that wasn't what I was muttering.

I didn't know it at the time, but a photographer for the *Times* of London had been in the photo pit near my chair on the court, and he took snaps of me reading Bridgette's letter. He used such a long lens that you could see every line of the letter, starting right at the top. Neil Harman, the tennis writer for the *Times*, is one of the journalists with whom I always got on well. He told me later that they had the shot, and I asked him not to print it. Neil and his editors had a lengthy, heated discussion about whether they should print the picture of me reading the letter and all the contents. Neil prevailed on them to refrain, out of respect for me and my privacy. So they printed the picture of me reading the letter, but they blurred the contents. It was a gesture I wouldn't forget.

A very harsh reality was setting in. Wimbledon, my last refuge, had turned into the focal point of my demise. My loss on the Graveyard Court was big news, and to some it confirmed what they down deep probably wanted to believe—that I was through. Given how often I had relied on Wimbledon to get me back on track, this was a novel situation for me. I had this sinking sensation and thought, *What the hell am I going to do to get out of this hole now?* Coincidentally, Andre lost in the same round, on the same day, to the up-and-coming Thai player Paradorn Srichaphan. But that was cold comfort—make that no comfort at all.

I felt utterly empty, and had no answers to explain it. Marriage may have had something to do with it, especially with Bridgette being pregnant. Maybe all these big life changes were subverting my focus, or putting me at war with myself. But I felt I knew what I wanted: my wife, our child, a good, clean, normal life—and to squeeze every drop of potential out of my career. I had spent more than a decade beating people for a living, putting all of my mental, physical, and emotional energy into the task. I beat people. That was what I did, that was who I was. I had to ask myself, *Am I still that person?*

When I returned to our house after the Bastl match, I actually felt like crying. That freaked me out, too, because I'd always taken losses in stride. Heaven forbid, it was just a damned tennis match. But still . . . As we returned to Los Angeles, there was no longer any question: the wheels were falling off, and the worse it got, the more I had to think of the "R" word—retirement.

Despite all the problems I experienced in the first half of 2002, I never really thought about hanging it up. But I was coming up against one of the most spirit-killing problems any player has to face:

the growing, inescapable chorus of critics who seem obsessed with putting you out to pasture. In politics, there's this concept called "the Big Lie." Basically, the idea is that no matter how outrageous, illogical, or untrue something is, if you shout it out long and loud enough, on a large enough platform, people start to believe it.

The retirement discussion is like that. If enough people all around are constantly asking you if you're going to retire, suggest that you should retire, or speculate about when you're going to retire, you start thinking maybe you should retire. Unless you are completely oblivious to public opinion, you begin to second-guess yourself. *Gee, maybe you* are *fooling yourself. Maybe you should think about calling it quits.* In my case, those voices were growing louder, more insistent, and more impatient. It was harder and harder for me to ignore them, even though I knew they should have nothing to do with my decision-making process.

The Australian Open had been a disappointment, Davis Cup a shock, the French Open a nonstarter, and Wimbledon nothing less than a catastrophe. There was no silver lining anywhere. To top it off, the day we got back to Los Angeles we flicked on the television and there was this talking head from CNN, Jim Huber. They were doing a piece on Wimbledon, and Huber steps out and calls Bridgette "the Yoko Ono of tennis"—a reference to the Japanese artist who married John Lennon and was widely blamed for the breakup of the Beatles and a decline in the quality of Lennon's work.

I glanced at Bridgette and saw her go pale; she looked shattered. I felt horrible, because something new crossed my mind: maybe she *did* feel responsible for my troubles, no matter how silly it would have been to do so. The poor girl—all she had done, for months on end, was support me—even as she was going through all these changes, and this is what she got for her trouble. Some a-hole on CNN making a nasty remark that, if you think about it, wasn't even a valid comparison.

Bridgette wasn't exactly barefoot and pregnant. Still, we had gotten married shortly after she finished *The Wedding Planner,* and her film career at the time was rising—dramatically. A short while later she was totally out of her career loop, sitting around a house in London, and dealing with morning sickness, while I was gone all day, struggling with my tennis, and stressing out about it when I was at home.

That schmuck Huber probably just liked that remark. He probably thought it sounded cool, or it might get him a laugh. The guy could have said I should throw my rackets off a cliff after that performance at Wimbledon and jumped after them, and I couldn't have cared less. But what he did say got to me. It made me livid. I told myself, *Someday, I'm going to see that motherf#$@&%r again.*

If I had to find some crazy, even remotely positive thing in all this, it would be that the hardship brought Bridgette and me even closer, in that it was testing both of us in a kind of marital trial by fire. If we got through it, Bridgette and I would appreciate each other that much more. Over the next days, we talked—we talked a lot—and I was never one to talk much. We acted like a family. We circled the wagons.

I realized that despite Jose Higueras's great abilities, I wasn't getting what I needed coachingwise. He had been up front with me; he was at a stage in life when, after the intensity of his relationship with Jim Courier, he wouldn't ever get so emotionally vested in a player again. But what was I going to do? I couldn't go back to Paul, not after cutting him loose the way I had. He had moved on, he had another job.

Bridgette and I kept talking about these things, and the "R" word became part of our dialogue. The debate was building inside me, and it all came to a head one night while we were lying around in bed. It occurred to me that maybe I was spinning my wheels, making life miserable for both of us, when we had so much to celebrate and be happy about. Thinking aloud, I asked myself: "Is it still worth it? What else do I have to achieve in tennis? Why should I put us through all this?" Bridgette just looked at me and said, "You're my husband, and I love you. I don't care what you do, but promise me one thing—when you decide to quit, when you do go out, promise me that you'll do it on your own terms."

That comment immediately put everything in perspective for me. It was like a huge weight was lifted off me, and the future looked less clouded. Some of the turbulence I'd been feeling melted away. I said, "You're right. I need to relax here and just get back to work. First thing, let's figure out this coaching situation."

The next morning, I got up and called the one guy I had left. I put my pride and fear aside and dialed up Paul Annacone.

Paul didn't say a word about the past; he just said he would do it, and could probably sort it out with the USTA, for whom he had been working. If the conversation had gone any other way, or if either of us ended up feeling weird about the situation, that might have been it for me. I had nowhere else to turn. Within days, we figured out a plan of attack for the summer. The one thing I could do to show my appreciation to Paul was offer him a serious commitment of my own: I agreed to hire him for two years, although it was hard to imagine that I would continue playing for that long—especially if things didn't work out.

We went back to the basics in our first training sessions shortly after Wimbledon. Paul lifted my spirits from the get-go. It was great to hear his voice again, and to tap into his way of thinking. It may sound crazy, but to hear Tim Gullikson say, with a sly grin and a twinkle in his eye, that my serve down the middle was like a Green Bay Packers power sweep, that meant something. And to hear Paul say he wanted me to go and impose myself on my rivals, that I should remember that I was Pete Sampras and they were not, that meant something, too. It meant more than I had imagined it would.

It may sound like I just wanted to get stroked, but there was something else in play. I worked so hard to suppress my own emotions, and to stay levelheaded, that it was extremely valuable to see that someone else—someone I trusted, who knew the game, and who had always been square with me—could still get emotional about my tennis. No matter how selfish tennis players are, it's also true that they spend a lot of their lives playing for others—for coaches, for parents, for spouses. Paul showed great faith in my game and that inspired me.

At the Canadian Open, I lost to Tommy Haas, a solid top-five guy at the time, in a third-set tiebreaker. At Cincinnati, I lost in the second round to Wayne Arthurs, the southpaw Aussie throwback, again in a third-set breaker. There's nothing wrong with your game when you're getting to third-set tiebreakers; the only thing lacking was my ability to make that final, confident push to finish off an opponent. But I was getting my self-assurance back, one stroke at a time.

But by then, the "R" word was firmly established as part of the dialogue about my career. It came up in every single press conference. I don't think the media should ever press a player on the retirement issue, at least not when he's struggling. It's almost an insult. But it's also an easy sound bite, and a tool for getting a reaction out of a player. I guess some of those guys just figure, Heck, let me take a shot—I've got a heck of a story if Pete says, "Yeah, as a matter of fact I'm retired as of now because you suggested it. . . . Why couldn't I see it myself?" Such fishing expeditions cost a reporter nothing, but they can exact a toll on a player.

But it wasn't just the press raising the "R" word. Ever since my loss to Lleyton Hewitt in that Open final in 2001, more and more players were weighing in on the issue. I was hardly surprised when Yevgeny Kafelnikov said I should retire, because Yevgeny was a pretty out-there dude. He was one of the first guys to buy a jet, which was a pretty extravagant thing for a guy who wasn't a regular winner at majors. He later told me that he once landed in an Australian airport without bothering to get clearance. When the plane touched down, there were police cars and SWAT team types all over the place. Yevgeny seemed to get a big kick out of that.

Yevgeny also bragged about how smart he was, getting his prize money in cash. He seemed to enjoy throwing his dough around. He once boasted about having dropped fifty thousand dollars on lottery tickets—at one pop. After leaving the tour, he turned up as a pro poker player. But back when we were both playing, our regular, good-natured exchange in the locker room consisted of him asking when I would retire, so he could win a few more Grand Slams, and me answering that I'd keep playing as long as he did, just to keep him from getting those majors.

In my last tune-up before the U.S. Open at a small tournament on Long Island, I lost a tight three-setter in the first round to the French player Paul-Henri Mathieu. I said in the ensuing press conference that I felt I had a good shot at the Open, I felt I might even win it. One of the guys in the room laughed, out loud. I started to get up from my chair. I wanted to go and punch the prick in the face. But I got hold of myself, swallowed back my pride, and sank back into my chair. I patiently answered the rest of the questions put to me.

I won my first match at the Open, beating Albert Portas pretty handily. After the match, Ian O'Connor, a reporter with the *Journal News* of Westchester, New York, came into the locker room to give me a surprising heads-up. He had called Pete Fischer during the match, and Fischer had pretty much trashed me, using words like "atrocious" to describe the way I'd played. Ian felt bad, but he wanted to both warn me and ask if I had any reaction to Fischer's comments.

I hadn't been in touch with Pete Fischer since around the time of his trial. He sometimes wrote to me from jail. The letters were increasingly long, rambling, and all but impossible to read because Fischer's handwriting was so bad. I tried to wade through some of them, but gave up quickly. I never answered him.

I'd come face-to-face with Pete only once since he was released from jail, and that was at the Los Angeles tournament. I was making my way along a path, avoiding eye contact (if you make eye contact with people, you never get where you're going because everyone wants to talk, get an autograph, take a picture), when suddenly Pete just materialized in front of me, stepping in my way.

I was startled. I just looked at him and said something inane like, "Hey, it's Pete Fischer!" That was it. I just kept walking. But I was a little rattled; it was like an apparition, coming back to haunt me. When I played my match that evening, I easily blocked out the knowledge that Fischer was probably up in the stands, watching. It was weird. As a little kid, I used to get so nervous, knowing he was watching. I wanted so much to live up to the standard he expected. But this time, there was no reaction or emotion, no feeling at all. If he was up in those stands, he was just some other guy, watching Pete Sampras play a tennis match.

Not long after that, I got a few more letters. I glanced at them and saw that they were very critical of my tennis. Again, I ignored them. I figured maybe he wrote them because he was angry that I never replied to his previous letters, or showed any interest in maintaining contact with him.

When O'Connor filled me in and told me how negative Fischer had been, I got angry. It was a low blow at a time when I was down. I thought, *You motherf#$@&%r . . . After all I've done for you, supporting you, giving you money, and now you're just constantly taking shots at me. That's it. I'm done. No more contact—at all.*

Looking back on Pete's impact on my career, I feel some ambivalence about the credit he always gets. I don't want to undervalue him or anyone else involved in shaping my game. But Pete loved to position himself as a mad genius—the guy who had created the tennis version of Frankenstein's monster. And that's an overstatement. Fischer was an important figure in my life, all right, and a strong force in my development. But genius? I don't know.

Pete has worked with a number of other people since my time with him, and nothing much came of any of them. He worked with a girl named Alexandra Stevenson, loudly proclaiming her "The Next Martina Navratilova." It was a familiar boast from the guy who had proclaimed me "The Next Laver." But Alexandra didn't pan out. I'll never dispute that Pete handled my development very well; a lot of other coaches, in similar circumstances, might have blown it. But at the end of the day, it's always the player swinging the racket. It's the player who has to live with the short- and long-term pressures of the quest to win, to excel. Fischer was less like a genius than the guy who catches a world-record fish. He may be an excellent fisherman, but there are a lot of those out there. He also happened to get lucky—once.

I had another bizarre incident to deal with shortly after the Fischer interview, and it became a big story early in the U.S. Open. After winning his second-round match to earn a spot opposite me, Greg Rusedski popped off in his press conference, saying I was no longer the same player as in the past. He suggested that I was a step slower, and he thought he had a pretty good shot against me.

Of course, the press threw that right out there when I met with them, and I famously answered that Greg was a guy with issues—in fact, I said, "Greg's issues have issues." That went over big—the press loves trash talk. But what the hell. Rusedski was a cocky guy who seemed arrogant and rubbed many people the wrong way.

Rusedski was born and raised in Canada, but once he got onto the pro radar he took advantage of his mother's British citizenship and emigrated to London. England, after all, was desperate to have quality players to call its own, and didn't much care how they got there as long as they had that U.K. passport. So this big, raw-boned, hard-serving Canadian kid moved to England and within weeks he'd decked himself out in a Union Jack headband and mastered this heavy British accent. He went around saying "telly" instead of "TV" and "petrol" instead of "gas." Usually when Greg said things I just shrugged and said, "Whatever." He was a funny character, and he presented a pretty broad target. So I took a shot.

I have to hand it to Greg, he subsequently pushed me to the limit. I'd won my first two matches at the Open decisively, but I needed every bit of confidence I could muster to stop him 6–4 in the fifth. I was lucky to have won two of my sets in tiebreakers against one of the hardest-serving guys in the business. Surviving that serving contest on the fast courts of New York was a confidence booster, because it reminded me of enduring all those Wimbledon matches with Goran Ivanisevic, or indoor battles with Boris Becker. It felt awful good afterward.

Despite all the turbulence and controversy I was dealing with, I didn't play the Open feeling any anger. Nor did I feel I had a point to prove. Down deep, those coals were burning, but I was focused on the task at hand. I was fit. I felt good. I had been written off, but that only makes someone like me more dangerous. I didn't fantasize about walking into those press conferences and saying, "I told you so," and in my mind little tiffs like the one I had with Rusedski bordered on comedy rather than high drama. As that Open played out, it was about one thing and one thing only for me: I wanted one more major. I had one more major in me; I knew that. That's what had kept me going, and why all that other stuff fell away so easily.

I don't really know why I felt so confident and calm, or why I needed a last Grand Slam so badly. It wasn't like I needed another major; I had the record. It wasn't like I hadn't passed the trial by fire at the U.S. Open; I'd bagged a few titles there. It wasn't like I told myself that I wanted to win one for Bridgette—I'd done that in a way that would be hard to top, when she sat in the guest box at Wimbledon and watched me break Emerson's record. It was just that some crazy conviction inside me said I had one more Slam to go. There's a ham actor in every player, and I wanted to have one last scene that brought down the house.

I felt good after the Rusedski match. Tommy Haas was playing great tennis that summer, but I beat him in a very close four-setter. Next came a guy I felt comfortable playing, young Andy Roddick. He'd tagged me once, but he played a straightforward game, and not too many guys who played that way scared me when I was in peak form. I lost just nine games to Andy. More important, it was a fast match that didn't wear me down—something I welcomed at that quarterfinal stage. I then put away surprise semifinalist Sjeng Schalken in another short match. I was back in the U.S. Open final, this time in much better shape than I had been the previous year.

At 4 P.M. on a calm and bright Sunday afternoon in early September, I looked across the net and saw the same person who had been there twelve years earlier, almost to the day, when I played my first Grand Slam final: Andre Agassi.

The Andre I saw in 2002 was someone very different from the kid I had seen in 1990, and it went well beyond the fact that the multicolored mullet had become a shiny bald head, and that lime green costume was now a fairly plain, conservative shorts-and-shirt tennis kit. I saw a seasoned, confident, multiple Grand Slam champion who was in full command of his game—a game that could hurt me. This was no stranger. This was my career rival. This was the yin to my yang.

Over time and through rivalry, though, our identities blurred a little and parts of our personalities had jumped from one to the other, like sparks sometimes do across two wires. We had a lot of shared history now. The sharp edges had been worn down and the contrasts muted. We were elder statesmen, celebrated champions, co-guests of honor at the Big Moment one more time. In many ways we were just a couple of nearly worn-out tennis players looking for one last shot at glory.

We were the oldest pair of finalists in the American Grand Slam in thirty-two years—I was thirty-one, Andre was thirty-two. We were no longer kids who, in different ways, resisted the responsibility that came with our talent and threw in the towel if you pushed them hard enough. We both had more to be proud of than ashamed about, but that wouldn't take the sting out of the loss one of us was going to experience in the 2002 U.S. Open final.

I had no sentimental thoughts or reveries going into the final with Andre; I didn't think at the time that it might be my last official match. There were no revenge or vindication motifs in my mind, no desire to gloat, no emotional moments spent contemplating my career or how I had arrived at another Grand Slam final. It was all about the moment for me, it was all about the tennis we would play over the next two or three hours, and that was always how I liked it best.

The atmosphere was electric; the entire crowd in Arthur Ashe Stadium seemed to expect something special. I always had a taste for big occasions, and I couldn't ask for much more than this. I rolled through the first two sets with some of the best tennis I had played in years, while Andre got off to a slow start. He was in immediate disarray, trying to cope with my pace and the pressure I put on his service games. I was coming very close to the level I hit in my 1999 Wimbledon meeting with Andre. The *New York Times* reporter Selena Roberts wrote that I was "popping out aces like a Pez dispenser."

In the third set, Andre finally got his bearings and we settled into a slugging match. When I served at 2–3, Andre made a furious charge and had three break points, but I managed to fend them off. We struggled on, and I felt a little heaviness creeping into my legs, while Andre slowly ramped up his game, shot by shot. At 5–6, Andre got to my serve again. I fended off one set point, but he earned another one. I drove a forehand volley into the net and suddenly Andre was back in the hunt, down two sets to one and encouraged by my apparent fatigue. The lights of the stadium were already on; each of our faces was sheened with sweat.

Andre would later say that one of the tricky things about playing me was that any opponent could play great against me and lose 6–4, 7–5—or play terribly and lose 6–4, 7–5. It was a reference to the way I often cruised along, unconcerned about the score or what the other guy was doing, because I felt I would hold serve and, as the set wore on, get my inevitable opportunities to break. Something like that happened in our last match. I knew I had to rally to keep the match from going to five sets, and I managed to lift my game to stop the bleeding. Once I was at an acceptable level, I awaited my chances.

We held serve to 3–4 in the fourth set, but then the script went awry and instead of holding and putting pressure on Andre's next service game, I found myself down two break points. If Andre converted either break point to go up 5–3, we definitely would go to a fifth set. And Andre was looking stronger as the match went on. I managed to fight off the break points to even it, 4–all.

Andre probably felt deflated momentarily; the situation was like our last Wimbledon final all over again. And I knew, at an instinctive level, that this was my moment. I had spent an entire career honing the ability to recognize and exploit moments like these, when for an instant my opponent's attention or resolve flickered. I was ready. Suddenly, I was in touch with my long-lost friend, the Gift. And it felt great. I broke Andre.

Minutes earlier, I had been in desperate straits, filled with foreboding as a fifth set loomed in the gathering twilight. Now, improbably but most definitely, I was serving for the match. I knew what to do next. I ended it swiftly, with a sequence of points that ended with an ace followed by a backhand volley winner.

I dropped the racket and slowly raised my arms. It was over, over and done, over and done for good. I didn't know it at the time, but it was my last U.S. Open title as well as my last match as a pro. My last match with Andre, as well as my last Grand Slam appearance. It was my last moment in a special sun that was fading as fast as the one that descended into the haze of a late-summer afternoon in New York.

I had been given a rare opportunity to go out on my own terms. I took it.

Epilogue

As I threw my arms in the air after winning what would be my last Grand Slam, I let out a primal simple scream that nobody seemingly heard or noticed. I hollered, "I f***ing did it!"

The match had proven to be the final and most daunting hurdle of my career. I'd experienced two years of adversity with people breathing down my neck. And I'd found one last ticket to that place where I was completely focused and sufficiently confident to get the job done. When it was over, I felt great. The first person I looked to was my wife, Bridgette, up in the player guest box. I had to get up there; she'd been such a critical part of my final push. I wanted to share the moment with her, and I also wanted the world to see me doing it.

I felt great. This was vindication, pure and simple. Weeks later, the late publisher of *Tennis Week,* Gene Scott, would write: "It just goes to show that at the end of the day, we didn't know who Pete Sampras was." Gene later told me that he meant that as a reference to the depth of my competitive character. I was very proud when I read those words.

I felt great. I had beaten my greatest rival on one of the biggest stages in tennis to win the title I would come to cherish most. As it turned out, Andre would have a little more fuel in his tank than I did, but he'd bought himself a few extra years by relaxing and taking a few breaks from the game in his prime. Andre would play deep into 2006, but my candle burned out quicker.

After that last major final, Andre and I agreed to stay in contact—

just in life. We agreed that it would be a shame, after all we'd been through together, to lose touch. Besides, we had a lot of things in common, including two kids each. We'd been players since the age of seven. We had a lot of history, a lot of life—a certain kind of life—in common.

My sister Stella and her husband were at the 2002 Open, and they joined our small core group, along with my trainer, Brett "Moose" Stevens, in a small victory celebration back at our hotel. We ordered a big room-service meal and drank champagne, and I felt great. That same night, Bridgette and I flew back to Los Angeles.

For the next two months, I woke up every day with a smile on my face. In just three months, I had gone from absolute misery—despite all that I had to feel great about—to absolute contentment. This was some example of closure, although I didn't think of it that way at the time. In fact, in the following weeks, I idly wondered what was next for me. I never thought I was done as a player. I felt I was still in great shape. I had no doubts about contending. I didn't feel like I was burned out. But as the weeks passed, I discovered I had no desire to play, and pulled out of all the fall tournaments on my schedule.

By the time the Christmas holidays rolled around, I was getting used to hearing the happy squeals of our infant son Christian. Paul Annacone, who was still my coach, made sure I got out to hit a few balls every few days, but soon it was time to think seriously about getting in shape for the Australian Open. I realized I wasn't motivated to do that, and I pulled out of that, too.

I made no decision or announcement about my future; I wanted to be sure that when I was done, I was done for good with no second thoughts. Two weeks before the 2003 Wimbledon, Paul and I started to practice. I thought maybe I would play it again. But after a few days of hitting, I knew I was finished. I had no urge to compete at Wimbledon, or even to go and see the old place that had been so good to me. I had no fuel left in the tank, and it seemed like the work couldn't be worth the potential reward. I knew it was time to call it a career.

Guys retire for different reasons. Sometimes their bodies don't hold up. Sometimes the game passes them by and forces them out. Sometimes they're just mentally fried and tired of the grind. Sometimes family figures into it. For me, it was none of the above. My game was still there. My wife was so supportive that if I'd laced up and run out a week after winning that last major, she would have been 100 percent supportive. She even said to me, "I hope you don't feel like you have to quit now that you've got a wife and family."

It may sound odd, coming from a guy who was often said to lack emotion, but my decision to quit was an emotional one. The love of the battle was gone from my heart.

The USTA had been in close contact with Paul, and after I pulled out of Wimbledon, they asked him if I planned to play the U.S. Open. If not, they said they'd like to give me a retirement ceremony. It seemed like the right time and place. I'd be able to take my family and say good-bye to tennis on my home soil, in front of some of my greatest fans, in a dignified and appropriate way.

So Bridgette and our families traveled to New York in August and booked into the Plaza. The magnitude of the occasion didn't really hit me until we went out to the National Tennis Center on the day of the ceremony—opening day of the U.S. Open. When I got there, it really hit me at gut level. I saw Arthur Ashe Stadium again, and I saw all the guys, practicing and milling around. I thought, *Wow, I'm really into this, just being here and having a chance to go out this way is a great honor. . . . It really is over.*

I became emotional during the ceremony that evening, but I didn't want to lose it so I kept my comments brief and low-key. I was touched and honored to see so many of my rivals present—Boris Becker had flown in from Germany just for the ceremony. It was like I was staring my entire career right in the face. The words Jim Courier, Boris, Andre, and others said felt really good. Andre was there, even though he had other things on his mind—like winning another U.S. Open title. I understood that—boy, did I ever. I really appreciated Andre's taking part.

All of the emotions of the previous twelve months hit me then. I was happy that I planned only a short speech because I also wanted to enjoy and savor the sights and sounds, almost like a spectator would. The more I drank in the atmosphere, the more convinced I was that I'd done the right thing. At moments I also felt a twinge of sadness, knowing that it really was over.

The next day, former president Bill Clinton called me, and I did one last round of media appearances on talk shows and such. Then we returned to Los Angeles. I didn't return to New York again until July of 2007, after my induction into the International Tennis Hall of Fame.

I still play and watch tennis. I'm partial to Roger Federer, although I respect the grit and courage of Rafael Nadal, too. I miss Wimbledon, but I knew I would. In 2007, officials of the club contacted me and asked if I wanted a wild card into the tournament. I politely declined. I felt I could still win matches there, but I didn't like the idea of going out to play guys I'd never even seen play before.

Late in 2007, I played a three-city exhibition tour with Roger Federer, who had closed to within two Grand Slam titles of my fourteen. Much to the surprise of pretty much everyone, I actually won the third match of the series. I enjoyed the occasion; it was a great chance for both of us to strut our stuff and give fans a glimpse of how we might have matched up. And I had a great time sitting around comparing notes and talking tennis with Roger. If I have a legacy, I hope it's that of a guy who gave his all to the game and fought with a champion's heart, a player who represented solid, enduring values, and demonstrated a great respect for the history and traditions of the game. It's nice to see that the mind-set didn't fade away with me; Roger has clearly taken up the torch.

I miss the majors—ten years from now I'll still miss them. I have so many great memories to draw on, and can still recall what it felt like to be playing matches at Wimbledon. In fact, I can easily conjure up the physical sensation of walking out onto Centre Court to play a final. I can sit here and think about it, resurrect all the emotions, sights, and sounds, and can actually get nervous all over again.

But don't worry, I can handle it. I always handled nervous pretty well.

About My Rivals

O ver the years, I had to answer the call against a staggering array of rivals—dangerous players who were capable of giving me fits and worse. Some of their names might surprise you. And some of them may not have been given their due, or their full measure of credit, elsewhere in this book. There were also some impact players in my era who just didn't figure heavily into my career high—or low—points. I'm including them as well, to try to give you an all-around sense of how I felt about most of the important players of my time. They're listed alphabetically by name, and I'm adding my head-to-head record against each man, along with my comments.

BORIS BECKER (12–7) . . . Like Goran Ivanisevic, Boris could go toe-to-toe with me on grass or fast surfaces because of his big serve. But overall, I felt I did everything just a smidgen better than Boris did. It was that simple. I didn't have any secret or special tactics. I knew we would go out and trade thunderbolts, and the player who was serving better, feeling the ball better, and playing with more confidence probably would win.

Two of Boris's biggest assets were his personality and his ego. He was a hugely charismatic guy, and he also walked with a swagger, especially at Wimbledon. He was such an icon in his own time that journeymen were intimidated by his very presence. But there was no intimidation and certainly no animosity or mind games when we played. We respected each other, and that showed in the spirit and tone of our matches. Our rivalry was always about good, power-based attacking tennis—and little else.

SERGI BRUGUERA (2–3) . . . He's one of the few guys I played more than once or twice who finished with a positive head-to-head against me. He once beat me on hard courts, I once beat him on clay. People tended to deride and dismiss Bruguera as a clay-court grinder, but he was better than that. He posed special problems that lifted him a healthy notch above the other baseliners. Sergi played from way back, which made him vulnerable to attack, but the guy moved like a deer. He was one of the best movers ever, and he could get to anything and take a good whack at it with a heavy, topspin forehand.

MICHAEL CHANG (12–8) . . . When we were juniors, Michael was the gold standard, and he really punished me when I abandoned the two-handed backhand. So I developed a mental block against Michael that lasted for quite a while. But also, right through my early years as a pro, I could be a little inconsistent, and that was the one unforgivable sin when you played Michael.

In those early years, Michael often made me hit that one extra ball that teased out an error, but over time, I became more consistent and I developed more power. Michael then became a kind of litmus test for me. If I was playing well, I could control and overpower him.

I beat Michael in one match that was absolutely huge—for him. That was the 1996 U.S. Open final. He was in the running for the number one ranking and it was his best chance to win a second major, thereby shedding the one-slam wonder label that some people applied to him. That label was unfair, of course, because of Michael's great consistency. He was always in the mix at the top of the game, where a true one-slam wonder tends to pop up out of nowhere—and go back there after making his stunning statement.

JIM COURIER (16–4) . . . Jim was an interesting case because there were definitely strategic, tactical things I did to offset the threat represented by his big forehand and huge fighting spirit. Jim was a great player, and our lopsided head-to-head is a tribute to some tactical things I was able to figure out and use to great advantage.

The big thing for me with Jim was getting my backhand to his backhand in rallies. If I wasn't really hitting my backhand well, he could push me back and I would end up fending off balls, hitting them up the middle where he could spank them with his forehand. When Jim got you into that bind, he was deadly tough. But that was the only way I felt he could hurt me.

What I really liked to do with Jim was hit my second serve out wide to his forehand—that's right, his fearsome forehand. You could accomplish two things by serving to Jim's forehand—force him out of his comfort zone, and get him off balance so that you could exploit that backhand. With Jim, like Andre, you had to keep that ball out of the middle of the court, from where he could dictate with his forehand.

Returning is different from rallying, and Jim didn't like to hit that forehand return because he had less time to wind up and tag it like he could in a rally. This was such a gem of strategy that when Jose Higueras agreed to work with me near the end of my career, he confessed that I had been the first player to recognize and exploit that weakness in Jim's game.

There was another reason to play Jim's forehand more often than was advisable—his backhand, while vulnerable, became pretty good if you kept going to it and he got in a groove. Stefan Edberg learned that in their matches, although it was also true that Edberg didn't serve big enough to hurt Jim.

Jim was toughest on clay, and his two French Open titles attest to it. But he wasn't a great mover. He made up for it by playing from inside the court (unlike, say, a Bruguera, who ran swiftly, east to west, behind the baseline) and making the most of his power.

The main challenge against Jim on clay was making the big shot that could turn the tables in a rally. On hard courts, you can go from defense to offense with one good shot. On clay, you need a few shots to do that, and that makes it tougher. On hard courts, I could have a backhand-to-backhand rally with Jim and turn it around with one swing; on clay I couldn't do that, so he had the upper hand. Jim's inside-out forehand was awesome, and he was always looking to set it up with that big serve.

STEFAN EDBERG (8–6) . . . I really enjoyed playing Stefan; we had a similar sensibility, in that we always wanted to attack, especially behind our serve. The key to playing Stefan tough was getting a hold of his serve. If I could dial in and hit my returns so that he had tough first volleys, I was okay. It was critical to keep the backhand return down low off his serve. That was tough for one-handed-backhand players like me, because you had to get over the kicker to do that, and if you didn't pull it off, he was all over the floater or above-the-net return. His volley was instruction-video grade, silky and biting at the same time.

In his prime, Edberg had a great serve—a big kicker that gave him plenty of time to get to the net, and once he was there it was tough to get the ball past him. He was always trying to rush you. The most deadly thing you can do to a guy is take away his time— make him rush or feel like you're swarming all over him. Stefan was very good at that. His volley was superb, especially on the backhand side, and he was a tough guy to lob.

Stefan had a strange forehand that he hit with an odd shoveling motion. He didn't have a lot of power on the forehand side, but he managed to keep the ball deep. He never developed the wrist action to get a lot of snap on the ball, but the funny thing is that the forehand was ten times better than it looked, and a lot of guys went down thinking they could attack that forehand and win.

By contrast, Stefan's backhand was a work of art—smooth, solid, and versatile. There were times when Stefan actually ran around his forehand to hit a backhand. One of Stefan's great assets was his self-knowledge. He knew what he could and couldn't do, and as he got older he evolved into a very strong competitor. He knew that to beat me, he had to get to the net. To that end, he tried everything, including the chip-and-charge. He did that selectively, to keep me off balance. He would do it for a few points, than abandon the strategy for a few games, then come back to it. At times, it was very effective.

Over the years, I also came to feel that if I stayed with him, I could slowly overpower him—in the end, he was more of a finesse guy than a power guy.

WAYNE FERREIRA (7–6) . . . Now there's a surprise for you, right? I'm not even sure why Ferreira gave me problems. He certainly never worried me the way some guys did. He moved well, returned well, and had a fine serve and a huge forehand, but most of all he came into matches with me with a really positive outlook.

The real question was why Ferreira could play me so tough but look so fragile, mentally, and falter against so many other, weaker, guys. But that's one for him to answer. One thing was for sure— there was no pressure when he played me. It was all gravy for him. I apparently motivated him and made him a real warrior, mentally. He beat me on a few occasions when I was really playing well, and all I could do was shrug and say, "That's Ferreira for you."

LLEYTON HEWITT (4–5) . . . He loved players who served and volleyed and tried to pressure him, so I played right into his hands—as he demonstrated in that U.S. Open final of 2001. Lleyton was one of the few guys who really could resist the onslaught of a high-quality attacker. It was very tough to get the ball by him, or to ace him. He was quicker than Andre, and therefore passed a little better. Lleyton relied on foot speed and quickness to outmaneuver opponents, and he was young enough to run and concentrate all day if need be. He was a lot like Michael Chang, right down to the way he loved having a target—a guy at the net, forcing him to select a specific shot and placement.

Lleyton was tough, too—street-fighter tough. But I never had trouble with that. Psychologically, this is a pretty rough game, and Lleyton's intensity rubbed a lot of guys the wrong way. He was always yelling, "Come awwwwwn!" I didn't mind that—it was his own energy he was wasting. For a period I felt that Lleyton might really dominate. His game translated well from surface to surface, and the guys had a hard time figuring out a strategy against him. He won the U.S. Open and followed it up with a win at Wimbledon, but then a few things happened.

For one, Roger Federer improved, and he figured Lleyton out cold. The game in general also improved while Lleyton was at the top. Guys were playing with a little more power, partly thanks to advances in racket technology, but fewer of them were playing into Hewitt's hands. Lleyton liked having a target, but in his era guys stopped coming to the net. Hewitt was a victim of his time.

As Lleyton became more and more vulnerable, he was having to work harder and harder to win matches. When you play with a grinder's mentality like Lleyton did, you rely a lot on mental intensity. But no matter how tough you are, it's hard to keep up that hard-working, patient style, week in, week out. Eventually it catches up with you and you get a little burned out. Then the vultures gather.

GORAN IVANISEVIC (12–6) . . . Goran's greatest asset was that huge lefty serve. It was just too damned good most of the time, especially on grass. It wasn't even a matter of that heavy slice a lefty can produce. Goran hit his serve with a fast, almost rushed action, and the result was a quick, heavy ball that stayed low.

Goran was smart—he knew that he wasn't going to win many baseline rallies, or even volley his way to titles the way Stefan Edberg could. He designed his entire game plan around that serve, and he designed it to win Wimbledon—the tournament where my own game worked best. Goran's second delivery was big, but I always felt I could find it, get some stick on it. That was partly because I wasn't that worried about Goran's second shot. I could play my return a little safer and still think I had a chance, which wasn't the case with a Rafter or an Edberg.

YEVGENY KAFELNIKOV (11–2) . . . I loved playing Yevgeny— except for that match in 1996 in Paris, where he beat me in the semifinals at Roland Garros. It may stand as the most damaging if not the most painful loss of my career. Yevgeny had nothing to hurt me with, although he rode herd on guys who were at all uncertain or intimidated by him. That ugly forehand was better than it looked, and his backhand was smooth.

PETR KORDA (12–5) . . . Korda was a little like Ferreira, except even more flashy and unpredictable. When he was off his game, he could lose to anybody. But he seemed to feel less pressure against top guys than his peers. It was like he had nothing to lose against players like me. He just swung from the heels, and if he was making his shots, you were in trouble,

RICHARD KRAJICEK (4–6) . . . I never really liked big servers, the guys who could do to me what I routinely did to them. Returning serve and hitting passing shots were not my strengths. I was okay with them, but having to do that over and over took me out of my comfort zone. Krajicek could really put the pressure on; if he had his serve going, he was very tough to break, and that put more pressure on my service games. Richard was inconsistent, mentally, on a week-in, week-out basis, but somehow he seemed pretty pulled together against me most of the time. He blew hot and cold, but against me it was always hot.

GUSTAVO KUERTEN (2–1) . . . Kuerten came out of Brazil, a nation with a very weak pro tennis tradition, and rocketed all the way to the top. He was a nice guy, and like most players with exceptional talent, he had his window. It opened for Gustavo in 2000, when he ended up going into the ATP Championships with a chance to fight his way to the prized year-end number one ranking.

"Guga" had to beat me in that event, and then take down Andre Agassi in the final in order to clinch the number one position. It was spelled out in black and white. He did it, and on a fast indoor court, where he had undistinguished results for most of his career. It's one of the all-time great efforts, in a situation that couldn't have contained more pressure.

Kuerten won at just one Grand Slam location, Roland Garros. But he won there three times to stake a legitimate claim as one of the Open era's finest clay-courters. He was a great athlete, with a pretty big first serve and a great forehand. But Kuerten had two big disadvantages on fast surfaces—his long backswing and how far back he liked to play. I always had good luck with guys who stayed well back of the baseline, even great shotmakers and counterpunchers like Kuerten. I had plenty of time to play my shots, and I could attack at leisure. I always felt I could attack and pressure Guga, especially on the backhand side, hence my positive head-to-head record with him.

I always liked Kuerten's attitude. He was easygoing and always seemed to be in a good mood, with a big smile on his face. His career was prematurely cut short by a serious hip injury.

IVAN LENDL (5–3) . . . It's not really accurate to call Ivan a rival, because he was on his way out of the game when I was on my way in. But I got to know him pretty well, and I consider him one of the greatest—and most underrated—players of all time.

The first few times I played Ivan I was overwhelmed by his sledgehammer game. He made me feel rushed, and at that early stage in my career I could be pushed back and kind of outmuscled by him. His forehand was huge and so was his serve. He hit with either slice or topspin on the backhand side. But by the time I played him in the U.S. Open in 1990, I was pretty strong myself, and felt I could handle his pace. He was still better in the backcourt, but even there he didn't have that big an edge. I felt I had a shot if I served well and found a way to squeeze out a break.

TODD MARTIN (18–4) . . . My pal Todd was one of those interesting guys who was tall (six-six) and had a big serve and good volley—all the makings of a great grass-court game. But grass also exposed his biggest physical drawback—he didn't move that well. Todd did well on hard courts and even clay because he had that extra second or two to get into position, and when he had that extra time to set himself up for the shot he wanted to hit, he was deadly. He hit an extremely clean, fairly flat ball.

Todd was also a very smart tennis player who knew his own possibilities and limitations. The rest of us were lucky that Todd was a little injury-prone, because that might've been the main reason he never won a Grand Slam title. He came awfully close a few times. He had one heartbreaking collapse, against Mal Washington in the 1994 Wimbledon semifinals. He could have used a little more confidence, but he had enough game to win a major. It just never quite worked out.

Todd was a gentleman, too, a straight-and-narrow guy with very high moral standards complimented by a wicked, dry sense of humor. He was a good friend, and one of my favorite Davis Cup partners. It was always a pleasure to play Todd—except for the fact that he gave me trouble. Todd was able to kick that second serve high enough to my backhand to make me uncomfortable.

Despite his size, Todd didn't really have a big weapon. His first serve was fine, but his second serve, while pretty big, wasn't huge. His forehand wasn't quite powerful enough to compensate for his relative lack of mobility. The backhand was solid. Like Michael Chang, Todd was a good barometer for me; when I beat Todd in straight sets, I knew I was playing well.

TOMAS MUSTER (9–2) . . . This blond Austrian was a real work-horse, and you had to respect him for the way he came back from one of the most devastating injuries that ever befell a tennis player: In Miami in 1989, a courtesy car backed into him and all but crip-pled him for life. It was amazing that he was able to come back and become the number one player in the world, even though he held that ranking only briefly.

Muster was a model clay-court grinder with a big, one-handed topspin backhand and an effective forehand. He didn't do much on faster surfaces, though. I always felt there was a little gamesmanship involved when Tomas played. One year in Cincinnati, he would exhale forcefully and audibly right before I hit my serve. The sound distracted me—it was like a locomotive letting off steam. He would do that every time, right before I struck the ball.

The mannerism eventually got under my skin. On a changeover, I asked the chair umpire if he could hear Tomas blowing—because it was loud enough for the chair to hear. I said it loud enough for Tomas to hear me, too, and he must have, because that was the end of it. He didn't do it anymore.

MARK PHILIPPOUSSIS (7–3) . . . Mark may be the most talented player of my time not to have won a major. He struggled with injuries; he blew his knee out one year against me at Wimbledon, after playing like a house on fire to win the first set. He beat me at the French Open and the Australian Open. Mark was a little bit in that Boris Becker mold. He had a massive game; his first and second serves were huge, his forehand was a big weapon, and he could really crank the backhand, too. He was also very comfortable attacking the net; that made him a really versatile, all-surface threat. But I didn't think he was a great mover; that was his biggest weakness. Still, he should've won Wimbledon. Coulda, woulda, shoulda . . .

Mark's problem appeared to be that deep down, he just didn't seem to want greatness badly enough. One year when he was rehabbing a knee with my trainer, Moose Stevens, Moose tried to set it up so that Mark and I could work out in L.A. But all Mark wanted to do was surf. Wavering dedication was a main theme in Mark's career. He liked his fast-lane, casual lifestyle and he seemed to enjoy his playboy reputation. He was even featured in a dating reality show. Fair enough, it was his life, after all. But it was a shame to see that big, big game go unfulfilled. Maybe he just never grew up; or when he did, it was too late.

PATRICK RAFTER (12–4) . . . Pat was a great volleyer who took me out of my comfort zone and forced me to hit too many passing shots and thread-the-needle service returns. In terms of hard-charging opponents, I preferred to play Stefan Edberg, even though Edberg won more Grand Slam titles and had a better record. With Edberg, you knew where the serve was going and you knew he was coming to the net. You knew what you had to do, and if you didn't execute it well enough, you lost. End of story.

With Pat it was different; he mixed it up a lot more, especially with his serve. He kept you on edge, made you get into guessing games. The serve to the body is one of the most neglected shots in tennis; everybody, including me, likes to smoke aces or unreturnables to the corners. But the kick serve to the body is a great tool, and Pat was a master at it. The way to beat Pat was to make him play. He liked set pieces—kicker to the backhand, first volley crosscourt, second volley (or overhead) for the winner. If you could disrupt the pattern and find a way to make him play points, you could get on top of him.

Pat won the U.S. Open twice, and in one stretch at Wimbledon he made the semis followed by two straight finals (he lost to me in one, then became the foil for Goran Ivanisevic's long-delayed triumph at Wimbledon). Pat retired—prematurely, many thought—shortly after that loss to Goran. But Pat was like one of those NFL running backs who averages six or seven yards per carry for five or six years and suddenly falls off the radar, averaging one and a half for the next few years. That happens because those backs just get beat up and softened up; they lose a little something. That's what I think happened to Pat.

Pat had to work very hard to win his matches, for reasons having to do with his style and technique. Many of the things I said about Lleyton Hewitt apply to Rafter as well, although they had very different styles and did their grinding in dramatically different ways. Rafter was a serve-and-volley daredevil, a great mover and athlete always flying around the court, lunging, spearing volleys, making those joint-bruising changes of direction. It's just awfully difficult to work that hard for four or five years and keep coming back for more.

Pat won matches by attacking the net and then, when receiving, scraping by from the backcourt, always looking for a way to get to the net. He hit his kicker with a lot of effort, kind of contorted. It wasn't as limber and easy a delivery as Edberg's. He worked very hard to hold, because even though he loved to rush the net, he didn't have a huge serve—hence the reliance on the kicker (or American twist). Unlike other successful attackers, Pat couldn't pop the aces and service winners to make his life easier. Pat fought and struggled for everything he got.

MARCELO RIOS (2–0) . . . Rios was an odd one, a surly, strange sort of guy who had a lot of talent but seemed a misfit and an outsider on the tour. It's hard to enjoy life and survive on the tour that way. Rios moved in an easy, natural way, with a terrific two-handed backhand and great shotmaking ability. He was like a left-handed Andre Agassi. He was a great striker of the ball and could take it early, but he didn't serve as big as Andre and his game lacked the heft that made you feel like you were really in trouble. I always felt like Rios had nothing that could hurt me.

Still, Rios was very creative and "handsy"—he could change direction and pace on his shots with ease, and he just had a nice feel for the ball, and the game in general. Some people touted Rios as the Second Coming, but I never saw that. He was extremely talented, but that took you only so far. Rios held the number one ranking briefly, although he never won a major. He made my life truly miserable in 1998 when I was trying to lock up that record sixth-straight year-end-number-one ranking.

MARAT SAFIN (3–4) . . . Marat played a great match against me in the U.S. Open final of 2000 to put up one of the most impressive Grand Slam wins in ages. Marat is a big, powerful guy who moves awfully well for a man of his size. His forehand is huge and his backhand is heavy and solid. He can volley, and probably should attack more than he does on fast surfaces. When he's on, he's just fierce; for a while, he was the only guy who could give Roger Federer a run for his money—and he could do it on most surfaces. But Marat has always blown hot and cold; he has the whole package except for the mental part.

There's a bit of Goran in Marat, both in his personality and in his big, go-for-broke game. He just never liked grinding, although sometimes you need to grind if you're going to win a lot of matches. Marat opened a huge window for himself when he made that statement by beating me in the 2000 U.S. Open, but he jumped right out of the window and didn't win another major until the Australian Open in 2005. For a guy with his talent, it was too long a time between big wins.

MICHAEL STICH (4–5) . . . Out of all the guys who were real or potential rivals, Stich was the one who scared me the most—just look at his superior head-to-head record. I didn't play Stich a lot—he didn't seem to enjoy life at the top, so he left the game at a relatively young age. But if he had played a little longer, and wanted it as badly as I did, he would have been extremely tough.

Stich had a huge first serve and a big second serve that he could come in behind confidently, because he was a gifted volleyer. He moved very well and could do it all—stay back, chip and charge, serve and volley. He really had an all-court game and, among all the guys I played, the best combination of power, movement, and mental strength. Unfortunately for Stich, Germany was in love with his contemporary, Boris Becker. The rivalry between them was bitter and intense.

I always measured guys by the quality of their second serve, and that was the big difference between Stich and the other guys who could hurt me. He had a really easy, natural service motion, and while the Beckers and Krajiceks and Ivanisevics had days when their second serve was deadly, Stich was the one who seemed able to do it most consistently. It's a pity he quit the game so soon, although it made me breathe a huge sigh of relief.

That about does it, although you may be wondering whose strokes I would use to create the ultimate tennis player. Let me give it a shot. If you were building a composite player out of the guys who were my main rivals, I'd say you'd take Agassi's backhand

and Ivanisevic's first serve. Throw in Stich's second serve, Rafter's or Edberg's volley, and Hewitt's or Chang's speed. The forehand would be Ferreira's, Becker's, or Agassi's. I'd take Jim Courier's mentality, although Chang and Edberg (late in his career) were mentally tough as well. For an all-court game, I like Becker or Stich. I'd go with Agassi's service return, although I would take a really close look at Hewitt's and even Chang's, too.

Acknowledgments

I would like to thank my parents, Sam and Georgia, and my siblings, Gus, Stella, and Marion, for their never-ending love and support.

I would like to thank my coaches Paul Annacone and the late Tim Gullikson for being such instrumental figures in my career—as well as true friends.

I would like to thank my team during the heart of my career, which included my racket stringer and tuner, Nate Ferguson; my fitness trainer, Pat Etcheberry; my physio, Todd Snyder; and my personal trainer, Brett "Moose" Stevens.

I'd also like to thank my coauthor, Peter Bodo, for understanding my personality and game and for making the job of "opening up" so much easier for me.

And finally, to my fans . . . thank you for your continued support throughout my entire career. I have and always will appreciate you!

New York *Daily News,* 116
New York Times, 269
Nicholson, Jack, 60
Nick Bollettieri Tennis Academy
    (NBTA), 34, 37, 62, 123
Nike, 52, 121, 135, 141–42, 146, 237–38,
    251–52
    "Air" shoe campaign of, 115, 120,
    142, 251
Noah, Yannick, 65, 200
Norman, Magnus, 187
Novacek, Karel, 79

O'Connor, Ian, 263, 264
Olympic Games, 89
    of 1992 (Barcelona), 80, 85
Ono, Yoko, 253

Palos Verdes, Calif., 5–6, 20–21, 48
Palos Verdes High School, 19–20, 53
Paris Indoors, 54, 63, 105, 156, 208, 224
Paris Masters, 54
passing shots, 169, 174, 242
Pepperdine University, 52
Perez-Roldan, Guillermo, 92
Perry, Fred, 95, 215
PGA, 54
Philadelphia, Pa., 3, 31–32, 40, 45, 56, 92
Philippoussis, Mark, 157, 173, 175, 197,
    201, 214, 225, 287–88
Pioline, Cédric, 91, 104–5, 173, 185,
    193–94
Portas, Albert, 263
Potomac, Md., 2–3, 5

Queens Club, 56, 79–80, 93, 108, 138,
    190, 214, 233

Rădulescu, Alex, 194
Rafter, Patrick, 104, 112, 197, 203,
    213, 225, 227–29, 234, 235, 246,
    288–89, 292
Rehe, Stephanie, 13
Reneberg, Richey, 148, 151, 173

Rios, Marcelo, 108, 205–6, 208–9, 290
Riviera Club, 15
Roberts, Selena, 269
Roche, Tony, 250
Roddick, Andy, 63, 134, 234
    PS vs., 233, 250, 267
Rod Laver Arena, 157–59, 186, 216
Roland Garros stadium, 40, 58, 92,
    108, 137, 138, 162–65, 186, 187,
    193, 284, 285
    Philippe Chatrier Court Centrale
    at, 198–99, 216
Rolling Hills, Calif., 6
Rolling Hills High School, 19–20
Rose, Charlie, 230
Rosewall, Ken, 18, 31, 76, 237
Rosset, Marc, 71, 85
Rostagno, Derrick, 56
Rusedski, Greg, 197, 208, 265–66
Russia, 55, 81, 105, 148–53
Russo, Bobby, 150, 152
Ryder Cup, 134–35

Sabatini, Gabriela, 159
Safin, Marat, 213, 225, 232, 234, 236,
    246, 252, 290–91
Salinger, J. D., 19
Sampras, Bridgette Wilson (wife),
    223–24
    courtship and marriage of, 231, 233,
    253, 260
    film career of, 223, 233, 260
    pregnancy of, 253–54, 258, 259–60
    relationship of PS and, 253, 256–58,
    259–61, 267, 272, 273, 274
Sampras, Christian (son), ix, 253, 273
Sampras, Georgia (mother), 2, 8–10,
    48, 181, 228, 229–31
    Greek heritage of, 9
    nurturing and compassion of, 8–9,
    128
    PS's relationship with, 8–9, 10, 12,
    128, 293
    toughness and resilience of, 9–10

drug scandal in, x, 195–97
emotional vs. cool deportment in,
    85–86, 112–14, 129–30, 210–11
equipment revolution in, x, 14, 109,
    201
expense of training in, 10, 12, 21, 51,
    82
growth of international competition
    in, x
handshake in, 26, 50
ideal characteristics in, 6, 13, 15,
    26–27, 291–92
indoor, 31–32, 39, 53, 54, 55, 56, 64,
    105, 159, 160, 182–84, 203, 266
mental and psychological game of,
    25–28, 43, 44, 46–47, 66–67, 77,
    83–84, 87–89, 92–95
night matches in, 35, 157, 159
1968 start of Open-era in, 5
prize money in, 32, 36–37, 52, 55,
    105, 106, 120, 121, 263
scoring system in, 191
seeding system in, 28, 135, 143
slowdown of speed in, x, 112, 138,
    191, 202
televising and filming of, 17–18, 171,
    184, 220
Tennis, 37, 182
tennis balls, 158
    softening of, 112, 138, 191
    spinning of, 14, 15, 17, 30, 39, 219
tennis boom, 5, 31
tennis bums, 34
tennis camps, 18
tennis courts:
    clay surface of, 4, 28, 34, 40, 53, 79,
        80, 84–86, 92, 93, 106–7, 110, 111,
        137, 148, 149, 156, 160, 198–200,
        285
    grass surface of, 3, 23, 40, 53, 57, 77,
        80, 87, 92–103, 111, 191–92, 200
    hard surface of, 4, 40, 53, 57, 78, 80,
        84, 94, 104, 106, 159, 186, 200
    HAR-TRU green clay surface of, 198

indoor carpet surface of, 53, 54, 55,
    182
Plexicushion surface of, 159
public, 4
Rebound Ace surface of, 159
tennis rackets:
    abuse of, 22, 208, 211
    customization of, 110
    graphite, 110
    grips on, 4, 99, 110
    head size on, 111, 201, 250
    placement of, 77, 95
    stringing of, 110, 131, 167
    technological changes in, 14, 109, 201
    weighting of, 14, 110
    Wilson Pro Staff 85, 109–11, 250
    wooden, 13–14, 109
tennis shoes, 120, 142, 159
Tennis Week, 181–82, 272
thalassemia, 158, 181–82
tiebreakers, 85, 97, 98, 100–101, 109,
    152, 165, 177–78, 183, 191, 195,
    198, 202, 224, 229, 244, 247
Times (London), 113–14, 257–58
Today show, 230
Trinity University, 52

Ulihrach, Bohdan, 162
United States Tennis Association
    (USTA), 52, 54, 65, 78, 133, 147,
    152, 216, 250, 261
    geographic divisions of, 25, 28
    junior division of, 25, 28, 34
U.S. Open, 3, 5, 6, 54, 204–5, 289
    of 1989, 29, 35–36
    of 1990, 29, 41–48, 50–53, 56, 58, 61,
        91, 232, 286
    of 1991, 49, 57–62, 65, 80
    of 1992, 71, 80–84, 86–87, 89, 97, 99,
        156, 228
    of 1993, 91, 104–5, 193
    of 1994, 91, 115–16, 135
    of 1995, 119, 138, 144–46, 152, 184,
        239, 240